T0244360

DIGITALLY INVISIBLE

DIGITALLY INVISIBLE

How The Internet Is Creating the New Underclass

NICOL TURNER LEE

BROOKINGS INSTITUTION PRESS
Washington, D.C.

Copyright © 2024 by The Brookings Institution

PUBLISHED BY BROOKINGS INSTITUTION PRESS
1775 Massachusetts Avenue, NW
Washington, DC, 20036
www.brookings.edu/bipress

CO-PUBLISHED BY ROWMAN & LITTLEFIELD
An imprint of The Rowman & Littlefield Publishing Group, Inc.
4501 Forbes Boulevard, Suite 200, Lanham, Maryland 20706
www.rowman.com

86-90 Paul Street, London EC2A 4NE
Distributed by National Book Network

All rights reserved. No part of this book may be reproduced
in any form or by any electronic or mechanical means, including information
storage and retrieval systems, without written permission from the publisher,
except by a reviewer who may quote passages in a review.

British Library Cataloguing in Publication Information Available

Library of Congress Control Number: 2024937365

ISBN 978-0-8157-3898-5 (cloth : alk. paper)
ISBN 978-0-8157-3899-2 (ebook)

♾™ The paper used in this publication meets the minimum requirements of American
National Standard for Information Sciences—Permanence of Paper for Printed Library
Materials, ANSI/NISO Z39.48-1992.

I am invisible, understand, simply because people refuse to see me. Like the bodiless heads you see sometimes in circus sideshows, it is as though I have been surrounded by mirrors of hard, distorting glass. When they approach me they see only my surroundings, themselves, or figments of their imagination—indeed, everything and anything except me.

—Ralph Ellison, *Invisible Man*, 1952

This book is dedicated to my father, the late Francis Lee Turner, and my mother, Eleanor, who are my forever role models.

Contents

Preface

Around the end of 2017, I started this book before the COVID-19 pandemic revealed the depth and breadth of both our domestic and global digital divides. In 2020, two weeks before a global public health crisis literally froze the world, I completed a "digital divide tour" that took me to seven cities and small towns across the United States to understand how people experienced and coped with their available internet access. The places that I visited between 2018 and 2020 included Cleveland; Garrett County, Maryland; Hartford; Marion, Alabama; Phoenix; Staunton, Virginia; and Syracuse. In each location, I was invited by a friend or a mutual contact who welcomed me into the community. Quickly, I found myself interviewing local people, and randomly interacting with a variety of others while walking down the sidewalks of Main Street in small rural towns, sitting in locally owned restaurants and shops, or engaging in small talk on the benches at large affordable housing complexes in much larger cities.

All the ethnographic research for the book was done before the COVID-19 pandemic upended life as we knew it and created greater dependence on the internet and related resources. But even before the pandemic shined a spotlight on the vastness of the U.S. digital divide, the people I talked with had a lot to say about their experiences and connections online, and more specifically about their high-speed broadband "access," which is a modern fiber-optics technology that makes it easier to download online media while engaging in a multiplicity of other online tasks with various people in the same or different locations.

My personal and professional experiences with the U.S. digital divide started more than thirty years ago. In the late 1990s, while a graduate student, I was part of the community technology center movement that began around the time when being connected to the internet became increasingly important for government agencies, and at a time when a prior volunteer opportunity on Chicago's North

Side turned into a longer-term endeavor. These periods in my life are shared throughout the book because they have informed my current perspectives on the digital divide. Chicago eventually became a more permanent home after finishing graduate school, and it also was central to my "personal growth," as volunteerism at one small computer lab evolved into having more than five hundred public access computers at various centers around the city and south suburbs before I relocated to Washington, DC, seventeen years later.

Each computer lab that I opened was purposely designed and built and was highly committed to bringing technology access to low-income communities of color, which—without the necessary tools to transition them from analog to online experiences—were becoming increasingly invisible in a rapidly connected world. That was then, and the book now extracts from years of on-the-ground experiences and numerous publications years later while working at the Brookings Institution, a global think tank in Washington. Before Brookings, other organizations gave me the freedom to express my love for research and community technology, including the Joint Center for Political and Economic Studies, the only think tank focused on the Black community in the nation's capital. While developing the first media and technology institute there in 2010, I coauthored the first national minority broadband adoption study, which was widely cited by government, civil society, and research colleagues. Titled "National Minority Broadband Adoption: Comparative Trends in Adoption, Acceptance and Use," the research was the first empirical study to describe the experiences of Black and Hispanic populations, who were, at that time, late internet adopters when compared with whites.[1]

As I reflect on how much time that I have spent working on behalf of communities and individuals deserving of first-class, digital status, these cumulative lived experiences raise awareness about the critical intersectionality between race, place, and space—variables that have been gravely missing or discounted in early and current discussions about the U.S. digital divide. In my sociological research, I have found that the study of such intersectional ties helps to explain the unequal and often unfair experiences and outcomes of certain groups in American society that have been witnessed during periods of history when people of color seek fair and equitable opportunities in the areas of employment, housing, voting rights, and now digital access. In particular, the research argument of this book rests on the confluence of various social and geographic contexts, politics, and public policies that are critical to how we understand the role of race, place, and space in determining who has technology access, and at what level of quality. Without such a framework to better understand why the concept of the digital divide has been with us in the United States for decades, it is difficult to discern the reasons for its persistence as well as the causes, effects, or both. For example, historical policies to close the digital divide have primarily focused on access to broadband through new and expanded infrastructure deployments and affordable services. The effects that disappearing analog systems have had on more vulnerable populations—like the transition from old rotary telephones to smarter devices, or the rapid migration of jobs and other critical services to online platforms are also strong. And the lack of a broad political consensus to address these harder questions of how structural inequalities have exacerbated digital disparities by policymakers and advocates have led them to think about the problems as three primary areas to accelerate high-speed broadband—availability, affordability, and accessibility—which narrow and discount larger issues, including how the digital divide affects our global competitiveness. For example, students without universal access to the internet and related resources are both deterred and limited in their pursuit of widely vacant opportunities in science, technology, engineering, arts, and mathematics (STEAM) because they lack the bare minimum requirements to participate.

Along these same lines, the conceptualization of the problem as one that is primarily focused on wires and computers obscures what it really means to be digitally invisible, especially at a time when being connected to the internet influences one's social and economic well-being. It is a social determinant that will either establish pathways to global competitiveness or keep one trapped in waning analog existences that are unpromising in an increasingly digital world.

No matter how much money the federal government has spent or will do so in the future, or even the intensity of on-the-ground activism to promote digital equity, these narrow approaches cannot overpower and dismiss the strong effects of race- and place-based discrimination, which I believe are both core to the conception and persistence of the U.S. digital divide.

From job opportunities that slowly transitioned from the classified sections in newspapers to online career portals like Monster.com in 1999 and emergency remote education for school-age children in 2020 at the start of the pandemic, our society expects that individuals be connected—despite not always making it easy for them to find available and affordable high-speed internet. New subgroups of invisible populations are also emerging among the millions of people without accessible internet access that include small farmers who struggle to compete against agricultural monopolies where being connected enables precision technologies, and the people from rural America who have chosen to live in geographic isolation from urban areas suffer—whether rich or poor—due to the lack of competitive, local broadband options.

The Digitally Invisible

The people to whom I refer as "digitally invisible" live in communities throughout rural America where there are more cows than people. The digitally invisible are also contained within geographically redlined urban and suburban areas where structural racism has resulted in rapid disinvestments and slow economic growth, insufficient job markets and opportunities, and inadequate housing options.

Digitally invisible populations are those who struggle to maintain conspicuous identities amid substantial and documentable systemic barriers, and who cope with the poverty, health disparities, educational inequities, labor force abandonment, disabilities, and ageism that have become more complicated considering the rapid disappearance of analog activities. People of color who live among the categorization of being digitally invisible have been further racialized by disparities in connectivity because not having available and affordable broadband makes it more difficult to escape and navigate through the explicit barriers of and implicit discrimination that has led to their geographic, and socioeconomic, isolation.

Not being connected to the internet or having sufficient devices to engage in online media and applications leaves certain people and their communities in digital deserts, which mirrors the experiences of many of the people and communities spotlighted throughout the book. Their stories provide insights into what it is like to be digitally invisible and call out their struggles to maintain their profiles in more elevated and convenient online spaces. Though not entirely monetary, the economic and social tax incurred by people who are not part of the new information-rich economy and ecosystem are steep and deepen (rather than eliminate) existing historical practices fueled by racism and discrimination.

In other words, the digitally invisible are trapped by their demography, geography, and circumstances, which limit their abilities to work or learn remotely in a world no longer bound by the physical bearings of classrooms, apartment complexes, farms, or other business establishments.

Indeed, being online is integral to the series of social and economic determinants that both qualify and quantify decent livelihoods for all Americans, and people around the globe for that matter. Yet marginalized and more vulnerable populations—who remain traumatized and exhausted by the persistence of racism, geographic, political, and social exclusions—are left to fend for themselves, despite public policymakers' decades-long concerns and awareness about the lack of universally available and affordable internet access.

For example, during my digital divide tour in 2019 I met people in Garrett County, Maryland, with strong Amish and Mennonite religious beliefs, where the topography of acres of green land and farms dominates the density of people living in this massive agricultural area. There, the growing declines in farming due to narrowing federal funding and waning generational interest have resulted in productivity impasses for landowners who, in turn, have resulted in greater economic losses. With most of the young people forbidden to work outside the family, this has caused strains on these communities by threatening their cultural efficacy and social mobility. The physical size of Garrett County and the distance between its cities and towns have also made it more difficult for case workers to deliver efficient social services and care to the more needy residents—some of whom are from these religious communities. The normal turnaround for case workers to travel to client homes involved 2 long hours by car, especially to the farthest points of the county. Two hours of travel back to the main office in the city of Oakland was required for inputting client notes into wired computers—often leaving two weeks to pass before case managers returned to the client's home to address the problem. Without ubiquitous internet access throughout the area to administer services, the residents suffered, alongside the helpless and often hopeless case workers. Many residents of the county also did not own adequate and operable transportation to make it into Oakland, and on top of that, ridesharing services like Uber and Lyft were largely nonexistent without working cars to withstand the long distances of travel and unsteady internet access to receive or order the services. Essentially, what poverty and geographic isolation looks like for the families in Garrett County today is about the choices and opportunities that they cannot engage to make their lives easier to navigate.

Unfortunately, what I encountered in Garrett County, and in other rural cities and towns that were part of my tour, is not what an inspired and inclusive twenty-first-century communications ecosystem looks like. Rather, it clearly portrays the experiences of the digitally invisible who some would consider abandoned due to insufficient connectivity. Garrett County had also become the poster child for Maryland's struggle to contain opioid addiction and related deaths—another challenge that was impossible to address by case and health workers who could not keep steady appointments with residents in need, or engage in real-time, remote health services, like addiction recovery, on a regular basis. Despite the vastness of its greenery, the county was literally dying due to the lack of sustainable broadband and the provision of remote health care for needy residents. Mind you, these experiences in Garrett County, which is just three hours outside Washington, happened before the pandemic, and I can only imagine how quickly the conditions worsened for the people still living there.

During my visit to the much larger city of Syracuse, I met Debra, a Black resident of a senior-assisted public housing development there, whose apartment complex was on the other side of downtown—demarcated by an active expressway that distinguished the communities. Debra was the self-appointed manager of the small, first-floor computer lab in the building, and she helped other seniors acquire email addresses to searching for jobs and updating public benefits. Every day, she stared out the largest window in the lab, worrying about the city's recent plans to demolish her building—a place she had called home for decades. This was part of a proposed plan to redress years of Syracuse's housing redlining practices, and it came along just as she and the other residents were beginning to acclimate to the new digital normal. These circumstances made her worry more about the fate of her computer lab that have given life to the seniors who used it, and to her.

Years before the pandemic, when President Joe Biden unveiled national stories of students sitting in the parking lots of fast-food restaurants, middle and high school students from predominantly Black neighborhoods in Hartford walked daily to the local McDonald's restaurant to do their homework because of its open Wi-Fi access.

In 2020, the lack of residential broadband access for these students worsened as longer-than-expected school closures progressed at the onset of the global pandemic. Now, the Hartford Public Schools, like so many other large districts, are currently mitigating learning losses that have especially affected Black and Hispanic students. Statewide, third- to eighth-grade students lost seven months of learning in mathematics, and nearly five months in reading, according to a series of reports from Harvard University's Center for Education Policy Research and other national research partners.[2] These Hartford students are behind a year in math, and seven months in reading post pandemic, which seems much too low when compared with other students in the state. But these setbacks should have never happened if the city's schools had been on par with the wealthier districts, and the transition to emergency remote learning had been smoother.

From rural to urban America and from the young to older people, the digital divide has disproportionately affected numerous populations. But such consequences were widely familiar to policymakers, civil society, and industry leaders before the global COVID-19 pandemic. That is because the United States has been dealing with the digital divide for a very long time—almost three decades or more, to be exact.

Six Presidential Administrations

As a researcher at the intersection of technology and society, journalists regularly contact me to ask about the digital divide, especially when the issue is part of groundbreaking news on their beat. The interviews usually start with this first request, "First, Dr. Turner Lee, tell me what you know about the digital divide." Part of the inquiry is to wrap their hands around a complicated issue, and the other part is because they have not googled my publications before the interview. After being asked the same question on multiple occasions by reporters in recent months, I have realized that most people started the clock on the digital divide around the onset of the global pandemic in 2020, when millions of people were asked to stay home as part of voluntary quarantines. But this is not when the digital divide first appeared.

Over the last six presidential administrations (technically starting with President Ronald Reagan), the United States has had the political interest and will of many leaders who stood up either legislation and/or public policies for more ubiquitous broadband infrastructure or established programs to promote a digital equity agenda that focused on an available and affordable internet, as well as low-cost devices and basic computer training.

In the mid-1990s, Larry Irving, who most consider to be "the father" of the concept, was appointed as assistant secretary at the National Telecommunications and Information Administration (NTIA) at the U.S. Department of Commerce by President Bill Clinton. Working for Commerce under the late

Secretary Ron Brown, Larry, who is also a friend, warned the country about a growing digital divide and the lack of access to the technology at a time, when now-outdated 386 computers connected to the internet via telephone modems. He laid the problem out in a very binary manner as a deluge between "haves" and the "have nots," and he defined the digital divide as the impasse between the people who had the resources and connectivity to get online and did, when others were not so lucky. In 1995, under his leadership and at the request of Clinton to have more research, the NTIA published a series of white papers that adopted the title "Falling through the Net: Haves and Have Nots in Rural and Urban Areas"; in each part of the series, aspects of the digital divide were documented and shared alongside predictions about the consequences for those without the internet when it came to accessing online content for economic and social self-sufficiencies. That same year, Larry delivered a speech before large foundations like the Markle Foundation, the RAND Corporation, and other organizations that held similar concerns about the digital divide, where he reiterated the onset of internet privilege: "Information technologies can widen the gap between the affluent and the poor. By the year 2000, 60% of the new jobs in this country will require skills that are held by only 20% of the existing population and those skills basically were technology and computer related. If we don't get access to technology to people across this country, at an earlier age and more ubiquitously, we are going to have increased social problems . . . increased poverty. We need to start addressing this."[3]

Ironically, it took another twenty-seven years—and the global pandemic—for Larry's concerns to really resonate with the public. That is why I also argue in the book that political partisanship has largely worsened stifled Congress's efforts to make the internet available for all because members of Congress, and those in the White House, have successfully politicized the digital divide and have supported years of the same shovel-ready approaches to broadband infrastructure and digital literacy programs. In fact, more time has been spent by policymakers on blanket and/or wholesale telecommunications issues that to this day remain unsettled, like debates over who controls the internet or the perpetual blame of insufficient deployments of internet service providers (ISPs). In my opinion, these and other debates have overridden serious inquiries into what is needed to make digitally invisible people less hidden so that they may thrive rather than survive in our global society. Over the years, the energy behind closing the digital divide has lost oxygen in crowded debates over other tech policies that are more focused on reeling in the power of existing and emerging telecommunications and Big Tech firms, and not necessarily on how they affect everyday people. At the writing of the book, Biden's Federal Communications Commission (FCC), the agency responsible for oversight of the nation's communications, issued draft rules to settle the score on the long-standing net neutrality debate to apply stricter regulations to ISPs, which have been accused of being selfish with their connectivity, despite some breakthroughs in their low-cost broadband programs during the pandemic. Time will tell where these rules will eventually land, or whether they will, again, be contested by incumbent ISPs and Republican legislators.

In 2020, when the global public health crisis blindsided the world, despite the predictions of people like Larry Irving about the state of digital inequality, the circumstances of online access worsened for certain communities, while the market value of incumbent and start-up technology companies increased, especially in online advertising. Despite our nation's constant dealings with the digital divide for decades, many leaders (even those from civil society organizations) caught amnesia when talking about the digital divide as if they had never seen it before. There was also an immediate disassociation between what is taking place among existing and emerging technologies, and the impact on people, particularly those whose lack of internet access make it virtually impossible to realize the benefits of the former.

As he often does, Larry resurfaced and wrote a poignant op-ed titled "The Digital Divide May Be News but It's Not New," which was published in the *Morning Consult*, a daily Washington journal, at the onset of the digital divide frenzy.[4] In it, he outrightly shamed policymakers for blanking out on how to address digital inequities after decades of political, industry, and community investments. As one who has also been part of community, national, and international discussions of both the digital divide and equity since the 1990s, I completely agree with his contemporary reflections and also the frustrations that linger decades after Larry's tenure ended at the Commerce Department.

The modern-day digital divide is hauntingly the same early juxtaposition between the affluent and the poor where having internet access has continued to be more of a privilege for the former, and for the latter—a dealbreaker in our increasingly digital economy. What also makes the contemporary digital divide so much more critical is how it manifests some of the same symptoms that leave people relegated to second-class digital status in the United States. That is, it further widens inequalities—many of which are encoded by race, class, gender, and other federally-protected categories—when people without internet access are unable to benefit from twenty-first-century services, including remote health care and work, distance learning, and online civic engagement. You might wondering why I keep homing in on these points in this preface.

I am incessantly driven by the argument that, in the end, the new digital divide is about people. Particularly, the people who have been left alone to fend for themselves while traditional analog or in-person economic and social structures disappear. It is about how certain technologies and their applications have exacerbated the erasure of more vulnerable groups. Whereas some would suggest that the modern digital divide is about the saturation of fiber-optic networks and more affordable low-cost, monthly broadband service options, that is only part of the narrative, and though widely critical to the development of robust networks, these points are perhaps not the most significant reason for broadly expanding our communications infrastructures.

The Biden-Harris Administration

In November 2021, President Joe Biden and Vice President Kamala Harris promised to change the narrative and the progress toward widespread, national internet access by including high-speed broadband networks in the nation's largest infrastructure investment legislation since President Franklin Delano Roosevelt's New Deal legislation—a point of comparison constantly touted by the Biden-Harris administration. The Infrastructure Investment and Jobs Act, later known as the Bipartisan Infrastructure Law due to the overwhelming support on both sides of the aisle, included an original budget of $65 billion toward the expansion of U.S. high-speed broadband networks. The NTIA was charged with the largest allocation of the dollars—$42.45 billion—for the Broadband Equity, Access, and Deployment (BEAD) program, which would be given to states and recognized U.S. territories to support broadband infrastructure deployments in unserved and underserved areas. The main qualifications for funding were that states used the resources to invest in networks for underserved and unserved areas without high-speed broadband service offering download speeds of 25 megabits per second (Mbps) and upload speeds of 3 Mbps. The Biden-Harris administration deemed that these types of internet speeds allowed for basic connectivity for video or music streaming in 2021. In 2021, the Infrastructure Investment and Jobs Act and the Consolidated Appropriations Act also enabled the creation of the NTIA's Tribal Broadband Connectivity Program, which provided $3 billion to support tribal broadband infrastructure, and, as of the time of my writing, $2.76 billion has already been deployed. Additionally, in fiscal year 2022 (beginning in 2021), the Bureau of Indian Affairs' National Tribal Broadband Grant awarded another nearly $2.7 million to indigenous nations and tribes. The U.S. Department of Agriculture was also provided with $8.37 billion in funding across forty-three programs, including $1.9 billion for the ReConnect Program, which offers loans and grants to expand high-speed broadband infrastructure in rural America.

In the third year of the Biden-Harris White House, the federal investments in broadband assets substantially increased when, in June 2023, an additional appropriation of $42 billion was added to broadband infrastructure funds to advance the quality of service and speed in rural and suburban areas. The combined federal appropriations starting in 2021 were now up to more than $1 trillion, with most of the funds still going to severely unserved and underserved rural areas as part of the BEAD program by the fall of 2023.

In addition to infrastructure, the original bipartisan law in 2021 also allocated a separate pot of money to the NTIA—a total of $2.7 billion, to be exact, for digital equity programs that encouraged adoption and use among disadvantaged populations. Federal monies were also apportioned as part of the bipartisan infrastructure bill to the FCC for the $14 billion program called the Affordable Connectivity Program (ACP), which was in place to provide low-cost broadband programs for eligible consumers, and, at the time of writing, had surpassed more than 20 million enrollments. Later in the book, I share additional federal expenditures that are being made toward broadband access from the U.S. Department of the Treasury with designated pandemic-relief funds, and grandfathered broadband programs housed at the NTIA and FCC that support deployments in high-cost areas, like rural and target programs for connected health care delivery, before the newly adopted infrastructure bill. On top of this federal goodwill, various states have also done their part to add to the coffers of broadband activities and programs when Congress authorized direct funding to them during the emergency public health crisis.

Without question, Biden, Harris, and their administration have greenlighted the largest federal appropriations when compared with their predecessors. The combined totals across agencies and programs exceed trillions of dollars, although an exact number of cumulative is not easy to glean due to a lack of spending dashboards. In comparison, President Barack Obama spent less than a tenth of these current investments on high-speed broadband around the time that the 2009 American Recovery and Reinvestment Act was enacted. With such tremendous federal investments under the Biden-Harris administration, if we fail to close the digital divide, once and for all, it will not be because we did not have the resources.

Before the pandemic, the FCC reported that more than 14 million people were without access to broadband in their home or community. Companies like Microsoft suggested that the FCC's number was an undercount, and there were probably 100 million people without internet access. The people most stricken by these digital inequities are disproportionately people of color and indigenous populations, low-income, less-educated, rural, older, foreign-born, disabled, LGBTQ+, and most likely an intersection of many of these attributes. But even with the long history of reporting on how these populations are not sufficiently connected, policymakers forget to confront their parallel experiences of structural isolation and discrimination.

For these reasons, there will be a high chance that despite the current political will and backing, the United States will not entirely redress decades-long digital inequalities. That is because our national approach to righting digital wrongs often relies on the maintenance of the same partisan formulas for federal investments, which is largely embedded in a "build it, and they will come" approach, where more supply of broadband networks is valued over consumer demand. Further, when politicians, industry, and civil society organizations have addressed digital inclusion and equity, they have traditionally done so in ways that bypass the more fundamental question of how the nation will ultimately handle universal service and access to the nation's most advanced communications infrastructure, and how this deposit into the digital infrastructure translates into more equal and sustainable futures for American households and workers. For example, in more recent White House efforts to promote what it considers newfound digital equity, an eerie silence has resonated on the state and future of America's universal service program, which by law guaranteed rotary phone service in the homes of every U.S. household to carry not only voice calls but also emergency services, like the three numbers 9-1-1. Since the last revision of telecommunications policies in 1996, the concept of and provision for universal service in the United States remains outdated and stagnant, while efforts to close the digital divide have appeared to be strikingly redundant and political.

Right now, the United States needs to reclaim and prioritize the notion of universal service that originated with Theodore Vail in the early 1900s; he had been the leader of the American Telephone and Telegraph Company, which later became AT&T.[5] The language then scribed into the Communications Act of 1934 went on to state that "all people in the United States shall have access to rapid, efficient, nationwide communications service with adequate facilities at reasonable charges."[6] Back then, the focus was on ubiquitous telephone service that had value for families in the United States, including access to nationwide public safety resources like 911, which was created in 1968 and later became a standard in the world of three-digit numbers. In 1984, President Ronald Reagan, a Republican, created the Lifeline program to scale up national use and affordability of basic telephone service to qualified individuals by discounting their service to $9.95 per month. Since the early days of the program, low-income rural, urban, and Tribal consumers have benefited from Lifeline, an initiative that over the years somehow became recognized as the "Obamaphone," or a novelty of the Obama administration, which is entirely false. When the Communications Act of 1934 was subsequently updated in 1996 under President Bill Clinton, the statute was subsequently revised to modernize Lifeline to include mobile wireless phone, and also to establish the Universal Service Fund, an independently administered program under the FCC's jurisdiction that still supports four government programs focused on achieving widespread and available communications, especially in hard-to-serve areas like rural America.

The Universal Service Fund was largely attributed to a time when static telephony was still the predominant form of communication (predating broadband), and the incumbent telephone companies bore responsibility to pay a "telecommunications tax" (which they ultimately passed on to consumers) to ensure program funding. From its inception to today, the Lifeline program has been largely undersubscribed, with a capture rate of less than 40 percent of eligible individuals, which appears to be a waning resource compared with the more recent Affordable Connectivity Program mandated under the Biden-Harris infrastructure bill, which risks elimination by Republicans opposed to any type of national social safety net for broadband access.

However, for decades, technological advancements have numbed the effectiveness of telephony at a time when high-speed broadband has emboldened new ways to communicate. Yet the concept of and funding for universal service has also been overlooked in recent decades, resulting in the festering digital divide due to unraveled traditional communications structures and regulations.

If we are more honest with ourselves as a nation, the United States has significantly failed to honor its commitment to universal access as prescribed in the early 1900s by Vail. But in doing so, the country not only has created rather digitally desperate circumstances for people and their communities but also is quickly eroding our nation's global effectiveness in a highly competitive digital economy in the areas of production and workforce talent. Without all-in and forward-thinking approaches to universal service, the interests of innovation and private sector companies have relegated ordinary citizens to being consumers or commodities of existing and emerging technologies, instead of involving them as workers, producers, and innovators. This is wildly playing out among some of the more recent technologists, who are introducing tools like artificial intelligence (AI) and generative AI, like ChatGPT, that treat people more like commodities and exploit their personal data for profitable gain. And this continues to happen when technology and society converge, because under our historical and current frameworks for technology policies, lawmakers reward the innovators and shortchange the people who should be beneficiaries of enriched economic opportunities.

Throughout my time spent on the digital divide tour from 2018 and into the early months of 2020, the people from urban, rural, and indigenous Tribal lands did not have agency over how they wanted to be connected to technology, which is a far cry from what policymakers, industry, and some civil society organizations believe that they need, as demonstrated by steadfast supply-and-demand formulas. Hence, the tragic reality of the digital divide has been its focus on garnering the public and private sector will to build more broadband networks, improve the quality of its service, and reduce monthly subscription costs. This is another point that I will continue to assert throughout the book.

In June 2023, I attended a press conference at the White House where President Joe Biden suggested that he would be "the guy to finish the job" compared with his predecessors, who were unsuccessful in breaching digital inequities.

But if history is a marker for predictable activities, it is not guaranteed that more people will get online. In fact, such presumptions may ignore the possibility that some people and communities do not want to be online due to religious or some-times extreme distrust of the internet, especially among people like the Amish or older populations. There is also some folklore in confident proclamations to close the digital divide that bringing such access will eliminate or downplay the realities of the other America, a concept coined by the sociologist Michael Harrington in his groundbreaking book, like poverty, racism, and class, whose social structures are needed to justify concepts of wealth, white supremacy, and privilege.

What I am trying to say here is that the strategy for how we have traditionally defined and approached the digital divide does not also correlate more connec-tivity with social mobility, which leads to people to being less poor, geographi-cally isolated, or safer in an increasingly digital economy. With such high stakes for global digital competitiveness, having more infrastructure is not a victory in the United States without parallel investments in people to ensure that there will be evolving and astute workforces and entrepreneurs who are prepared for the next iteration of the digital revolution.

When we fail to fully close the digital divide, tremendous vacancies persist in positions related to cybersecurity, computers, and data science because the people who are eager to learn are inadequately prepared due to living in areas where having utensils at the dinner table were assumed and not given. The lack of digital infrastructure sustains pedagogical models that are sternly rooted in traditional practices of analog learning, leaving certain students and communities behind. Without internet access and a device, it is almost like having a book without paper, a statement later shared by a principal in a Black rural town that I visited.

Existing models focused on available, affordable, and accessible broadband are fundamentally misaligned with how many people, especially those from more vulnerable populations, get online. In the Biden-Harris plan, federal funding did not go toward the expansion of commercial wireless or cable services for people affected by the digital divide, despite a large percentage of Black and Hispanic households being dependent on their smartphones or television cable service for their primary gateway to the internet. For the last five years, we have invested an incredible amount of political and economic capital in 5G technology, which is the latest and fastest iteration of commercial wireless technology. Yet, the omis-sion from the Biden-Harris broadband efforts is like placing thorns in the sides of communities that continue to barely float rather than swim in the digital economy—where access to mobile is, in fact, more affordable and reasonable than a residential broadband connection.

In this book, I talk a lot about a young man named Joseph, whose mobile phone was turned off when we first met in Staunton, Virginia, in 2018. Due to the lack of provider options and his mobile provider's data caps, he shared the difficulties of finding work as a day laborer, mainly leaving him the middle of the month without operable service. When I returned to his home more than a month later, his phone was still shut off and he was still out of work.

While some advocates might suggest that it is for this reason that we require a granular focus on telecom policies like net neutrality, most political operatives, especially now, still compare the acceleration and urgency of high-speed broadband with the rural electrification movement, and, as a result, current public policies privilege fiber-optics for high-speed broadband over other useful technologies, like wireless, satellite, and cable. But two things should stand out in this analogy. When we speak about the early growth of electricity, we are erring on the side of one type of technology—which, by the way, because of its expensive nature could quickly absorb the extraordinary federal investments. Preferencing one technology over another reduces options for making networks work for people wherever they live and however they choose to connect. Modern communications systems are much more dynamic and diverse than traditional telephone service, yet we continue to rely on bifurcated frameworks and outdated regulations when it comes to a more advanced U.S. communications infrastructure.

Further, Black men and Black people more generally did not benefit from rural electrification efforts, or from the New Deal, for that matter. They were often overlooked, or in places and spaces that were not direct beneficiaries of such benefits that are points that I share in the final chapter of the book. I find that idolatry of and nostalgia for New Deal programs, and of the rural electrification movement are, by far, unrealistic under contemporaneous circumstances. Politely speaking, the comparisons with historical moments like rural electrification and New Deal policies may be lazy substitutes for the lack of widespread fortitude to update old public policies, and engage what we have learned with the expansion of more sophisticated technologies.

I hope that the book and its findings change the trajectories for America's most vulnerable populations and their communities, from the modernization of the stale universal service program in the United States through contributions to reform that all inclusive companies add to the groundswell of digital activities. I also implore the United States to embrace technology within classrooms, and to find ways to advance local, public, digital infrastructure beyond just schools and libraries to include faith-based organizations, social service agencies, community-based organizations, local hospitals, and community health clinics, as well as small businesses that desire to bring high-speed broadband, training, and other resources to their establishments.

Finally, the United States must be creative in accomplishing these tasks by making the digital divide everybody's issue—not just the incumbent telecom providers that maintain central visibility in these debates, but drilling down the importance of digital equity and urgency within adjacent industries that now leverage technology for more advanced business models in the financial, automotive, retail, and hospitality sectors, and in government agencies. We do not normally think of these industries as tech-driven, but digital transformation efforts over the years have transitioned them to be more reliant on online platforms. In the end, it will be these industries that will require resources beyond basic digital literacy programs to embolden the next generation of scientists and other STEAM workers—as well as administrative assistants, customer service agents, and even mechanics—who will be required to leverage technology to do their jobs.

Throughout my own three decades of doing this work, it has become clear that the efforts to close the digital divide have been driven by various trade-offs that the country has made, and those intricately involved in the work, continue to make between tending to the immediacy of closing the problem and deeply exploring how we advance true and inclusive internet equity. Too many people outside Washington grapple with what being a first-class, digital resident means. Efforts to solve the digital divide should be positioned as a path to potentially heal some of the nation's most systemic inequalities that exclude individuals and their communities from fully engaging online platforms and related resources that improve their quality of life. I also hope that the book puts policymakers, industry leaders, and those who stand at the reins of civil society organizations on alert that the partisanship and paternalism about the digital divide has stifled progress for certain people and their communities, as well as the nation overall.

Without the tools communities need to be effective and competitive in and outside of our society, everybody loses—not just the incumbent and new broadband service providers that tend to be the focus of debates on the future of telecommunications and the Big Tech companies being blamed for its further demise. The global pandemic revealed a scroll of everyone else equally affected by physical social distancing, and the explosion of a plethora of digital goods and services. The same circumstances applied to individuals and workers who lived in communities with limited broadband access and who did not have options for where and when they could work, like Joseph in Staunton.

That is why we need to shift the conversation from solely being about the digital divide, which, it turns out, will be the first inning in a longer series of activities needed to democratize technology. While dispersing resources, the United States requires great deliberation about its existing policy frameworks and definitions that have led to internet privilege—issues that the country has been dealing with far too long. I know this because my exposure to racism began at birth, and to the digital divide around the late 1990s.

Notes

1. Jon P. Gant, Nicol E. Turner-Lee, Ying Li, and Joseph S. Miller, "National Minority Broadband Adoption: Comparative Trends in Adoption, Acceptance and Use," Joint Center for Political and Economic Studies, February 2010, https://www.broadbandillinois.org/uploads/cms/documents/mti_broadband_report_web.pdf.

2. See Education Recovery Scorecard, a collaboration of the Educational Opportunity Project at Stanford University, the Center for Education Policy Research at Harvard University, and Stanford CEPA, https://educationrecoveryscorecard.org.

3. "User Clip: Larry Irving on Digital Divide," C-Span (Clip of "E-Mail Accessibility," November 21, 1995), June 7, 2023, https://www.c-span.org/video/?c5073707/user-clip-larry-irving-digital-divide.

4. Larry Irving, "The Digital Divide May Be News, but It's Not New," Morning Consult, August 31, 2020, https://morningconsult.com/opinions/the-digital-divide-may-be-news-but-its-not-new/.

5. Milton Mueller, "Chapter 2: Universal Service: A Concept in Search of a History," in *Universal Service: Competition, Interconnection and Monopoly in the Making of the American Telephone System* (Syracuse: University of Syracuse, 2013), https://surface.syr.edu/cgi/viewcontent.cgi?filename=1&article=1017&context=books&type=additional.

6. Federal Communications Commission, "Universal Service Fund," https://www.fcc.gov/general/universal-service-fund.

Acknowledgments

No book is fully credited to the author alone. And for this book, that is particularly true. I formally started writing this work three years ago, but it is the product of decades of conversations, mentorship, research, and constructive revisions, as well as sometimes unhelpful but meaningful feedback.

At the Brookings Institution, Darrell West, senior fellow and author, edited multiple versions of this book with such detail that I cannot even begin to thank him for his incredible time spent reading, editing, and coaching me over the years. Each time, Darrell offered insightful comments about technology, governance, and politics that I hope shine through in these pages. His unwavering and timely support (and regular text messages) throughout this project made this book possible. Similarly, the Governance Studies program at Brookings offered me the space and time to write this book. I am grateful for my colleagues Camille Busette, Brigitte Brown, Courtney Dunakin, Tracy Viselli, and Molly Sugre—and fellow scholars at the Center for Technology Innovation for their support, guidance, and patience during the process when I was juggling administrative responsibilities, other research, and the book manuscript. I am very appreciative of the amazing support from the team at the Brookings Institution Press—Yelba Quinn and Alfred Imhoff—along with our communications colleagues, especially Andrea Risotto and Tracy Viselli. Writing a book of this depth would not have been possible without my other distinguished team members, the research assistants, who have helped me over the years. I want acknowledge Jack Malamud, Xavier Freeman-Edwards, Mishaela Robison, Lulia Pan, Samantha Lai, Caitlin Chin, James Seddon, Aiden Hizkias, Matthew Brown, Shezaz Hannan, Brian Schwartz, Jake Schneider, Jack Karsten, and the many other researchers and interns who supported me on this three-year journey. Many of them have gone on to graduate schools or to other their professional endeavors, but their suggestions, facts, and notes throughout the book. My gratitude also extends to Amber Von Schassen, my other wonderful editor and story developer, who edited many versions of the book to bring honor and value to the individuals and communities mentioned throughout. We met when she was a Brookings research associate with my colleague E. J. Dionne. She believed in the scope of the work from the moment that I shared it with her, and a couple of years later, she went on the journey with me to complete the final manuscript. She, too, sent many text messages and emails to coach me through a time-intensive process that did not seem like it had an end. Her encouragement and enthusiasm kept the project in motion at times when I was being pulled in so many directions. I am forever indebted to her objective feedback and insights.

I also want to thank the various donors and others who have believed in my work since I started in telecom, more than fifteen years ago. This book was completed independent of their support, and the views and opinions are my own. But there are so many individuals among this group who allowed me into their worlds from the public and private sides of philanthropy, which helped shape my research questions and data collection, including the MacArthur Foundation and McGovern Foundation. I am also grateful for previous jobs and opportunities, and to the people who gave me the chance to work in this space including Ralph Everett, former president of the Joint Center for Political and Economic Studies, and Rey Ramsey and Ben Hecht, my mentors at One Economy. I also want to personally acknowledge the mentorship of the Reverend Jesse Louis Jackson, Senior, the founder and president of the Rainbow PUSH Coalition, and his current and former staff members, including John Mitchell, Kimberly Marcus, and my late and eternal friend, Bishop Steven Smith—all of these individuals under the guidance of Reverend Jackson instilled the urgency of now to ensure digital access and equity for people of color, particularly those who had been relegated to invisibility through disenfranchisement.

I want to also extend my thanks to the many people who shared their stories about their online experiences as I trekked across the country for the Digital Divide Tour. They trusted me and allowed me to tag along, and I hope that I have captured their range of emotions and perspectives in the book. I would not be in this position to talk about the digital divide had it not been for the many people who supported me from the early days in the community technology movement and beyond. I am particularly grateful to people who have since passed but left an indelible mark in this passion that I have for digital equity, including the late Don Samuelson, Charles Shaw, and Charles Benton. To the wide net of mentors, and friends—including Aldon Morris, Rhonda Levine, David Honig, Maurita Coley, Michael Powell, Bill Kennard, Larry Irving, Julia Johnson, Kristal High, Marie Sylla-Dixon, Mignon Clyburn, Tanya Lombard, Donna Epps, Marc Morial, Kevin Branch, Charlyn Stanberry, Muriel Cooper, Vickie Robinson,

Heather Gates, Jessica Rosenworcel, Pierre Clark, Bruce Montgomery, Narda Jones, John Palfrey, Vilas Dhar, Eric Sears, Jon Gant, Dominique Harrison, Antonio Williams, Fred Humphries, Howie Hodges, Nilda Gumbs, Carolyn Brandon, Deb Lathen, John Gibson, Fallon Wilson, Fredrick Harris, Camisha Parker, V. Mishaune Sawyer, Rhonda Cheatham, Hannibal Navies, Charlie Firestone, Joe Waz, David Redl, Jillian Spindle, Abigail Bouzan Kaloustian, Katherine Smith, Roger Wilson, Leo Sosa, Harold Feld, Susan Allen, Antonio Tijerino, Demetria Gallagher, Joseph Miller, Chanelle Hardy, Sean Mickens, Hazeen Ashby, and so many others, including my extended family members of aunts, uncles, cousins, and "play cousins," who encouraged me to work in the space as a researcher, practitioner, activist, and now author. This long list of friends and family members includes people who did not always agree with my arguments but who pushed me forward to continue the work. If I have missed anyone, I send my apologies way in advance.

I also would not be here at all if it was not for the high expectations in the late 1990s to the early 2000s of the Northwest Tower Resident Board, the Homan Square Community Foundation and the entire North Lawndale community, the Chicago Housing Authority (especially Adrienne Bitoy Jackson and Cass Miller), the city of Rosemont when longtime Congresswoman Robin Kelly was assistant city manager, and other places that I was able to share with in their larger redevelopment efforts, including in Washington, among great legislators like retired Congressman G. K. Butterfield, and current members of Congress, Congressman Jim Clyburn and Congresswoman Yvette Clarke.

Family must be in your corner to cope with the mood swings of a writer, as well as the intense social isolation during the process. Fortunately, my loving and supportive husband, McArthur Gardner, provided me with both the space and love to finish the book. He was there for me to sort through ideas, even when the scope was beyond his wildest imagination. My husband, along with my two beautiful children, Keith and Chloe Lee, have been tolerant and patient with me over the last three years as I completed my work on this project. To my children, they never stopped believing that the book would get done, and I am grateful for their patience in the time spent away from home. The love and support that they both shared during this time meant more than they will ever know, along with suggestions for making the content more interesting to their age groups. I also want to extend my appreciation to my immediate family—my mother, Eleanor Turner; my sisters, Frances Turner and Tene Greenwood; as well as my brother-in-law, George Greenwood. The three years that it took to complete this manuscript meant a lot of rainchecks on significant family events, especially as the world changed during the pandemic. My immediate family's care was never ending, along with the love from my in-laws, Pearl and Joseph Taylor, who better understood the woman whom their son married.

Equally important to everyone who has sown into my life is my late father, to whom this book is dedicated. The memories of my father, the late Francis L. Turner, are infinite. He was an architect whose creative genius and love for his people inspired me to pursue equity and social justice, all while guiding me on how to design computer labs to be safe and inviting spaces for historically invisible communities. Because of him, I am, and so is this book.

I

History on Repeat

Opportunity for all requires something else today: having access to a computer and knowing how to use it. That means we must close the digital divide between those who've got these tools and those who don't.

—President Bill Clinton,
State of the Union Address,
January 27, 2000

1

The Digitally Invisible

Heavy snowfall rarely intimidates people living in Chicago, especially when winter pushes into the month of February. But on this night in the late 1990s, the temperatures dropped as fast as snowflakes and expedited my cleanup of the 800-square-foot, first-floor computer lab at the Northwest Tower Apartments. The lone high-rise building overlooked the city's downtown with the Dan Ryan Expressway, or I-94, drawing a hard line between two very different communities. One is known as the city's downtown area, with its corporate buildings and exclusive shops. On the other side of the expressway was the Northwest Tower Apartments in a predominantly working-class, heavily Latino neighborhood with sprinklings of locally owned businesses. The residents of the apartments were the exception to the community's demographics. They were all Black people living in one of Chicago's many affordable housing developments.

I was introduced to the Northwest Tower's computer lab by a man named Don Samuelson, a white gentleman in his early sixties known for wearing a tightly wrapped trenchcoat and thin-rimmed glasses that were always glued tightly behind both of his ears. He owned the property management company that maintained the Northwest Tower Apartments, which was one of several federally assisted buildings in his portfolio.

In the 1990s, I was as a graduate student at Northwestern University, whose campus was nestled in the affluent suburb of Evanston, Illinois, just 30 minutes north of the computer lab. A few months before that wintry February night, Don was on campus to meet with one of my professors and talked fervently about his idea to bring "neighborhood networks" to low-income housing developments that offered free internet access and computers. During the meeting, I took notes for my professor, and immediately after followed Don to the parking lot, where we talked for a couple hours about what he shared. He established a computer lab at the Northwest Tower Apartments not too far from downtown Chicago, and asked if I would volunteer. I agreed, and I showed up the very next day to a first-floor room that appeared to be a former walk-in utility closet—a visual that stood in stark contradiction to what Don had described in our conversation. There were no staff, only four refurbished computers and a broken utility table in the middle of some collapsed cubicles.

Over the next four months, I kept showing up—three to four times per week, to be exact—until the Northwest Tower's resident board voted me in as the lab's first official director, a position that came without a salary. For reasons unknown to me, they were not renewing Don's contract, but desired to keep the computer lab open. Being the lab's first official director was exciting, and mandated additional responsibilities beyond those of a volunteer, like opening and closing the lab at the same time daily, with shortened hours on Saturday (we were closed on Sunday). I was also responsible for the upkeep of the four barely operable computers and software, even though that was outside the range of my experience. On top of that, my income was far lower than Don's, as a nearly impoverished graduate student who lived off a monthly student stipend. But that did not stop me from using my personal credit cards to purchase ten new Gateway 386 personal computers (PCs) and a new Hewlett Packard desk jet printer without an extended warranty because it exceeded what was available to spend.

I vividly recall the day when the Gateway PC boxes, with their trademarked black paw prints stamped all over them, arrived at the first-floor security desk of the building. A group of residents, including the teens, helped to bring them in two at a time due to the room's size, where we proceeded to connect the new PCs to the older computer monitors, discard the open boxes, and then repeat the process for the next two until they were all installed. In fact, the entire building was elated on the day that the computers arrived; residents peeked into the lab on their way to the elevator and shared smiles with the group of us who hauled in the units. The next morning, members of the resident board had the custodian repaint the walls in the computer lab and replace the broken utility table with one from the basement storage closet to match the decor of the new equipment. The custodian also tightened the screws on the leaning cubicles.

However, the outdated computers were not the only problem that we encountered as we updated the space. The internet was running over a telephone line via an ethernet connection and was slow to the point of crawling—making the new computers like a brand new car on a road with many potholes. In the 1990s, households with limited incomes had no other choice but to rely on dial-up, modem access through plain old telephone service (POTS). Faster connections via digital subscriber lines (DSL), or the internet over the copper wires of telephone lines, were not available in the late 1990s to low-income communities, despite being available for subscription in wealthier ones—mirroring the redlines of the Dan Ryan Expressway that stood between Northwest Tower and the city's downtown.

It was not until the early 2000s that high-speed broadband networks entered the market to replace traditional dial-up services and, years later, DSL. Copper telephone lines and other fiber-optics for digital communications soon enabled what was called T1 lines, which were mainly used by businesses and government entities. Broadband powered by Asymmetric Digital Subscriber Services was a still relatively new technology, first launched by the British company Telewest, but when it was fully deployed became groundbreaking and easily outperformed traditional telephone services. That is because it ran over high-speed fiber connections, which meant that someone could be talking on the phone while simultaneously downloading data over the internet, especially movies or large data files.

For Northwest Tower residents, having DSL access was a much better alternative to the traditional telephone modem for connecting the new computers to the internet. Plus, we knew that high-speed broadband access was either not available in our community from the incumbent telephone companies, or was too expensive for what we could afford. But we somehow found out about a potential new entrant to the market. A start-up telecom company based in Milwaukee was leasing space on the building's roof to place its cellular satellite dishes, and it was preparing to launch a new DSL service in Chicago. During the meeting with their sales representative, the resident board and I asked to be this firm's first pilot location and negotiated an affordable monthly cost. Lab users immediately experienced the difference in how fast the new computers worked. Before high-speed broadband, DSL served the residents just fine, because they were able to seamlessly connect to first- and second-generation online search engines like Mozilla and Firefox before Google dominated the market.

Five months after I became the lab director, the hardware and service upgrades motivated the residents and me to aspire to even bigger dreams for our center, which led to a "wish list" that was handwritten, bulleted on a big posterboard sheet, and hung on one of the four walls. If we ever had money, the residents desired new computer monitors, general office supplies (e.g., paper clips, paper, and ink), and a new Macintosh computer to support a Hip Hop station for aspiring rappers, music producers, and songwriters. We, and especially me, also wanted paid staff. At this point, the residents had given me a nickname—the "computer lady"—because of the numerous hours spent at the lab daily.

In many ways, our wish list was how we honored Don's vision for an established neighborhood network program, which the U.S. Department of Housing and Urban Development (HUD) formally established a year or so later in 1995 under President Bill Clinton's administration. The new Neighborhood Networks program encouraged property owners and managers of HUD, and of the Federal Housing Administration's insured and assisted communities, to open on-site technology centers for promoting self-sufficiency among residents. The Northwest Tower computer lab was recognized as one with a formal certificate a few months later, and the residents and I stayed hopeful that someday HUD would provide the financial resources for us to fulfill our posted wish list. We just did not know when.

Kiahna's Story

I regularly came to the computer lab almost daily, especially after the hardware and internet upgrades, which is why I was still there on that very snowy February night sometime in the late 1990s. Earlier that day, I had taught three separate computer courses to adults: "Learning the Basics of Microsoft Office," "Getting an Email Address," and "Résumé Writing." When school was dismissed earlier in the afternoon, dozens of K-12 students stormed into the lab for homework help and online entertainment. Everyone had finally left the lab, and I was anxious to be next, especially as the weather conditions worsened.

But not too long after I buttoned up my heavy coat, put on my hat and gloves, and turned off the entrance light, Kiahna, a middle school student, busted through the heavy metal door with her backpack straddled on one shoulder, and the boney top of the other one exposed as her coat hung limp on it.

"Miss Nicol, don't leave," she pleaded. "I have a paper due tomorrow for school, and I need help."

"Have you seen the weather outside? I need to get out of here before I get stranded on this side of town," was my response with my own backpack in a sturdy position on my shoulder.

"Miss Nicol, please, please don't tell me that you're leaving," she said, as she plopped her heavy backpack on one of the tables that I had just cleaned, forcing me to switch the light back on. "I have a research paper for school and need to use the computer to turn it in tomorrow."

Like the other students who regularly hung out at the lab, Kiahna had a way of getting what she wanted from me. Her wide, teethy smile set against her caramel complexion was always disarming, and I was generally known by the kids as being a general pushover, especially when they called me "Miss Nicol" despite my not being that much older than them.

Throughout the months, many other students exhibited last-minute desperation to complete their homework. Kiahna was no different. Our students knew we had the resources in the computer lab to get the job done. HUD's regional office had recently donated a half-dozen donated Microsoft Encarta CDs that were the digital version of printed encyclopedias. The large sets of same-colored, hardback books were only available in libraries or at schools if you could not afford a set at home. Growing up Black and middle class, my mother, who was a junior high school teacher, made sure that we had a full set of them on the bookcase in the living room, which made doing homework both easier and void of excuses in our household.

It was 9 o'clock that night, and Kiahna knew that getting to the library was not an option, and she was pressed to present to her teacher a typed research paper using the new computers and printer in the lab. While I was totally supportive, she did not realize that I had my own school deadline, including an annotated outline due to my department chair first thing in the morning. But that did not stop me from taking off my outer garments and powering up one of the ten new workstations, and the printer. The "computer lady" was back in action.

Around midnight, Kiahna typed the last sentence on the keyboard and printed her final paper. She jammed it into her heavy backpack and bolted out the same heavy metal door that she barged into a few hours ago, and she headed to the elevator to make it upstairs to her grandmother's apartment, who was a long-time resident of the building.

"You going to be OK going up by yourself?" I asked her as I resuited up while holding open the door of the lab.

"Yes, my grandma knows that I was down here," she said, with a huge smile on her face. "Thanks, Miss Nicol." Grandma knew like the other adults in the building that the computer lab was a safe space where the kids in the building regularly congregated.

Soon, she disappeared on the elevator, and later in the week finally popped her head through the heavy door of the computer lab to announce that she had received a "B" on the paper. She also warned me about another big assignment due next week, to which I urged her to come in earlier because I was exhausted the next day. What she did not know was that it did take an hour and a half to make it back to campus in the snow, and I stayed up another two hours to finish the outline for my professor.

The night that I spent with Kiahna was a glimpse into how my life was organized in the late 1990s. Graduate school classes came during the day, followed by computer courses and tutorial assistance for students seeking homework help. Five to six months after stepping into the Northwest Tower computer lab quickly turned into two years, which did not feel burdensome at all, as the resident board and building residents befriended me and exhibited care for an impoverished graduate student through prepared meals every now and then, and shared wisdom about their city with a transplanted New Yorker with no immediate family members nearby.

Two years into my role, the resident board surprised me by reimbursing previous computer purchases, which was timely, as some of my credit cards were prepared for legal action for nonpayment. Leftover monies from an expiring HUD Drug Elimination grant were approved for the disbursements and extended to the items on our wish list, which lay crinkled and yellowed on the wall. We purchased new monitors, and we finally built the soundproof Hip Hop station in a very small closet in the first-floor space. George Gilmore, HUD's regional director at the time, later found more resources and partnerships for software and programming for us. He was another man whom I quickly admired on this journey because he cared about our small computer lab.

The Early 2000s

In 1993, during the Clinton administration, HUD signed a memorandum with the U.S. Corporation for National Service to deploy paid members of its AmeriCorps Volunteer in Service to America (VISTA) program to multifamily housing. Eligible paid volunteers could work in HUD Neighborhood Networks like ours, and, later, community technology centers, when Clinton enacted and expanded the National and Community Service Trust Act of 1993.[1] Not since Clinton has the Corporation for National Service received such attention and funding to expand its reach into local communities, either urban or rural, while establishing financial and education incentives for participants. As part of their service, AmeriCorps VISTA members received a nominal stipend for one year of service to nonprofits, gained eligibility to apply for federal jobs, and received some monies to be allocated to educational expenses.

Our lab secured an Americorps VISTA member, whose name was Simeon. He was a graduate student from Romania studying at the University of Illinois–Chicago, who spoke very little English and had his first baby on the way. Simeon came every day during the week for about three to four hours, and quickly learned that he was probably the first European-born person that building residents had ever met or seen. But he soon gained his stripes working at an inner-city computer lab after being playfully locked out of the room multiple times or trapped in the adjacent bathroom by the rowdier young people in the building—especially on days when I was not there. When Simeon finally caught on to their antics, he threatened to expel them from using the lab after school, which was not what they wanted to hear because this was, indeed, the place to be for building residents of all ages.

Starting in the late 1990s and going into the early 2000s, the internet became an essential resource for adults looking for work. Beverly, a resident, had lived there for several decades with her two middle school boys, and was a regular student in the lab's computer courses, especially after her case worker told her that she needed to go online to recertify her housing benefit and show proof of searching for a job. In 1996, Clinton signed the "Welfare to Work" bill during his first term that required adults on public assistance to either be actively looking for a job two years after receiving benefits or be enrolled in some type of training course. Program participants had to regularly update their activities with their case managers on a weekly basis. During the day, when the lab was relatively quiet because the young people were at school, Beverly sat glued to her favorite PC, and waited for a dozen or so emails to trickle into her inbox after the screeching connection of the computer modem to the internet, and the loud greeting from the portal that announced "You've Got Mail."

When Jobs Went Online

Beverly and other adult residents in the building started to struggle when the classified sections in newspapers shrank—seemingly in a period when the internet was becoming more commercialized. That required Simeon and me to change the focus and direction of our courses from teaching basic digital literacy skills like learning how to turn on a computer or acquiring an email address to showing people how to create résumés and apply for jobs online, as well as instructional modules on navigating government websites for public benefits. Of course, our new content resulted in a significant increase in lab usage by adult residents, and by others from the surrounding community who had heard about the classes.

In 2000, 25.5 percent of unemployed job seekers looked for a job online, compared with 76.3 percent of job seekers in 2011.[2] Conclusions from a national minority broadband adoption study that I later coauthored in 2010 at the Joint Center for Political and Economic Studies found that African Americans who earned less than $20,000 were more likely to go online in search of job opportunities, at 92 percent, and those without a job (87 percent) were equally dependent on the internet in the late 2000s to find some type of employment.[3] People highly dependent on the internet tended to be those without an undergraduate or graduate degree, and that number has steadily increased as more job postings migrated from print to online media.

While Beverly and other adult residents were in a mad dash to get online for these activities, if they could not find anything they were qualified for or was worth applying to, they took one of the courses at the lab to comply with the work mandates and quiet the annoyances of case workers, and other social service providers, that sometimes came to the building at least twice a week.

However, online job applications were not the easiest to complete for adults with low literacy skills or limited digital literacy. For example, Beverly could not read, despite spending hours in the lab searching for jobs and purchasing things off websites—which she did through her memory of the graphics and branding associated with certain companies. She also relied on Simeon, who spent a significant amount of one-to-one time with her, and later her two boys, who stayed when the time dedicated to homework help ended.

Beverly was not alone. We had others who required more attention, and sometimes it was due to the accessibility of the applications, including font size, the specificity of online questions, and the like.

When Simeon's Americorps VISTA year ended, we were all saddened because not only was he a committed instructor and tutor but he was also a trusted friend to many residents at the lab, and me. In addition to his instructor role, he helped residents with job searches, offered insight into the robust resources of the World Wide Web, and took the time to teach the seniors some of the words from his native language. The AmeriCorps VISTA program's partnership with HUD also completed, but fortunately we secured support for very nominal stipends from other grants provided from the Commerce Department of the State of Illinois that were starting to add resources around Clinton's newly funded policy efforts to close the digital divide for low-income populations. One of the residents whom I hired was a very tall, like NBA-draftable height, young man named Vincent, who had recently graduated from Xavier University in Louisiana. He grew up in the building and returned to Chicago for work. Despite some of the residents still judging him on his past activities at the building (which some referred to as "poor choices"), his accomplishment of becoming a college graduate made other residents proud, including me, which is why I hired him. His younger brother, who at the time was in middle school, was also one of my most reliable and trusted students. He often stayed late to help with cleaning while most of the other kids, including Kiahna, ran to the local playground. Hiring Vince was a dream come true for me because the demand for center resources increased after Simeon's departure, especially among adults.

More of them were enrolling in the courses and using the resources for job searches and applications. I will never forget the September 11, 2001, terrorist attacks on the United States, for a variety of reasons. I got married to my first husband a mere four days after the attack on New York's World Trade Center. Despite producing two wonderful children in that marriage, I should have known then that it was not going to last, due to more than half of the guests not showing up because of airport lockdowns and primal fears. Beyond my own recollection, the date of 9/11/2001 was one of the many saddest periods in U.S. history, when terrorists in broad daylight intentionally attacked New York City's World Trade Center, and the Pentagon in Washington. In Pennsylvania, courageous passengers subdued the terrorists on assignment and took down the plane in a deserted field to stop a day of pure evil. With the younger George W. Bush just months into his first term, his administration swiftly created the Transportation Security Administration (TSA), which created new jobs for workers without college degrees. Enacted during the 107th Congress, the TSA was directed to protect the nation's airports with uniformed officers who examined passengers and luggage for prohibited materials, and screened travelers against lists of those deemed national security threats. An individual only needed a high school diploma or

GED, and the pay, as well as benefits associated with civil service work, were intriguing to Northwest Tower residents, who flooded the lab to apply. There were two ways to submit your résumé—going to a job fair at the airport, which was a hike on public transportation, or going online to the hiring portal to submit an application.

The TSA jobs were perhaps the first and largest migration of viable work opportunities to the internet, as well as the first major disruption to low-income communities, who for the most part did not have technology access—let alone the resources of public computer labs except for local public libraries. A few months earlier, the residents and I were joyous at our newly equipped computer lab with new PCs and printers. During this period, residents had a lot of anxiety and skepticism about what it took to apply. That is, we were becoming weary of a technology that was more difficult to understand and navigate for essential activities, like finding and securing a job. Even credentials that included Microsoft Office certification were becoming preferred and required by employers of low-skilled workers, who needed everyone to understand how to use a computer and the internet. Around this time is probably when certain communities started to be erased by new technologies.

The Homework Gap

Government public benefits (e.g., food stamps, public housing and Section 8, energy assistance programs, and Medicaid) also began transitioning to online portals, which also exacerbated the limitations that many residents felt at the time. This was happening before federal, state, and local policymakers were talking about open government—an area that I later researched with colleagues in 2011, when it was found to be less participatory and accessible to low-income populations.[4]

Kiahna's need to use the computer lab for homework help predated the concept of "the homework gap." Jessica Rosenworcel, then an appointed commissioner to the Federal Communications Commission, who was grappling with the digital divide, emphasized the importance of the internet for education in 2015. Around that time, some members in the U.S. Senate were hoping to advance the Digital Learning Equity Act to increase resources in classrooms for innovative learning, and to bring more internet services to nontraditional anchor institutions, including local affiliates of the Boys and Girls Clubs, and park centers that were not covered by the existing E-Rate program. This federal program funded schools and libraries to ramp up their internet services and online resources. In a press statement supporting the act almost a decade after I met the students at Northwest Tower, Commissioner Rosenworcel shared: "The homework gap is the cruelest part of the digital divide. Today, too many students are unable to complete their school assignments because they do not have Internet access at home."[5]

In 2022, Rosenworcel was appointed the FCC chair by President Joe Biden. She has not strayed from her early mission to close the homework gap, and has worked diligently as an advocate for vulnerable populations, including those from indigenous tribal communities.

The New Digital Normal

It is safe to say that in the early to mid-2000s, the growing dependence on the internet forced people like Beverly and Kiahna into compliance with a new norm of online versus in-line communications. Early on, there was—and continues to be—a belief that technology lowers the barrier for more vulnerable populations. But the digital transitions that Beverly and Kiahna experienced ran somewhat counter to this idea. It was starting to become more difficult for low-income populations and their communities to get online for critical services. My former boss, Rey Ramsey, who cofounded One Economy, one of the most effective nonprofits addressing the digital divide back then, always used to say that it was society's responsibility to ensure that no one is left offline. In 2006, One Economy launched the Public Internet Channel, which was designed to be a website with English and Spanish language content that shared geographic information on safety/emergency services, education, health, financial services, and civic engagement.[6] The cochairs for the new online channel were former U.S. senators John McCain and Barack Obama. This was before they ran against each other for president.[7]

The Importance of Universal Access

Here is where a conversation about universal access to communications seems most appropriate—one that should have happened as the internet became the conduit for essential services even before the 1990s. But how different administrations handled this issue of universal access is important to discuss, especially because public policies were guided by their politics. While former president Reagan, a Republican, made traditional telephone services more widely available and affordable to eligible consumers as the fortieth president, the forty-first, elder George H. Bush, and another Republican, did very little in telecommunications policy to benefit constituents during his term. His administration was largely known for his veto of the 1992 Cable Act, which required that cable operators carry local broadcast stations without charge and allowed the latter to collect retransmission fees on aired content.[8] From 1989 to 1993, Al Sikes was the chairman of the FCC under Bush, and he told *Politico* in an interview that "we were an all-analog world except for the computer sector."[9] And given this, the elder Bush administration focused more on the backhaul and backroom deals with the private sector and various government agencies to make computing faster and more robust, while

continuing Reagan's light-touch, regulatory approach that seeded the early innovations in communications services.

Despite his later focus on the digital divide, in his first term, President Bill
Clinton also took aim on the media ownership rules initiated under Bush and
signed into law the Telecommunications Act of 1996—the first major update
since its constitution in 1934, when the telegraph was created. The updated
Telecom Act not only deregulated the cable television industry but also allowed
local telephone companies to provide cable services, required v-chips in TVs
to enable parental blocking, increased the number of TV stations broadcasters
could own, and banned the transmission of indecent content to minors on the
internet, which later became known as the Communication Decency Act.

Unfortunately, the outcomes of the act's rewriting led to massive media consolidation, cross-ownership of media outlets that furthered media conglomerates,
and challenged First Amendment liberties, setting off a range of constitutional
battles over what constituted inappropriate and obscene materials. When it was
over, the Telecommunications Act of 1996 significantly changed the existing
marketplace. In addition to formally establishing the Universal Service Fund (USF)
at the FCC, it set forth rules that increased competition among telephone
companies, which was not well received by the Baby Bells that were part of
an earlier mandated divestiture from AT&T in the 1980s. Under the Telecom
Act, they could enter the long-distance market if they opened their networks to
internet service providers (ISPs), competitive local exchange companies (CLECs),
and companies offering DSL and other local and long-distance telephone services.
That was how the Northwest Tower residents and I were able to access DSL services
from a smaller and less-known provider. Clinton's rules espousing greater competition rules came to a screeching halt under the younger Bush's presidency in the
early 2000s, and many of his policies were reversed at the start of his term.

But the Clinton-Gore administration did much more than the first Telecom Act
update; it deepened the focus on the national digital divide, and appropriated funds
to address disparities early its their first term. Again, this was around the time when
Larry Irving became the assistant secretary of the National Telecommunications
and Information Administration (NTIA) in the 1990s, and when he officially coined
the term "digital divide."[10] Some more to say about my friend Larry before he
took the position. He had worked for the late Texas U.S. representative Mickey
Leland, who was known for being an antipoverty advocate. Both Leland and the
late commerce secretary, Ron Brown, for whom Larry first worked, were killed
in a tragic airplane crash while on official business. In the early part of his first
term, Clinton directed his Cabinet and agency secretaries to take on the issue
in their programmatic and funding efforts—starting with the NTIA, which
was an agency originally conceived by President Richard Nixon as the Office of
Telecommunications Policy in 1970 before President Jimmy Carter renamed it.
Irving, because of his mentors, was perhaps the best person to work on this,
alongside B. K. Fulton, another leading strategist.

The NTIA began defining and quantifying the problem of the digital divide through longitudinal indicators and measurements that would report out the status of the digital disparities in a series of white papers issued by the agency. One of the many white papers published over the next five years provided the first new empirical data on internet and device use, along the lines of a binary definition of the issue. One paper specifically called out the problem: "For many groups, the digital divide has widened as the information 'haves' outpace the 'have nots' in gaining access to electronic resources."[11]

Together and separately, the NTIA reports established that demographic differences in wealth, education, race, household type, and geography were main indicators of the lack of access to computers and computer modems, which was how internet access was measured at the time. In the late 1990s and early 2000s, the digital divide was measured by one's access to telephones (for dial-up), PCs, and the internet. Getting online was determined by the quality of and access to telephone modems that enabled data communications over voice services, including POTS, DSL, and T1 modems that ran over fiber-optic or high-scaled copper wires, which were often reserved for businesses with greater bandwidth needs. All three data services were considered part of the dial-up sphere and were not cheap to engage because local and long-distance calling services were subjected to metered pricing, or cost per minute. At that time, YouTube video services, Facebook/Meta social media networks, and Google were either nonexistent or were in the very early stages of development.

On top of the emerging empirical research, the Clinton administration created and funded channels for digital literacy programs back in the early 2000s. First, he developed the HUD Neighborhood Networks program, and later established support for community technology centers in low-income neighborhoods. After expanding the services at the Northwest Tower computer lab, I redirected more of my time into the development and management of community technology centers, where I met so many enthusiastic and hardworking leaders and community experts, who became part of a larger national movement to accelerate technology access and relatable tools for local people where they lived.

In February 2000, the federal initiative to increase access to the internet, connected devices, deployment of high-speed networks, digital literacy, and expanded online content was led by Vice President Al Gore. The former administration also set forth $2 billion in tax incentives to generate private sector involvement in computer refurbishing and other programs and allocated $380 million in new and expanded public-private partnerships.[12] They also directed funds to the E-Rate program, which had special mention in the Telecommunications Act of 1996 to provide funding to schools and libraries.

By 2001, the issue's attention and new funding enabled me to start my second computer lab—the Homan Square Community Technology Center, which was part of a community redevelopment plan spearheaded by the late real estate mogul and philanthropist Charles Shaw, in collaboration the City of Chicago, private investors, and other funding sources. The Homan Square redevelopment plan was a critical next step for the North Lawndale community on the city's West Side. With high rates of returning ex-offenders to the community, and the lack of robust educational and employment resources, the community was ripe for a refreshed economic strategy. Dating back to 1988, when Eugene Sawyer was in office as Chicago's mayor, Charlie pitched the Homan Square redevelopment project to revitalize North Lawndale and targeted the long-vacated, original Sears Roebuck catalog headquarters. Realtor Shaw, whose landmark work was the first high-rise condominium at Navy Pier, wanted to repurpose the area to house a community center with a city-run park district, high school, and affordable housing—ideas that were soon embraced and executed with the help of the next mayor, Richard M. Daley, and Congressman Danny Davis, who represented Illinois' Seventh District and had his office down the street from the abandoned lot.

While I was working at Northwest Tower, Charlie's development team approached me to build and manage the computer lab in the new community center, which was uniquely timed around the same time of increasing federal and state investments in technology. With a $100,000 grant from Shaw and his partners, we built a slightly larger space than the Northwest Tower computer lab (about 1,000 square feet) in a small corner of the massive new construction and equipped the lab with Citrix mainframe computers to lower the costs of equipment and maintenance. These "dummy terminals" allowed us to essentially load all types of software from tax preparation programs, certified computer training, and homework help on one main server in the lab's closet that turned out to be both innovative and cheaper for us as a nonprofit.

During the ribbon cutting ceremony for the opening of the new facility, which took place on December 15, 2001, just months after 9/11, my second computer lab was up and running—this time serving the predominantly Black community of Chicago's West Side. Another difference: I had traded in the moniker "computer lady" for "beauty shop queen" because when you entered the Homan Square Technology Center, you were welcomed by comfortable chairs for friendly conversations and fiery debates in the foyer before venturing to one of the more than twenty Citrix computer terminals, monitors, and two printers with warranties. I still did not take a salary at the new Homan Square lab. Here, we also had the money to finally hire staff, like Roger, who was a former owner of a small telephone beeper shop in the community who later helped us design and launch the first wireless community network that propagated at a location in the community center and gave free internet to those within a ten-block radius of the building. Many others were part of the journey, including Jillian from Alabama, who was a college student at the University of Chicago and became our work-study employee and taught adult computer courses; and Abigail, or

Abby for short, from Bucknell College, who later managed the administration of grants to the center, with the assistance of Kathy, who grew up in North Lawndale and was both the office manager and glue for our small-scale operations, as she managed sign in-sheets and other data entry responsibilities. She also stayed behind on many evenings, including those when I was navigating between Northwest Tower and here.

The 2000s were ripe with resources for community-based organizations to build and manage local computer labs, which had far exceeded the initial support we received from HUD, and Mr. George Gilmore. In fact, we quickly took advantage of the plethora of grants and other resources for staff, equipment, and software donations, and other things that we simply could not afford to buy.

As the mid-2000s approached, I went on to build additional labs with a group of friends and colleagues where we later focused on getting more adults the training that they needed to stay competitive and employable in an increasingly digital world, which was the focus of our third and largest computer lab, at the Charles A. Hayes Center, which was named after a famous Black labor activist from the South Side. Funded by the Chicago Housing Authority, the goal of that center was to prepare residents from the city's public housing developments with transferable computer and interpersonal skills before their homes were demolished and replaced by new mixed-income developments with much stricter work requirements. One of the last computer labs that I ever built, which I think was the fifth center, was in the south suburb of Rosemont, Illinois, which was about 30 to 45 minutes away from the city. There, I met the second-term Congresswoman Robin Kelly, who worked with the city's manager before she became the first Black women to serve as chief of staff to the Illinois state treasurer, and soon after a member of the Illinois House of Representatives, before coming to Washington.

Back then, the Clinton-Gore administration had a grand plan to accelerate technology access to stave off activities that were quickly restricting their full participation in our twenty-first-century economy. But that was until the money ran out, and newly elected policymakers shifted the focus to capital investments in infrastructure—a feat in which the federal government did not directly partake, but rather cleared the path for deregulation.

The Near to Final Death of Analog

As the backdrop for the transformative abilities of digital technologies, traditional analog communications were slowly being picked off. The Merriam-Webster dictionary defines "analog as" "a mechanism or device in which information is represented by continuously variable physical quantities." The key word in this definition is the word "physical," meaning that which we can see or touch is primarily available in analog properties, like a physical record player whose needle requires contact with the surface on vinyl media to play, or photocopiers that need pieces of paper or other physical media to be placed on large glass screens or inserted into paper feeders for duplication, or facsimile transmission.

In communications, analog relies on POTs to send and receive electrical frequencies to transmit voice calls or, later, data. In the 1990s, telephone service and use were the norm, not the exception. In fact, I still to this day remember my family's phone number as "NE6-2437," which was punched into the numbers found on physically held or stationary rotary phones.

Traditional analog was siphoned off by technological innovation over the decades. In the music industry, vinyl records replaced cassette tapes, before saved digital media on pressed CD-ROMs and later DVDs were wedged out by digital music recorders, like the iPod that curated and stored clips in cloud processing systems instead of on physical plastic discs. Today, and honestly for right now, music streaming platforms, like Spotify and Apple Music, rely on none of the previous media, and instead enable music to be played across a variety of internet- and Bluetooth-enabled devices, from voice-controlled Alexa devices to smartphones and stand-alone speakers.

Compared with the rapid and ongoing digital disruption in the music industry, the death of POTS took longer, and in some places is currently on life support, as more incumbent telephone companies have not been able to fully retire their copper services, especially in some very rural areas. In the late 1990s, competition from Voice over Internet Protocol (VOIP) did try to disrupt the voice communications market by using basic internet connections for phone calls. President Clinton appointed William Kennard as his new chair of the FCC to investigate the start of internet-enabled platforms, services, and devices. During his term, Kennard invoked a "first, do no harm" approach to the internet's evolution, and encouraged a more deregulatory approach to motivate private investments in emerging technologies and networks, which is why the Clinton-Gore period was known for its early efforts to commercialize the internet.

But such advancements toward more digitized services and platforms were actually widening disparities for those who could not easily get online. In particular, the patrons of my computer labs soon realized that not being versed in a new technology later determined the quality of their lives in employment, education, health care, and civic engagement. Despite the fact that many building residents were still heavily dependent on their rotary phones with large and small buttons, more government services were migrating online than in earlier times, which made the workloads at the community technology centers very urgent, and forced staff to be more creative, especially as the resources under Clinton were dwindling as the gavel was being turned over to President George W. Bush.

What Policymakers Soon Figured Out About the Digital Divide

When President Bush pressed beyond the aftermath of 9/11, he shifted the focus from the digital divide to large-scale networks to distinguish the country's global competitiveness. The Bush-Cheney administration also pierced the legacies of analog technologies with the congressionally mandated Digital TV (DTV) transition that directed a quick turn-off of analog systems in favor of digital-only transmissions for television. Appointed by Clinton as an FCC commissioner, and then elevated to the role of chair by Bush, Michael K. Powell, the son of the late distinguished general Colin Powell, led the DTV transition, and facilitated the free market growth of the internet—a process begun by his Democratic predecessor as chair, William Kennard.

The Bush-Cheney administration also took on the Lifeline program, and almost two decades after the first change to the program in 2005, it apportioned the program funds to cover prepaid, wireless benefits, which again confirms that this was not the "Obamaphone" that Republicans have professed over the years.

Because the DTV transition took more than eleven years to complete, President Barack Obama had to be the one to finish the job; and once again, as any good Democrat would do, he returned to the digital divide issue—this time through his administration's ConnectAll initiative, which was a national promise to provide 99 percent of the nation's schools and libraries with high-speed broadband. Obama also pivoted back to making telecommunications policies front and center for the White House, in his fervent desire to guide the direction of existing and long-standing debates on internet control and governance, or what became internationally known as net neutrality, which will be more thoughtfully discussed in the concluding chapters of the book.

Obama's two terms as president also codified him as the first social media president, due to his usage of Facebook and Twitter in his campaigning and engagement with the public. But while he went to the internet to talk to the masses, millions could not hear him due to their lack of basic access and the affordability of that access. That is, there was still a digital divide—one that was further widened by the dearth of analog options to conduct critical and essential activities and business, and one that was somewhat unrelated to dogmatic concerns about internet control, or net neutrality, that consumed most of the time in office of the Obama-Biden White House, and was inherited by a new FCC leader, Tom Wheeler—who is now my colleague at the Brookings Institution.

When Donald J. Trump took office as the forty-fifth president of the United States, he followed Obama's increased social media use (despite not adhering to the archival rules set forth by the National Library of Congress for his tweets), and he utilized social media for just about everything, from advancing his own political agendas and personal vendettas, and furthering a polarized world based both on political beliefs and technology access. Weeks into his term, his appointed FCC chairman, Ajit Pai, who reversed the prior administration's net neutrality decisions, eliminated programs to advance digital equity and returned to most Republicans' view on digital access that networks should be built and expanded into rural areas where most of their constituents lived and voted.

Trump also countered Chinese 5G competition by denouncing China's global dominance of the supply chain and pulling out all Chinese equipment in telecommunications to reduce foreign spying and espionage, along with competition with American companies. He returned the tech and telecom sectors to deregulatory states, advanced mobile technologies by removing barriers to build out like local permitting, and created some of the most generous tax breaks for corporations, especially the tech sector—all while allowing for greater technological discovery among Big Tech companies that put profit over people.

Trump was perhaps the only U.S. president who experienced what the digital divide looked like in full view during a state of distress, when the COVID-19 pandemic forced millions of people online due to the early mandates for physical social distancing. But he failed to apply federal resources to the problem until it was too late; and when he did, those monies came through pandemic emergency relief programs that were not enough to minimize the great disruptions of not being connected to the internet for millions of Americans, including his own constituents.

By the time President Joe Biden was elected, the pandemic was still in high-gear, and thousands of insurrectionists and election deniers stormed the U.S. Capitol on that fateful day on January 6, 2022. The Biden-Harris administration was also presented with more powerful and wealthier Big Tech companies, which at the beginning of Biden's presidency made it more difficult to focus, especially as civilians came to rely on these companies for commerce, health care, public information, education, and other activities that normalized the circumstances of the pandemic.

In the early part of his term, Biden allocated millions of dollars through either an executive order or congressional enactment to a range of federal programs targeted to spur job creation, business development, and educational supports of laptops and internet service. In November 2021, he persuaded the divided 117th Congress to fund the largest Infrastructure Investment and Jobs Act, or the Bipartisan Infrastructure Law, of which broadband deployment and access constituted $64 billion of a $2 trillion budget to also repair and expand the nation's roads, bridges, water, and transportation systems. The act, as shared earlier in the book, was sold as the largest and latest New Deal program to restore the U.S. economy and start the process of building a more cohesive democracy. The Biden administration's broadband program, "Internet for All," is the largest federal appropriation toward high-speed broadband.

Here is more perspective on the comparisons in federal spending on digital inclusion efforts. In 2000, Clinton allocated a little under $3 billion toward digital access, particularly programming and established the first federal program to support digital access, the Technology Opportunity Program (TOP). In 2009, the Obama administration allocated $7.2 billion in resources for digital equity through the American Recovery and Reinvestment Act, which were divided three ways: for the creation of the first National Broadband Plan ($333 million), the reestablishment of the Broadband Technology Opportunities Program ($3.8 billion), and enabling the Rural Utilities Service ($3.3 billion) to expand broadband access.

By his third year in office, Biden had quadrupled every previous federal investment and added to the existing USF and other agency resources allocated to broadband infrastructure. As part of his Infrastructure Investment and Jobs Act, the Biden-Harris administration allocated $64 billion to high-speed broadband under the guise of the Internet for All program. The NTIA was given $45.2 billion, which was divided in an 80/20 split. Eighty percent of the dollars went to states and localities to build out of fiber-optic networks in unserved and underserved communities under what is called the Broadband Equity, Access, and Deployment (BEAD) Program, and 20 percent (if not closer to 15 percent) allocated through the Digital Equity Act programs to promote equity and inclusion in local broadband communities. Of the $45.2 billion, $2.7 billion was appropriated for digital equity, as mentioned in the preface.

While unprecedented broadband investment in infrastructure went to states, localities, and Tribal lands to expand and build new fiber infrastructure in unconnected and underconnected communities, the United States did not have a sufficient and accurate map of where existing broadband assets already were, despite the prior congressional charge to the FCC to do so. Congress gave the FCC until January 2023 to issue updated maps, given that the formula for the state distributions were being made from the data found on the broadband maps. When the deadline came, the broadband maps though still not fully complete, were shared with some advocacy organizations arguing that the lack of census-level data foreclosed on highly disadvantaged communities, some of which were unserved by competitive broadband options. Some of these same groups also found the maps to be void of listings of community assets, like the anchor institutions that were primarily used by students and residents to get online during the pandemic. What was also missing from the maps was public and affordable housing.

Since the Biden-Harris administration also wanted to ensure that all states and localities received some portion of funding toward the expansion and creation of high-speed broadband networks, it was also not considered that some of these states' governors were not attuned to the task at hand after many decades of internet neglect, and for states with densely populated urban areas, a fiber-only statutory requirement was not going to solve their digital equity challenges, primarily because a large majority of their residents were mobile dependent to get online.[13] Some could argue that the preference for fiber-optic deployments was in line with the administration's nostalgic references to electrification—where the conduit was the major focus. I will say more about this toward the end of the book.

Under the Biden-Harris administration, similar competitive capital investments and programs targeted to infrastructure were led and appropriated out of the U.S. Treasury Department, the U.S. Department of Agriculture, the FCC, and other broadband programs at the NTIA—all at the same time. Combined, these investments were, in theory, more than enough to close the digital divide, as the Biden-Harris administration professed. Vice President Kamala Harris shepherded this portion of the Infrastructure Investment and Jobs Act, alongside U.S. commerce secretary Gina Raimondo and NTIA assistant secretary Alan Davidson, to meet the five-year period to deploy the trillions of dollars in BEAD monies, starting with initial draws to the states starting in the summer of 2023, was historically different from previous administrations.

The Internet for All program's other heavily invested program was the $14 billion Affordable Connectivity Program (ACP), which was an extension of the pandemic relief for families struggling to get and stay connected to the internet and was under the purview of the FCC. During the public health crisis, the Emergency Broadband Benefit (EBB) offered to eligible individuals enrolled in existing social service programs—like SNAP, veterans, and households of students on free and reduced-price lunch—a $50 discount toward monthly broadband service, and a one-time $100 subsidy to purchase of an internet-enabled device. The EBB was supported through an approved $3.2 billion in federal appropriations as part of the American Rescue Plan.[14] When it rolled out in May 2020, the Universal Service Administrative Company, which is responsible for USF, reported that over 4 million eligible consumers had claimed the benefit, including households with school-age children eligible for a free or reduced-price lunch. In addition to the EBB, there was also the $7.17 billion Emergency Connectivity Fund, which was also passed as part of the American Rescue Plan to help schools and libraries acquire Wi-Fi hot spots, modems, routers, and internet-enabled devices for students, staff, and library patrons.[15]

When the bipartisan infrastructure law was enacted in early 2022, the EBB program transitioned to the ACP, with the monthly service benefit reduced to $30. By the beginning of 2023, more than 15 million people had enrolled in the program and were receiving benefits, and that number was nearly 20 million by the beginning of June 2023, and has grown exponentially since its inception.

Because the midterm elections ushered in a Republican majority in the House of Representatives in 2023, who have historically rebuffed any type of social support programs, the ACP and infrastructure spending have been under attack. They have already hosted a series of congressional hearings on the oversight of public infrastructure dollars,[16] and the capacity of the NTIA and FCC to manage such large appropriations. On top of these interrogations, the ACP is set to either expire at the end of 2024 or when the funds run out (which could be in April 2024), with limited likelihood for reauthorization by the current House majority unless the White House directly intervenes. In October 2023, it pushed Congress for an additional $6 billion to keep the program afloat through December 2024, at a minimum. But it does not appear likely that the program will be permanent. In February 2024, the FCC froze all new enrollments as the program monies ran low. This is always one of the risks of making the digital divide about programs. It never gets seen as a critical part of America's DNA or a key factor of economic competitiveness.

Biden's infrastructure bill was and probably still is heavily dependent on the collaboration between the private sector, government and, when appropriate, civil society organizations, especially anchor institutions of schools and libraries to help accomplish the feat of closing the digital divide. As a result of the size of the federal appropriations, the NTIA has hired more staff and consultants in all fifty states, and in the District of Columbia and Puerto Rico. A new cadre of what I call "digital divide moguls," or heavily paid consultants, have helped states with their proposals for multiyear funding. Incumbent broadband service providers have awakened the giant of new subscribers as the companies driving low-cost, broadband programs like ACP with some ISPs become fully able to fund a household's internet service at its most basic tier with government support. Small and medium-sized fiber communications companies have tapped into BEAD money for new and expanded networks and are heavily invested in the ACP's permanence for new customers to support their capital-intensive endeavors.

Though the digital divide is extraordinary in its size, time will tell if President Biden can close it once and for all—particularly when the formula is still focused on a binary understanding of the issue, which leads with demand over supply, or networks over customers. In the 1970s, the sociologist and antipoverty researcher Michael Harrington coined the term "the Other America" as the focus of his transformative book that details the forgotten and invisible people in communities of underinvestment and underutilization, despite the nation's economic growth.[17] His most significant critique of antipoverty programs was that they were not necessarily designed and executed with wealth and economic self-sufficiency in mind. Rather, antipoverty programs served to preserve the status quo, and to keep people resigned to the corners of their communities through the most minimum of social safety net programs to keep them afloat. We call these interventions lifesavers that are returned at the end of a boating trip, or, in this context, when one administration decides to implode the progress of the other.

Of course, some naysayers have already called out Biden's herculean effort by suggesting the lack of transparency on just how much money was being spent on broadband infrastructure, his bet of investments on very expensive fiber technologies (the backbone of traditional telephony), or the glaring deficit in digital equity funding. All these could result in a not-so-perfect storm come the 2024 election or not, as states began to spend federal dollars.

Nevertheless, on June 26, 2023, the president, vice president, commerce secretary, and infrastructure czar all declared "Happy Broadband Day" as they announced an additional $42 billion in broadband spending.[18] This time, the monies were targeted to areas with poorly functioning broadband service or non-competitive options for subscriptions. Such additional spending was amplified during an event at the White House, where stories of rural communities without access dominated the discussion, along with a subsequent press release announcing that red states—including Texas, Alabama, and Mississippi—had gotten most of the BEAD funds. All this was before the Biden-Harris administration's team announced that they were hitting the campaign trail letting people know that they were getting the job done. With oversight over the agency with the most skin in the game, Secretary Raimondo started the event with these remarks: "Today, we're celebrating the biggest investment in broadband to help us finish the job and finally close the digital divide in our country once and for all." When Biden arrived on the stage, he pointed to Senator Joe Manchin (D-WV), who sat in the audience, and acknowledged him for being his close friend and the person who helped close the deals made in the Bipartisan Infrastructure Law.

A few things of note as the administration added to the coffer of existing infrastructure funds. Fiber is not technology-neutral, leaving low-income people in urban areas who are highly dependent on wireless or cable out of the picture. Funding fiber in rural areas may mean that the same people who have been disconnected before, during, and after the COVID-19 pandemic may remain in the dark when it comes to the upstream and downstream benefits of being online. Some broadband service providers may get even more rich, while others may find themselves bankrupt if they are unable to maintain and upgrade newly built networks. And what about emerging wireless technologies, like 5G, which promise to be gamechangers for communities of color, and are more likely to make the internet available on their phones than at a fixed location?

The Early Practices of and Lessons from the DTV Transition

When I think about the mix of federal investments and communications, I want to return to the DTV transition in the United States, where the switch from analog to digital services rewarded the innovators and their companies, and penalized people, who became consumers of color television sets largely made in China.

In 1996, Congress authorized the distribution of one additional broadcast channel to every full-power station to start the process of broadcasting digitally while slowly migrating from analog systems. Almost ten years later, in 2005, it passed the Digital Transition and Public Safety Act, which requested that the analog portion of public spectrum be vacated by April 7, 2009, for use by public safety departments; and out of the budget reconciliation bill from which the act was passed, billions were to be raised from federal spectrum auctions to support the Treasury in its funding of consumer education, subsidies for digital converter boxes, and interim public safety emergency communications during the transition, among other things. Congress gave the Bush administration's FCC the authority to transition the nation's broadcast infrastructure to only digital transmissions.[19] In fact, the date February 17, 2009, was set as the day when all television would be broadcasted digitally, leading the way for the evolution of TV, including High-Definition TV (HDTV), and national emergency communications.

The DTV transition was not cheap. More than $1.5 billion was earmarked to the NTIA to supply coupons to consumers to purchase $40 digital converter boxes from retail big box stores like Walmart and Best Buy.[20] This allowed 1.5 million coupons for consumers to be dispersed. At the time, Meredith Baker, now CEO of the country's largest commercial wireless association, was acting administrator at the NTIA and was leading the converter sales, as well as the spectrum reallocations from analog to digital services. FCC chairman Powell was responsible for a successful and effective transition process for millions of Americans, especially those soon to be left stranded by dinosaur analog systems. But as the process evolved, he, too, realized how messy it was, stating in an October 2011 press release: "The DTV transition is a massive and complex undertaking. Although I'm often asked what the FCC is going to do to 'fix' the DTV transition, I believe that a big part of the problem were the unrealistic expectations set by the 2006 target date for return of analog spectrum."[21] He ended up developing the new DTV Task Force, to help "re-examine the assumptions on which the Commission based its DTV policies and give us the ability to react and make necessary adjustments."[22]

When the original February deadline arrived, so too did the leadership return to the Democrats under President Barack Obama. He asked Congress for more time to meet the DTV transition deadline, which led to the date being set as June 12, 2009, to address the more than 6 million people that the Nielsen Company reported were not yet ready to make the switch. The DTV Delay Act in 2009 also came under the leadership of the new FCC chairman, Tom Wheeler, and NTIA assistant secretary Larry Strickling, who had to fix what the Democrats complained was a Republican debacle that did not give citizens sufficient time for preparation. During this period, the NTIA also ran out of funding for converter coupons or saw many of them expire without anticipation of the delay, which left the Obama administration with the additional challenge of finding more resources to make everything work.

But what is both interesting and enlightening about this period in our nation's history is that the people who were ill prepared then are the same people who are not connected to available and affordable technology access now. When the DTV transition was finally completed and in compliance of the June deadline, Nielsen reported that 2.9 million households were left in the dark, compared with the earlier figures of more than 6 million households, and they were primarily people of color from low-income communities, older Americans, and those from rural areas.[23]

In the end, the television industry evolved, and it created opportunities for new innovations in the space that have generally benefited consumers, the private sector, and government. For example, HDTV has led to more improved television technologies, including greater advancements in color pixelation qualities like 4K and soon-to-be 8K technologies, and enhanced abilities for the transmission of high-speed broadband connections for video streaming, which is the parallel invention of what we have seen for the music industry. The DTV transition also supported the evolution of emergency communications for public safety and establishing greater resiliency in national security threats to the nation's communications infrastructure since the 9/11 terrorist attacks on our soil.

If anything was learned from the DTV transition, it was that it was necessary for economic competitiveness in the global TV market and helped define the technical specifications for all TVs imported into the United States from other countries. This was a larger discussion couched within the debate over the concepts of "digitalism," and "digital convergence."[24] And despite the DTV transition leading to incompatible global standards, it was done and, at least in the very beginning, created manufacturing jobs that were mainly located in China— which is a shameful lesson that we should avoid repeating as robust broadband creates direct and indirect economic development opportunities.

Digital Access for Global Competitiveness

For current efforts to eradicate digital disparities to be effectively executed—where the switch is flipped off on digital disparities—they must be part of a national plan, and it is imperative that they position universal access as the central tentacle and intelligence of America's global economic competitiveness. Having the Internet for All program is important in theory, but what is even more compelling is ensuring that internet access provides financial stability and wealth to individuals and communities by giving everyday people avenues to equitable education, training, service, and productive growth in their own communities.

Recasting a new definition of the digital divide includes such aspirations and goes beyond a traditional understanding of it as related to the conflicting lifestyles between the "haves" and the "have nots" or the "privileged" and "underprivileged." All this construction does is reiterate what the sociologist Harrington referred to as those on the other side of society struggling to catch up to people with the resources needed to thrive in the twenty-first-century economy. Without both, a conversation and a narrative buster on how to motivate Americans to leverage digital resources to improve the quality of their lives, we will be relegating the nation's most vulnerable populations into more consumptive rather than productive roles in the digital ecosystem. These roles make equity unattainable and untenable, and exacerbate other forms of deception and exploitation.

Without a reversal in the social service framework in which we traditionally couch digital access issues, we continuously disadvantage America's ability to be a leading innovator in technology, and technology-adjacent occupations, products, and services. Here is where large-scale investments in broadband internet do not repair the existing traumas of how race, place, and space show up in scenarios of housing discrimination, education and health care disparities, gentrification, and the production of new and emerging technologies tend to be separate from innovation.

When I attended the White House briefing in June 2023 for that memorable press conference, I admittedly was shocked that most of the room was full of white men in tightly buttoned gray, black, and some noticeably tan suits who appeared to salivate at Biden adding $42 billion to the existing coffers. But minutes after the president's remarks, a young, white woman who sat next to me said unprompted, "I don't see any other veteran groups in this room, and you would think that they were invited." She was right, and then we both noticed the visible absence of civil rights and social justice organizations seated in this prominent room at a critical time in history, as were the nonexistent references to how we were going to democratize technology access in America's urban communities that are significantly plagued by noncompetitive and unaffordable broadband. That was when I realized that history was about to repeat itself, with another round of the politicized digital divide. This time, the remarks catered to the looming 2024 presidential election, where Biden and Harris will require bipartisan, and largely Republican, wins on their massive infrastructure spending bills. The day after that press conference was the first stop on the Biden-Harris reelection tour.

With history as a darn good predictor of outcomes, Biden's assertiveness to close the digital divide may, once again, fall on partisan ears. And if there is a leadership change in 2024, the forthcoming policy will likely obliterate its legacy as states start deploying their projects.

Why This Is Not Your Grandmother's Digital Divide

In 2020, when the global pandemic essentially shut down our quasi-analog lives as we knew them and mandated physical social distancing, not being online became a serious inconvenience for millions of people in the United States and a major liability for millions of other who could not connect due to the lack of access to infrastructure and essential resources like internet-enabled devices. For the latter, that lack of connectivity scarred businesses, which were forced to permanently close due to their inability to transition to online platforms, a personal horror for individuals with existing health disparities and co-morbidities who could not get or stay well because of their inability to engage remote health care, and to many K-12 students who have fallen behind in math, science, reading, and other critical studies essential to an educated and prepared labor force. For these latter groups, they are whom I consider to be "digitally invisible"—the people who are left to fend for themselves as they often find their communities, still stuck in analog existences, decaying as the rest of the country paves a different path forward. When digital access concerns arose in the middle of the summer of 2020, there was nothing political about actively participating in the robust digital economy—except when policymakers made it as such. Thus, the fact that more monies were being distributed and poured into the digital divide to assuage a group of policymakers from rural states who already benefit from the bulk of previous and current funding was laughable to me, and a dire reminder that urban residents—who were more likely to be digitally invisible from Black or Hispanic communities—would not greatly benefit from the exorbitant government spending.

When I was in high school, my English teacher assigned Ralph Ellison's book *Invisible Man*. Published in 1952, the book is narrated in the first person by a Black male protagonist who shares what life is like within a racially divided society and the constant struggle to be seen as a human. Throughout the book, the narrator is denied opportunities to fit into economic, social, and political circles, even after attempting to blend into various situations. On one occasion, he is asked to deliver a fiery speech by what he refers to as the Brotherhood, but is later criticized for his inflammatory delivery by the white men who invited him. Countless similar events fuel the narrator's disappointment, converting his invisibility into vigilance, and subsequently violence, as he is restrained from realizing his true aspirations in a world that has already discarded them. During one of his culminating rants at a protest in Harlem, he falls into an underground bunker, and no one knows that he is missing, while he ponders the meaning of his life while alone and buried.

Reading this book in high school explained for me the dual identities that Black and other people of color face in a world founded on principles of racism and structural inequality. As you can tell, it also inspired me to tell the truth about the often complicated and unrewarded journeys of individuals desiring to upend the status quo and present revolutionary thoughts and practices that contribute to lasting social change. Ellison's signature book surfaced the importance of people telling their own stories—whatever the subject—because it is often their experiences sitting in places of invisibility, whether physically or emotionally, that compare with the same bunker where the narrator found himself.

In America and around the world, many invisible people exist, and their lives are defined by someone or something else. Depending on where people find themselves along the continuum of their race, place, and space, there are many invisible people in our society who have been forgotten or avoided, either causing them to stay put or pursue social justice in hopes of being seen by those in agreement with the status quo. In the 1960s, the historic Civil Rights Movement gave racially invisible people voice and structure to effectuate some lasting and other temporary changes in equity. More recently, the Black Lives Matter movement did the same as members took to the streets, raising the awareness of police malfeasance and brutality, while calling the names of individuals killed by their excessive force, including Eric Garner, Sandra Bland, Breanna Taylor, George Floyd, and, more recently at the time this writing, a young Black man named Tyre Nichols, who was killed by cops—Black ones, in fact, from a special unit taskforce still obliged to maintain the sordid and unfair practices of law enforcement.

Some new technologies proactively have enabled visibility among communities with limited options to narrate and expose the traumatizing consequences and constructions that systemic racism emboldens, including people of color, women, and those from LGBTQ+ communities. Smartphones with cameras and widely accessed social media platforms have disseminated shocking images and videos that have enabled contemporary social movements, and that have brought the deeds of many bad actors, including white supremacists and rogue cops, to prosecutorial justice.

But outside these moments when technology is used to inspire participatory activism and movement building, especially among racially and other marginalized groups, it can bury the experiences of everyday people and force them further into social, economic, and political invisibilities. Online connections are essential gateways to more robust livelihoods. The internet gives communities access to critical functions, activities, and critical conversations.

As I discuss in the next chapter, when the 2020 global COVID-19 pandemic halted in-person physical interactions, many people found themselves in digital deserts, unable to connect to employment, education, government, and health care resources. Now, as explained above, many of these same people are catching up to a society that essentially discounted how critical equitable access to the internet would become.

Unbeknownst to many, digital invisibility was a pervasive reality before 2020, especially among low-income, less educated, older, disabled, rural, and foreign-born populations, who also happen to be people of color, and are not sufficiently connected to the internet or lack an internet-enabled device, despite prior political will and investments. Despite all that the United States has done to advance digital readiness and make internet architecture faster, bigger, and bolder, some have argued that more than a quarter of people in the United States are not sufficiently connected to good-quality internet service, or at all. The moral of this and other stories is that millions of people are digitally invisible and therefore are left behind, and this number may not include unaccounted-for online workers.

I have already started to raise awareness about making our efforts to close the digital divide solely focused on providing disadvantaged populations with access to computers or giving large companies financial or regulatory incentives to construct more high-speed broadband networks. The United States has done that—again and again—over six presidential administrations. The previous approaches to closing the digital divide render many of the same outcomes from supply-and-demand formulas that still deliver marginalized experiences and services to vulnerable populations and their communities.

Ultimately, the main character in *Invisible Man* was forced to acknowledge the barriers impeding his full participation in society—primarily his racial identification. Once the truth surfaced from his stories, he changed his perceptions to create a new path forward. For more than three decades, I have worked in communities on issues focused on closing the digital divide, and narrowing the gaps that exist between vulnerable populations and innovation. I, too, have been invisible. That was until I started to share my own experiences, starting with my early involvement with community technology centers in the 1990s. Unfortunately, that invisibility persists because many of the issues have remained unchanged. The manner in how we approach and resolve them will determine our social and economic inclusiveness, as well as our global competitiveness in the increasingly technical world.

James Baldwin wrote in his book *The Fire Next Time* about the riots in Harlem in the 1960s: "Not everything that is faced can be changed, but nothing can be changed until it is faced." With the largest investment in the history of funding broadband from the Biden-Harris administration, our solutions may be well resourced to accomplish a massive feat of contiguous connectivity like what fueled rural electrification, but it may barely change the trajectory of wealth and equity among people systemically affected by racism and discrimination, or further racialized because of digital exclusion.

My Research

In this book, I rely on an ethnographic approach to study this problem, along with related factors and variables. Between 2018 and 2021, I interviewed dozens of people about broadband access, went to their homes, businesses, and schools to learn firsthand about their plight. I took road trips and flights across the country to places where people are already invisible—socially, economically, and politically. These represented a diverse range of localities: rural, urban, Black, white, Latino, old, and young community residents, schools, and places of business.

To complete the book, I embarked on what I called a "digital divide tour" of the United States and visited more than a handful of cities to survey their digital access and use. They were Cleveland; Garrett County, Maryland; Hartford; Marion, Alabama; Phoenix; Staunton, Virginia; and Syracuse. My last visit and interview took place two weeks before the global pandemic shed an even uglier light on the millions of the people without online access and offered a more granular perspective on their experiences.

The goals of this research approach were to start with people who were either seeking to eradicate digital disparities or were affected by them. I met with every-day people who have stood behind the distorted mirrors that Ellison wrote about in his novel. These are the people whose lives are tucked quietly but not neatly into rural areas of the country, in low-income and public housing communities that are often demarcated by the redlines of expressways and railroad tracks.

As I said in the preface, digital disruption and its intersection with poverty and geographic isolation have maintained second-class, digital status for consumers that have become more like the subjects of technologies that facilitate their dis-appearance from the institutions and resources fueling the nation's workforce, educational, and health care systems. And with the emergence of AI powered by machine learning algorithms, generative artificial intelligence trained from large language models, or the country's increasing dismissal of the concept that individuals have a right to online privacy, their statuses will worsen before they get better. Forcing us to confront the notion that digital invisibility could pos-sibly resurge another round of Jim Crow segregation—only this time online—a concern raised in recent years by fellow sociologist Ruha Benjamin.[25] That is why we should only be welcoming transformational solutions toward equitable and more universally available and adaptable high-speed broadband that move to eliminate and confront our nation's historical challenges, and do so in a way that makes a difference instead of sitting on top of old frames of reference and approaches.

In the preface, I have already shared short vignettes about the people whom I met. But the book goes into more detail about their experiences and those of other people who generously gave their time to speak with me. Chapter 2 narrates how the pandemic steepened existing digital invisibilities. Chapters 3 through 7 amplify the voices and experiences of people from across the United States where digital access sits differently for them, like Dr. Cathy Trimble, a principal in the rural South, whose students' iPads became books without paper when the state's emergency broadband funds fell short during the pandemic.

In chapters 8 and 9, I argue how government continues to rely on old play-books for universal service, which require major modernization to fully address the scope and breadth of digital inequities and espouse the need to centralize people and their agency in future solutions. How we decide to define and con-front the digital divide will be consequential in the future for the handling emerging technologies, especially in their encroachment on individual privacy and community freedoms. If we want to really close the digital divide, we need policies and programs that do not undermine the prospects of a more just and inclusive path toward digital equity, which center people and communities in current debates.

Decades after I met Kiahna, Beverly, and the countless other people described in this book, the United States is still leaving millions behind and making it virtually impossible for far too many individuals to carve out better lives for themselves and their communities. Not only is the country failing to provide opportunities, but it is also squeezing the air out of exhaustive regulatory debates that will do little to impress digital equity. As the narrator in Ellison's novel observed, being invisible robs people of their dignity, hope, and potential, and endangers our entire society.

Notes

Part I epigraph: Bill Clinton, "The 2000 State of the Union," speech, Washington, 2000, https://clinton.presidentiallibraries.us/exhibits/show/sotu/2000-sotu.

1. Domestic Volunteer Service Act Amendments of 1993, Pub. L. No. Public Law 103-82, 107 Stat. 785 785 (1993). https://www.govinfo.gov/app/details/STATUTE-107/STATUTE-107-Pg785.
2. Jason Faberman and Marianna Kudlyak, "What Does Online Job Search Tell Us about the Labor Market?" *Economic Perspectives* 40, no. 1 (2016), https://www.chicagofed.org/publications/economic-perspectives/2016/1-faberman-kudlyak.
3. Jon P. Gant, Nicol E. Turner-Lee, Ying Li, and Joseph S. Miller, "National Minority Broadband Adoption: Comparative Trends in Adoption, Acceptance, and Use," Joint Center for Political and Economic Studies, February 2010, https://www.broadbandillinois.org/uploads/cms/documents/mti_broadband_report_web.pdf.
4. Jon Gant and Nicol Turner-Lee, "Government Transparency: Six Strategies for More Open and Participatory Government," Aspen Institute, February 28, 2011, https://www.aspeninstitute.org/wp-content/uploads/files/content/docs/pubs/Government_Transparency_Six_Strategies.pdf.
5. FCC Press Release, "Commissioner Rosenworcel's Statement on Digital Learning Equity Act," September 22, 2015, https://www.fcc.gov/document/commissioner-rosenworcels-statement-digital-learning-equity-act.
6. CBR staff writer, "U.S. Senators and One Economy Launch Public Internet Channel," Tech Monitor (blog), June 11, 2006, https://techmonitor.ai/technology/us_senators_and_one_economy_launch_public_internet_channel.
7. CBR staff writer.
8. Paul Farhi, "Bush Vetoes Cable TV Legislation," *Washington Post*, October 4, 1992, https://www.washingtonpost.com/archive/politics/1992/10/04/bush-vetoes-cable-tv-legislation/8697e4ca-5cdb-475c-8cf5-3061d7548425/.
9. Cristiano Lima, "George H. W. Bush's Legacy on Tech & Telecom," *Politico*, December 5, 2018, https://www.politico.com/newsletters/morning-tech/2018/12/05/george-hw-bushs-legacy-on-tech-telecom-442744.
10. NTIA, *Falling through the Net: Defining the Digital Divide: A Report on the Telecommunications and Information Gap* (Washington: NTIA, 1999).
11. NTIA, p. XV (Executive Summary).
12. White House, "The Clinton-Gore Administration: From Digital Divide to Digital Opportunity," February 2, 2000, https://clintonwhitehouse4.archives.gov/WH/New/digitaldivide/digital1.html.
13. Emily A. Vogels, "Digital Divide Persists Even as Americans with Lower Incomes Make Gains in Tech Adoption," Pew Research Center, https://www.pewresearch.org/short-reads/2021/06/22/digital-divide-persists-even-as-americans-with-lower-incomes-make-gains-in-tech-adoption/.

14. Federal Communications Commission, "Fact Sheet: Emergency Broadband Benefit," May 25, 2023 (updated), https://www.fcc.gov/broadbandbenefit.
15. Universal Service Administrative Company, "Fact Sheet: Emergency Connectivity Fund Program," https://emergencyconnectivityfund.org.
16. "Implementing the Infrastructure Investment and Jobs Act, Transportation and Infrastructure Committee," July 19, 2022, https://transportation.house.gov/calendar/eventsingle.aspx?EventID=405951; "Reviewing the Implementation of the Infrastructure Investment and Jobs Act, Transportation and Infrastructure Committee," March 28, 2023, https://transportation.house.gov/calendar/eventsingle.aspx?EventID=406231.
17. Michael Harrington, *The Other America* (New York: Scribner, 1997).
18. White House, "Fact Sheet: Biden-Harris Administration Announces Over $40 Billion to Connect Everyone in America to Affordable, Reliable, High-Speed Internet," June 26, 2023, https://www.whitehouse.gov/briefing-room/statements-releases/2023/06/26/fact-sheet-biden-harris-administration-announces-over-40-billion-to-connect-everyone-in-america-to-affordable-reliable-high-speed-internet/.
19. FCC: Consumer, "Digital Television," August 9, 2016 (updated), https://www.fcc.gov/general/digital-television.
20. Dibya Sakar, "Retailers Will Offer Digital TV Converters," Associated Press, December 11, 2007, https://www.seattlepi.com/business/article/Retailers-will-offer-digital-TV-converters-1258501.php.
21. Federal Communications Commission, "FCC Michael Powell Announces Creation of FCC Digital Task Force," press release, October 11, 2001, https://transition.fcc.gov/Bureaus/Mass_Media/News_Releases/2001/nrmm0110.html.
22. Federal Communications Commission.
23. Sam Sewall, "The Switch from Analog to Digital TV," Nielsen, November 2009, https://www.nielsen.com/insights/2009/the-switch-from-analog-to-digital-tv/.
24. Jeffrey A. Hart, *Technology, Television and Competition: The Politics of Digital TV* (Cambridge University Press, 2004), http://ndl.ethernet.edu.et/bitstream/123456789/11845/1/69pdf.pdf.
25. Ruha Benjamin, *Race After Technology* (Cambridge: Polity, 2019).

2

The Pandemic and the Digital Divide

The year 2020 was when being connected to the internet really mattered, and for so many other reasons than being close to family and friends. That year, the societal chaos prompted by the global COVID-19 pandemic was further accompanied by the paralyzing footage of an unarmed Black man, named George Floyd, whose death at the hands of Minneapolis police officer, Derek Chauvin, was one of the more violent acts of policing. It was recorded by civilians who watched as Mr. Floyd lay nearly lifeless on the city street just outside the convenience store where he was accused of passing a counterfeit $20 bill.

Floyd's death later at the hands of law enforcement drove protesters to the street, armed with signs that espoused in this modern age of history that Black Lives Matter still. My entire family saw the video on one of the many cable networks, and watched it over and over again on various social media platforms. The night of his murder, my fourteen-year-old daughter and I quickly joined the thousands of activists in downtown Washington who stormed down Independence Avenue, N.W., with our own Brown hands raised, chanting *"Hands up, don't shoot"* in synchrony with face-masked crowds.

On top of the public health pandemic, and this continuing endemic of racism, was the apparent resurgence of the digital divide, which I offer with some sarcasm, since many of us have known for years of its existence.

In the previous chapter, we discussed the six presidential administrations from both sides of the aisle who attempted but failed to close the digital divide. But in 2020, it took a dramatic pandemic to reveal deep inequalities in housing, health care, education, and employment, as well as to rouse public attention and ultimately influence executive leadership to commit billions to the cause.

What began as thirty days of social isolation and physical distancing in March 2020 became months and then years of pandemic mitigation at all levels of government and society. More than 500,000 had died by the end of the first year, and those numbers rose dramatically in subsequent years. If anything, time seemed to worsen the contagion as it created stubborn variants and perpetuated human suffering. By the summer, more than 40 million Americans had filed for unemployment and were prompted to go online to apply after long waits for telephone support. Large and small businesses in need of similar support were also directed to online portals that prequalified them for emergency assistance to float payroll and other capital expenses.

Students from kindergarten to college were seriously affected when in-person attendance largely stopped, and classrooms shifted to online learning. More than 50 million K-12 students who were enrolled in public, private, and charter schools were sent home in early March 2020 to stop the spread of the virus. The shift to virtual learning was sudden, and many quickly realized there was a wider digital divide than imagined. In April 2020, the *New York Times*'s editorial board published a piece called, "50 Million Students Can't Attend School; What Happens to Them?" which joined numerous other commentaries from think tanks, advocacy groups, and research organizations. Many writers joined the cacophony of individuals who became increasingly nervous as more than 195,000 school districts in the country shut down in-person learning, and quickly forced nearly everyone to adapt to online, internet-based platforms for students.[1]

Common Sense Media, an online advocacy organization for children, released a study that shared that more than 15 million K-12 students were without home broadband access, or access to an internet-enabled device, during the pandemic.[2] Nine million of these students were reportedly without both a residential connection and a device, and they were from predominantly Black and Brown communities, as well as geographically isolated within rural areas.[3] Colleges and universities, including high-ranking institutions like Harvard and Yale, faced their own challenges. While U.S. students were immediately dismissed to return home, international students were given the ability to shelter in place until borders opened for travel. But there were many U.S. students who left the comfort of university settings only to come back to impoverished communities and homes—without the necessities of food, waters, and access to high-speed broadband.

School closures were universal, affecting public, private, and charter institutions. And with the immediate shift to virtual learning came a sudden realization that more entrenched digital disparities were at play, and were neatly aligned with decades-long educational inequities—some of which have been percolating since the 1954 decision *Brown vs. Board of Education of Topeka*.

Front-page news stories shared how digital lapses affected vulnerable student populations. One photo that shook the nation appeared on the front page of the

New York Times: two young boys from California's Salinas City Elementary District sitting with school-issued laptops perched on a stoop at a local Taco Bell, tapping into their Wi-Fi to connect to their virtual classrooms. Just a few months into the pandemic, I witnessed the effects of the digital divide on students as part of a televised interview on a major news network. The reporter featured a mother of four children who sat cramped in her compact car, traveling from one Wi-Fi-enabled school bus to another in South Bend, Indiana. The segment showed her children all on their school-issued laptops, and a stack of food from the trips that this mother took to recover their free breakfasts and lunches normally provided during school hours.

And some of the nation's teachers were also found in what came to be called "digital parking lots." An *Education Week* article was the first to break these stories when it profiled educators without sufficient and available high-speed broadband in their homes to build lesson plans and instruct students in real time.[4]

What made the pandemic's obstruction of learning even more detrimental was that by the end of 2020, many students did not get online when mandated by various school districts. Not having the internet was clearly the problem, which led Trump to deal with the educational divide by advocating for school choice for low-income parents desiring better access to remote resources. But the nation was slowly finding out that low-income Black and Latino students were learning alone, and in some instances, were becoming the teacher in their households as their parents and guardians were working in jobs that remained in person, like retail cashiers, cooks, home health care aides, and other low-wage occupations. Unfortunately, these were some of the same people who were more likely to catch and die from COVID-19, given a variety of risk factors, particularly the nature of the job, the dense conditions of housing, and the lack of access to good-quality and consistent health care.[5] What further exacerbated the situation was that some schools started to physically convene students, while others waited or were hindered in their ability to reopen with the backdrop of looming public health failures. If these vivid portraits of what it was like to be poor, a person of color, and/or geographically isolated do not resonate against the importance of understanding digital crises along similar vortices, what else will?

Three months into COVID-19 mitigation, U.S. chief scientist Anthony Fauci acknowledged the role of health disparities among people of color that made them more susceptible to the virus. Black adults were *three times* more likely to contract the virus and die from it—largely due to unequal access to good-quality health care and institutions before the pandemic hit. Between March and July 2020, one out of every 1,000 children in New York City lost a parent or caregiver to the virus, which made the death count close to similar numbers reported during 9/11 when upward of 3,000 children experienced similar loss.[6]

In education, wealthier parents who were able to move their jobs online mitigated the pandemic very differently from impoverished people through home schooling, neighborhood-based learning pods, or quarantine bubbles, where these parents offered the space, time, structure, and technology to their children. Historically disadvantaged and less fortunate K-12 public students, on the contrary, who already had limited spaces in their community for play and lived in geographically isolated rural areas, were among those with limited to no home internet access or a capable device who were left to figure the shift to virtual learning out. Alone.

Some of the nation's largest school districts, including New York City Public Schools and Los Angeles County Unified School District, opted to cancel the rest of the academic year in early March after realizing that the households of students did not have adequate connections to broadband at home. My own school district—Fairfax County Public Schools, in Virginia, which is the nation's fourth-largest school district—discovered the intersection between the systemic inequalities of poverty and geographic location, which prompted it to delay the full rollout of virtual education.

In addition to disrupting the normalcy of instruction, many K-12 students—even those in private and charter schools—were deprived of the social activities that contribute to this socio-emotional development. In 2020, and then in 2021, many students never experienced the fall homecoming dance, senior prom, or formal graduation ceremonies associated with these burgeoning years. Instead, families were left to creatively celebrate these milestones through complementary minutes available on existing and emerging videoconferencing applications, or lawn signs C-O-N-G-R-A-T-U-L-A-T-I-N-G high school seniors in the COVID-19 cohort. My oldest was a high school senior when the pandemic hit. He was choosing colleges that he had never seen in person, catching up with friends on prom night over videoconferencing tools, and sitting in front of his laptop in hopes of gaining his last credits to finalize his college plans. The original photo invitations that were carefully worded with the photo that I searched my phone for hours to place in the right corner of the invite were reboxed and stored on a shelf somewhere in my house. The extravagant graduation party was cancelled, much like many weddings, fiftieth-birthday celebrations, and other milestones to which we so feverishly commit as markers for milestones. Maybe we will throw an in-person party when he graduates from college soon.

Compare this with the solemn tones of online memorial services as direct lines of communication and physical closeness that were also severed between family members, friends, and neighbors. In the United States, visits to nursing homes to elderly parents became "windowpane" interactions that gained prevalence as loved ones were left alone, or near death. My own family laid to rest several people in 2020, including one uncle, two aunts, one cousin, and a few close friends. Some were early fatalities of the pandemic, and others were left without adequate medical care as they battled preexisting co-morbidities, like heart disease and obesity.

I clearly recall those live streamed, and in some instances, recorded memorial services that were soon posted on social media and shared among family members.

Zoom occasions were often limited to 60-minute calls, where rushed sadness and disbelief turned into nostalgic memories before the complimentary time expired. "Don't forget to hug someone you love" was often the common farewell at these online memorials, as each one of us came to reality about the devastating effects of the 'rona.

The problem further revealed itself the following year, when the Biden-Harris White House pushed for more regular testing of individuals to stop the spread. But the primary way to schedule in-person appointments before at-home test kits were approved was through complicated online portals, which created challenges for those not connected to the internet. Later, the Biden administration began to promote vaccination availability at local pharmacies, government offices, public health clinics, and doctor's offices. But those appointments also had to be done online, creating additional barriers and burdens to individuals who not only could not connect but also did not know how to navigate these streamlined resources.

The year 2020 became known for its vignettes: For an exorbitant number of unfortunate and unintended fatalities. For startling numbers of high unemployment after forced temporary and permanent business closures. For K-college school interruptions at the start of the pandemic. For long lines wrapped around city streets as cars pulled into makeshift food pantries at local churches. And for memories that will percolate when one recalls everything that transpired at the time—which in many cases are posted and curated on the internet.

In the 1990s, the Grammy-award-winning artist Prince had a song called *Sign of the Times*; one lyric always stood out for me: "when a rocket ship explodes, and everybody still wants to fly." But there was no flying or escaping the realities of 2020. The virtual celebrations, the adaptations to remote work and schooling, the inevitable video calls to friends and family to avoid close contact—all amounted to the skyrocketing use of the internet to do just about anything, from shopping to medical visits to online dating.

Honestly, my family was one that pushed through the pandemic's disruptions. Not being able to appear in person did not stop my children from learning and engaging in other extracurricular activities. When the eight-hour school day ended, the next wave of virtual extracurricular activities began, with piano and vocal lessons, art, and academic tutoring. All these were activated via the small screens of their smartphones, or the wide views of laptops sitting on the edges of desks recently cleared of schoolwork. While they learned something over the course of the 12 hours in a day, I sat in a newly painted home office with an assortment of LED selfie lights, capturing every angle of my face for Zoom, and Facetime calls and meetings—more than I had ever taken while in person. My fiancé, who later became my husband, was out of the home, since he was a painting contractor, and was busy renovating spare rooms for people who were trapped inside during the pandemic. My family had virtual resources and just about everything we needed to be productive during the pandemic.

The shift to remote work among some blue-collar and mostly white-collar workers shed light on who was able to digitize their job functions, and who was not. For example, the lack of digital agility among some businesses left more than 100,000 small businesses permanently closed toward the end of 2020.[7] These closures were largely owned by people of color and women. Black businesses were nearly 40 percent more likely to shut down, due to already-struggling balance sheets, the inability to capture immediate federal loan assistance, and inadequate broadband connections, as well as flexible digital practices to allow for online payments and instant web pages to market services.[8] For the average American business without broadband access, the accelerated shift to digitization in areas that included online commerce and social advertising was complicated, which is why Big Tech companies like Amazon, Facebook, and DoorDash, as well as other tech-enabled businesses, experienced record profits over the course of 2020.

Through the months that quickly turned into years, people with accessible, available, and affordable access to high-speed broadband, downloadable applications, internet-enabled devices, and online exposure made it through. The children of well-off parents survived with learning losses that paid tutors could correct. Some employers ramped up their videoconferencing capabilities, cut some slack on their work-at-home policies, and some incentivized online collaborations and normalized videoconferencing meetings to weather the economic effects of employees and the demand for their products and services. Some businesses and organizations pivoted their business models from in-person to online platforms after experiencing the deleterious effects of being analog—meaning catering to in-person and more traditional methods of commerce. Not all businesses and organizations were easily adaptable to online formats. Emergency personnel still had to go into work, especially nurses and home health care aides. Certain service and hospitality industries were still obliged to clock-in daily, while an increasing wave of workers transformed into delivery drivers to accommodate the increased consumption and obsession with e-commerce.

Even government agencies, which are traditionally slow to migrate public benefit applications to online formats, found ways to develop the greater capabilities of existing online portals for unemployment benefits applications and other more mundane tasks, like paying property taxes, renewing driver's licenses, and other things. Well-capitalized private companies and entrepreneurs threatened into obliteration quickly caught on to the pandemic, digital revolution through the enticement of consumers to their websites, social media, and unique virtual experiences and placeholders that offered seamless transactions for everything from grocery shopping to interactive workouts, and live-streamed, first-look movies for entertainment. The Big Tech community, including some of the largest online companies like Facebook/Meta and Amazon, among others, took advantage of the physical and social limitations of domestic and global consumers, prompting other nontechnical companies to steer clear of traditionally analog business practices toward more real-time, in-the-moment applications, including peer-to-peer banking transfers, remote health care, and telehealth.

When it came to broadband service, the nation was prepared, as much of this work had been completed under the Bush-Cheney administration. The National Telecommunications and Information Administration's acting secretary at the time was Michael Gallagher, who as expected pivoted away from former chief's, Larry Strickling's, digital opportunity agenda. Instead, he focused his priorities on the supply chain. In a speech at the University of Washington School of Law, he described the administration's focus on broadband deployment and spectrum policy, which under his purview would ready America's global competitiveness in wireless markets.

During the Bush-Cheney administration, high-speed broadband continued to evolve, and steadily increased subscribership in 2002, when there were fewer than 200,000 subscribers. Four years later, in 2006, more than 13 million were actively signed up. To put this in perspective, over 40 million people are subscribed to high-speed broadband in 2023. But in the early days of the migration to broadband, people like Kiahna, Beverly, and others at Northwest Tower were left out. We could not access a robust internet and related resources in the early 2000s at the North Side computer lab. But the market-driven policy decisions under Bush largely enabled industries, like incumbent telecommunications providers, and early-stage content companies—like Prodigy, Compuserve, Yahoo, and later Google in 1998—to gain prominence as dial-up was slowly being retired.

At the end of the Clinton FCC, into the one controlled by Bush and the Republicans, the United States also saw the diversification of technologies, especially mobile applications, that later facilitated greater participation for consumers in online platforms. Most people may not know that Japan was the first country to enable mobile connectivity through the NTT Network, but no one really knew about its success because the country's closed market primarily benefited its citizens. Japan's efforts encouraged the first-generation (1G) of cell phones, which enabled mobile voice communications before the entry of second-generation (2G) mobile services that provided more sophistication in communications through more efficient and secure calling services, basic data services, and short message text services (SMS). Later mobile networks like 3G enhanced data transfer rates, and gave rise to basic internet, music streaming, and video phone calls. The last mobile technology before 5G was 4G LTE, which parlayed the growth of high-definition video streaming on smartphones and other multimedia and behavioral applications— more than 3 million combined, between Apple's App Store and Google Play. To date, the economy has responded quite well to these advancements in mobile technologies. Between 2006 and 2016, as the transition between the various Gs progressed, the digital economy grew at an average annual rate of 5.6 percent, accounting for 6.5 percent of the current-dollar gross domestic product.[9]

The capabilities of 4G LTE mobile broadband, alone, helped Steve Jobs, the founder of Apple, launch the first internet-enabled iPhone—nearly twenty years after Motorola's first low-power cellular phone. Later, other companies were conceived after the introduction of 4G LTE networks, including ride-sharing apps like Uber and Lyft, which quickly disrupted analog transportation systems by leveraging the the Global Positioning System location and navigation capabilities of smartphones. Social media platforms basically followed suit when Facebook's founders—Mark Zuckerburg, Eduardo Saverin, Andrew McCollum, Dustin Moskovitz, and Chris Hughes—migrated their app, which was primarily used on college campuses, to mobile platforms in 2007, leveraging subscription and online advertising models to convert 2.9 billion people into today's loyal users. In October 2021, Zuckerberg, the remaining founder, and the chief executive officer, rebranded the company as Meta, combining brands that now engage text, photos, videos, and a range of other multimedia capabilities and transitioning them into the next phases of artificial intelligence and augmented and virtual reality experiences that digitize real and imagined physical interactions.

The 5G Revolution

If we keep in mind that in the two to three years leading up to the pandemic, fifth-generation (5G) mobile networks were also being touted as the latest in mobile innovation, even prompting the Trump administration to announce its intentions to create a national 5G network after watching its rapid evolution in China—a thought of a government-owned, 5G network was quickly rejected by the privately owned mobile carriers. With expected download speeds as high as 20 gigabits-per-second, 5G could download full-length movies in seconds, while handling more specialized technologies and functions, including remote precision medicine, connected cars, virtual and augmented reality experiences, and the internet of things. More than 500 billion internet-of-things devices—from sensors, to actuators, to medical devices—could run off 5G networks concurrently, and the enhanced capabilities of smartphones and other internet-enabled devices by faster, mobile broadband networks were projected to enable more advanced communications services—some of which had not yet been developed.

Cinderella may be a good analogy for the explosion of mobile telecommunications. She eventually found both her other shoe and the prince, which has happened in a communications ecosystem no longer constrained by one type of technology over another. This explains why there are more than 6.3 billion smartphone users and 1.14 billion people who regularly use internet-enabled tablets around the globe, which has consistently grown at a rate of more than 36 percent in under a decade. But more important, these historic shifts at every juncture of technology's development have been better than the previous iteration—creating viable alternatives to traditional analog communications.

Mobile communications also followed similar paths to entry as other technologies. Between 2011 and 2014, IBM built the Watson, which would be the first-ever supercomputer designed to beat human contestants on the game show *Jeopardy*. The Watson would, indeed, be a starting point for current innovations in artificial intelligence and neural network technologies that are powering online search queries, solving with exponential intelligence concerns about the climate, health care, national security, and COVID-19. But as with any technology, the room for abuse and scarcity is also rampant, implicating other social problems and concerns from predatory and deceptive practices to the outright marketplace exclusion of more vulnerable populations.

By the time the Biden-Harris administration assumed office, the average broadband speed was almost triple the Federal Communication Commission's defined standard of 25 Mbps download speeds. This made the United States pretty much prepared for the changing online demands of COVID-19 through its long history of investing in resilient broadband networks, internet-enabled applications and devices, artificial intelligence, and other future technologies that have become generally purposed for societal needs and wants.

Internet service providers—including Verizon, Comcast, Charter, AT&T, and Cox—fared quite well in subscription rates and profits during the pandemic as more people came to rely upon them for online access in both wireline and wireless services. Technology companies like Amazon, Google, Facebook, and Apple all reported third-quarter earnings in 2020 that surpassed prior ones, and economic projections. At the end of 2020, Amazon surpassed $96 billion in earnings and $6.3 billion in profits, which allowed the company to add nearly 400,000 jobs. The company's resilience—and that of other small, mid-sized, and large competitors—indicated the digital resiliency that I spoke of earlier in the book that welcomed new entrants into the digital marketplace, like new tech start-ups that found new ways to support the digital marketplace.

Instead of creating huge economic gaps over the course of what would become nearly two years in pandemic mode built stronger bridges between people, communities, products, and services. However, while people like me were largely inconvenienced during the pandemic, the most vulnerable were severely constrained and even endangered in reaching their full potential and attaining equity in spaces that were not digitally inclusive. They were also more likely to be the workers who enabled digital transformation among a variety of existing and new telecom and tech companies in their warehouses and data centers.

That is why the conversation about the digital divide must be honest about its origins. From the late 1990s, when the commercial internet began to flourish, up until today, some of the same people have remained digitally invisible, like the modern-day version of Kiahna and Beverly, who are severely foreclosed due to the lack of internet access. Today, there are also others who join them because their distance from a robust digital infrastructure makes it impossible for them to thrive and survive in an increasingly twenty-first-century economy, including the farmers who have trouble getting online to order supplies, or the patients whose inability to access remote health care can be a determinant of their well-being and livelihoods.

The endless amount of time spent online during the COVID-19 pandemic also furthered existing political polarizations, and even fueled online hate movements, as white supremacist groups spread misinformation or false truths about stolen elections, long-lived Confederate monuments, polarized political speech, and the insidiousness of daily tweets from a president lashing out against election results, while he was supposed to be addressing our greatest public health scare. This is how then–president Trump chose to structure the norms for online engagement, which some have suggested led to the later January 6, 2022, insurrection to repeal Biden's election.

My point in this chapter is to reveal that the pandemic was another formative period in the development of the digital lives of individuals, communities, and institutions. But even as the internet became the backbone for many people to stay connected to their communities and their ideologies, it was still not widely available for a host of others, especially those in need of navigating through even tougher times. Sadly, this should not have come as a surprise to anyone because the disparities that we experienced from 2020 and beyond were widely consistent with what was happening before the pandemic raised public awareness.

Notes

1. Editorial Board, "50 million Kids Can't Attend School. What Happens to Them?" *New York Times*, April 20, 2020, https://www.nytimes.com/2020/04/16/opinion/coronavirus-schools-closed.html.
2. S. Chandra, A. Chang, L. Day, A. Fazlullah, J. Liu, L. McBride, T. Mudalige, and D. Weiss, *Closing the K-12 Digital Diver in the Age of Distance Learning* (San Francisco: Common Sense Media; and Boston: Boston Consulting Group, 2020).
3. Chandra and others.
4. Madeline Will, "Teachers Without Internet Work in Parking Lots, Empty School Buildings during COVID-19," *Education Week*, April 29, 2020, https://www.edweek.org/technology/teachers-without-internet-work-in-parking-lots-empty-school-buildings-during-covid-19/2020/04.
5. Rashawn Ray, "Why Are Blacks Dying at Higher Rates from COVID-19?" Brookings, April 9, 2020, https://www.brookings.edu/articles/why-are-blacks-dying-at-higher-rates-from-covid-19/.
6. Carson Kessler, "Thousands of New York Children Lost a Parent or Guardian to COVID-19, Study Finds," The City, September 30, 2020, https://www.thecity.nyc/health/2020/9/30/21494764/thousands-of-new-york-children-lost-a-parent-to-covid-19-study-finds.
7. Ursula Perano, "Study Projects Over 100,000 Small Businesses Have Permanently Closed," Axios, May 12, 2020, https://www.axios.com/2020/05/12/small-businesses-coronavirus-closures.

8. Khristoper J. Brooks, "40% of Black-Owned Businesses Not Expected to Survive Corona-virus," CBS News, June 22, 2020, https://www.cbsnews.com/news/black-owned-busineses-close-thousands-coronavirus-pandemic/.

9. Kevin Barefoot, Dave Curtis, William Jolliff, Jessica R. Nicholson, and Robert Omohundro, "Defining and Measuring the Digital Economy," U.S. Bureau of Economic Analysis, March 15, 2018, https://www.bea.gov/system/files/papers/WP2018-4.pdf.

II

The Persistent Rural Divide

It's simple. A farmer can buy a million-dollar tractor with all the bells and whistles enabling it for broadband use. But without high-speed access, that farmer just bought another tractor.

—Remarks heard at a roundtable on rural broadband from
Bruce Rieker, vice president of government relations,
Nebraska Farm Bureau Federation, circa 2018

3

More Cows Than People

In 2021, Garrett County, Maryland, was vast—and empty. On the western-most edge of the state, nestled into the scenic Allegheny Mountains, the county had less than 47 people per square mile. Fewer than 30,000 people lived in the *entire* county. Between 2017 and 2021, the median income of the commu-nity was $58,011, and the share of those living in poverty was around 11 percent.[1] Most residents had at least a high school diploma, and many worked for the county's largest employers—health care and social services.[2] The non-Hispanic white population made up 96 percent of residents, while Black, Hispanic, Asian, and Tribal populations were the rest of county residents.

I learned about Garrett County, Maryland from Microsoft Corporation's president and CEO, Brad Smith, who talked about the area in a presentation on the state of rural broadband in the United States. He had recently published a book, *Tools and Weapons: The Promise and Perils of the Digital Age*, that detailed his personal struggles running a leading technology company amid disparate online connectivity, especially in rural America, where fiber tends to be the only viable path to getting people online.[3] During his presentation, he shared a new broadband initiative, which was later named Microsoft's Airband, focused on closing the digital divide.[4] Barry Toser, an executive at a mid-size broadband company, then took to the stage and shared a new partnership with Microsoft around a familiar, yet underutilized technology, called television white spaces.

I was immediately intrigued. Hearing these two prominent business leaders talk about new opportunities for improving rural broadband encouraged me to visit Garrett County, Maryland, which was physically located within the Appalachian region. I connected to Barry through my friend, Vickie Robinson, who works at Microsoft and found myself on the road, in my car, with the primary goals of learning more about television white spaces (TVWS) and the Airband project, along with seeing first-hand the experiences of actual people living in rural America.

Meeting Barry

What was normally a three-hour trip on I-270 from downtown D.C. took nearly five hours due to a snowstorm where thick flurries quickly coated and blinded the roads. Living in Chicago had not only made me more tolerant of the cold, but also a much better driver in these conditions. On the trip, I was accompanied by a Brookings staff photographer, who sat stiff under his seatbelt as the interstate became increasingly dangerous and harder to navigate. By the time we arrived at the Lake Star Lodge, the hotel clerk was long gone. It was 3 a.m., and she had clocked out earlier that evening, leaving the keys to our rooms in a box beneath a dense pile of snow. After a long battle to find the keys nestled under the postal box set at the top of the hill, we both called it a night.

"I'll see you tomorrow. Bright and early," I said to my colleague as I walked into my room. The interior of the suite resembled every thought that came to mind about a rural cabin—wood fireplace, sheepskin rug, and a view of Deep Creek Lake, which sat still with icicles forming on the top. Within a couple of hours, the sun rose, and a beautiful landscape greeted me through a tall, narrow window. Complete darkness had transitioned to a view of clear water and surrounding mountains with ice caps settled on their tops.

Despite an obvious lack of sleep, rural Garrett County took the cake for its grandiose scenic outlines seen from my hotel patio window, and a quietude one could not find in urban areas. The breathtaking view was encased with gawking birds awakening to the sunlight, clouds moving in slow motion across water, and snow fighting to stay crystalized as it sat between land and water.

These welcoming scenes were largely unknown to urbanites like me, who spent most of their lives in crowded cities and suburbs where streetlights hide any semblance of nature, and the sounds of cars mask the deafening silence bouncing off concrete structures. When I was a little girl, my family did make it to a place called Lake George north of New York City, but the cabin was among many on a crowded resort site with some, but not all, of Garrett County's beauty.

Since our tour guide, Barry Toser, was waiting for us in the lobby of the main building, I quickly packed up and texted my colleague, and we were soon greeted with Barry's huge smile, balanced by the width of small-framed glasses. Barry was from Northern Virginia, and from the high energy he exuded, he apparently had slept quite well the night before.

"Good morning, Nicol, you both made it," Barry said, still grinning from ear to ear. Small in stature, but big in enthusiasm, his early morning greeting was equally matched with the grandeur of the views.

Barry was one of the executives at the Declaration Networks Group (DNG), a small internet service provider (ISP) serving rural areas in Virginia, Maryland, and Washington State. The firm brings over a hundred combined years of expertise in telecommunications leadership and delivers high-speed broadband as part of its product, called NeuBeam, that uses a combination of advanced wireless technologies, including TVWS.[5] Over the years, the FCC permitted its use on mobile compatible devices and address other interference concerns, including line-of-sight issues due to tall buildings or satellite traffic. In 2019, the FCC approved and allocated bandwidth in unused channels between television broadcast and wireless spectrum for broadband services to address these and other concerns.[6]

This pivot was a critical victory for many ISPs like DNG and civil society organizations vetting alternative technologies to weaken the dependence on incumbent service providers and diversify options for broadband connectivity, including cable, fiber, fixed, or nonfixed wireless. The FCC's ruling also made it easier for DNG to explore other high-speed broadband solutions for areas with limited competition for services, starting with the partnership with Microsoft, which offered the company a road map, equipment, and hardware as part of its Airband Initiative.[7]

DNG's partnership with Microsoft started before the regulatory approvals of TVWS and enabled the inaugural NeuBeam service to reach more than 65,000 people in Accomack and Northampton counties on the Eastern Shore of Virginia and in Garrett County, Maryland, in 2018.[8] A year later, in 2019, DNG received additional federal funds from the FCC's Connect America Fund, to scale the delivery of broadband service to an additional 2,454 homes in the footprint.[9]

Garrett County is not very different from other rural areas that are working to bring high-speed broadband access to residents, but its topography makes it more difficult to deploy high-quality networks, alongside the low density of people to serve as potential customers for internet services. Before the pandemic, in 2020, 520,000 people in the state of Maryland did not have access to home broadband.[10] More than 390,000 Maryland homes did not have access to an internet-enabled device, including a desktop or laptop computer.[11] In Garrett County, in 2012, 75 percent of the county had broadband coverage, but only about 60 percent had home-based broadband service.[12] Coupled with the scattering of residents throughout the large county area and widespread poverty, lower-than-average broadband adoption rates were a reality that I would soon learn more about.

As fast as we had arrived in the lobby, Barry moved toward the door, signaling that it was time to start our tour of the county and a series of interviews that he set up. "We have a lot of land to cover," Barry said as we hustled to our separate cars. Barry was not underestimating the amount of time traveling to different locations in the rural terrain would take.

More Cows Than People

The drive to a local farm run by Jon Yoder felt like the longest 20 minutes that I have ever known. It provided sporadic glimpses of farm animals—mainly cows—sitting comfortably on the sides of the roads. I equated these rural areas as "the country," which was a phrase we used growing up in the city when we had to visit relatives who lived down South. My aunt, uncles, and their children lived in Rockingham, North Carolina—way off the beaten path of anything more commercial and populated. When I was eleven, I went in the summer, and remember seeing the fabricated homes and mobile trailers that sat on properties scattered with land and feeding grounds for cows, pigs, chickens, and, in some instances, goats walking freely on the side of the roads. But my aunt and uncle were not farmers; they were poor folks in the South living off the land that they were able to deed.

The Yoder Farm was quite different. It was a multigenerational, family-run enterprise that had acres of land with the front of the property adorned with a metal awning boldly naming it.

Jon, a short, white man with a long, shaggy beard and a tight brown leather jacket, waved our cars pass the large welcoming sign to the front of the house. From the looks of him, I felt like I was about to meet Santa Claus because the estate fit nicely into a scene from any one of the popular Christmas movies. But upon getting closer to the house, Mr. Yoder, who was still waving our vehicles into the long driveway, looked like a slimmer version of Mr. Claus as snow flurries furiously fell on his bearded stature.

He is a fourth-generation farmer, and one of many generations in his family from Garrett County. You could tell that he was well known here by the size of the land, and metal adornment naming his property when we arrived. The head of the expired deer mounted on one of the walls in his living room, which I would soon see, was also a pretty good indicator, along with his well-built home with exposed wooden beams below the ceiling.

Barry and I parked and were quickly ushered inside the house, where the smell of firewood greeted us, along with Mrs. Yoder and the couple's young daughter. They stood underneath that large, stuffed deer head that, up close, looked alive.

"Welcome to Garrett County," Jon said in a soft, welcoming voice, as he extended his hand to my colleague and me. After Barry explained the purpose of my visit, Jon did not hesitate to jump right in.

He was raised Amish in Garrett County before becoming a Mennonite at the age of six. Compared with the Amish, Mennonites differ slightly in their dress and adherence to traditional practices, such as using horses and buggies for transportation. Amish communities also tend to be less progressive in their use of technology, believing that it is a distraction from nature and not aligned with their religious beliefs and practices.

"This is mainly an Amish community, so the technology is pretty limited. But as farmers, we are on the back side of the curve, only until recently have we gotten good internet—thanks to Barry," Jon started to share and, of course, Barry responded with another wide smile.

Just as I thought, the Yoder family boasts a long lineage of farmers well known to the area. But the farming industry has not been insulated from production and economic shifts. Since the early twentieth century, farms have transitioned from labor-intensive wholesale production to smaller and more diversified businesses. The number of farms sharply declined, from 6.8 million in its peak in 1935 to approximately 2.02 million in 2020, according to the U.S. Department of Agriculture.[13]

Technology has widened the productivity gap of traditional farming with emerging technologies like precision agriculture that rely on the combination of networked technologies including the internet-of-things, sensors, Global Positioning System navigational tools, and other broadband-enabled tools. Yet for most farmers like Jon Yoder, their promise of these innovations has been blocked by broadband access problems, and also by the diminishing revenues from farming in general. Massive cuts in federal subsidies and diminishing profits for smaller farming businesses have not only affected general services and production but also their abilities to modernize.

"We, farmers, are still trying to figure out how to use the technology," Jon stated. "People talk about precision agriculture, which I think will be great. But until Barry and NeuBeam came along, I could see the last mile of internet from this window, and it wasn't coming to my farm."

What makes DNG's broadband solution unique is the use of small-mesh networks that target specific access points on Jon's farm, while providing internet to his home—again, via TV white spaces. With larger farms outnumbering and, in some cases, outperforming smaller family-owned farms, the need for new or enhanced online connectivity to rural industries is imperative. The economic competitiveness of the farming business rests on online access, particularly for people like Jon, who need basic internet access to order farming supplies and market their products outside the county.

"For our businesses to survive, they will have to be connected," Jon continued. "It helps me to make money and even get the weather app so I know how to decide my workflow, like watering the crops. If the app says it's going to rain, I won't water or mow [that day]." This might seem simple to those of us with readily available internet, but for a farmer who long lacked access to modern amenities, the availability of the weather app was transformative for his agricultural business.

Television White Spaces

Television white spaces, which Barry's group uses to provide internet to these communities, is not a new technology and was already being used by a small number of ISPs before Microsoft positioned it as a competitive technology. When I was in Chicago, I heard about TVWS from two young white media activists—Harold Feld and Dharma Daily—who approached me at my computer lab on the West Side of Chicago with the idea of offering Black, low-income residents what was then considered the internet over the vacant broadcast spectrum which was only available via Channel 37. I must admit that back then, I was not convinced of its efficacy with the heavy congestion of the city's airwaves. But here I was now—many years later, in 2019—hearing the praises about TVWS from a Garrett County farmer. Harold is now a spectrum genius, and Dharma, a respected researcher who has been working to close the digital divide for decades like me.

"This TV white space model is definitely one of many directions that rural areas can take to solve this problem," Jon shared, with tamed enthusiasm for closing the digital divide. "We definitely need more options out in rural America—whether it be cellular, satellite, or fiber. The key thing that matters to most of us farmers are cost, speeds, and data caps."

He supported DNG's NeuBeam product: "I can work from home and do some things that I just wasn't able to do before, like ordering equipment and finishing paperwork. And it's affordable, which matters." For the few words she did share, his wife echoed his sentiments and pointed to how they are able to connect their daughter to educational resources available online.

Hearing from a local farmer not too far from where policy gets developed, affirmed why we really need to close the rural digital divide once and for all. It is the basic connections that matter for businesses to order supplies, or the more robust applications that help Mennonite families keep their children exposed to resources outside Garrett County—despite the community being somewhat averse to outside influences.

Farming may be one of the last industries to be fully disrupted by technology. But it is clear from Jon Yoder's comments that solutions must meet his peers where they are, whether at the high- or low-end of connectivity or in a space where online services can drive profitability in a burgeoning digital economy. Jon also spoke about why the United States has a persistent rural broadband problem—largely due to the underestimation and misunderstanding of the supply-and-demand wants and needs of these rural communities.

I learned during my time in Garrett County that farmers were not the only rural businesses affected by not having broadband access. Josh, who we met later on the trip, was a local and owned the tire shop, My-O-Tire. As soon as we walked into his shop, his loud, burly voice that matched the size of his body hurled out praise for Barry as soon as we stepped into his shop. "Bring me more Barrys!" were Josh's first words.

Like Jon Yoder, Josh grew up in the county and married his wife, who had lived two towns over. He was not leaving the area and felt some relief in being connected to the internet. It meant that he, too, could order the right tire for his customers without sifting through a couple dozen print catalogs, and his wife could work remotely, which also meant that the couple could remain in the area for the indefinite future. DNG's NeuBeam product also helped him to complete basic tasks, like finding and ordering the right tires for customers. He shared: "In my business, you have no choice but to get things done. We were slow to get online. I used to go through every manual to find the right tire for a customer. Now, I can go online and just like that, it's ordered. Because of Barry, there are fewer people on the edges where there is no service."

It was the same idea Jon had shared with me just a couple hours earlier: They had long lived on the "edges" or the "last mile," but now, it seemed like that was changing with more stable internet. Josh, the mechanic, continued: "When I was growing up, we didn't have cable or antennas that worked. We played in the woods. We connected with friends by getting together in person. Garrett County is still a bubble like this and what's happening in D.C. won't get here [until] about six months. But, when [online] access increases, the lag decreases. It can help us here."

When the pandemic hit, I heard a rumor that Josh had to close the family-owned business but his wife was able to still work remotely—until DNG was hit with some COVID-19-related business challenges.

After meeting Jon and then Josh, I realized that being a twenty-first-century farmer or business owner in communities without broadband, or other digital resources, made them, too, part of the digitally invisible whom we do not often reference or talk about.

More Books Than Laptops

We left the Yoder Farm and arrived about 25 long minutes later in the gravel parking lot of the Swan Meadow School in the county's Gortner community. Swan Meadow is a historic, three-room school building built in the 1890s for local farming families of different faiths. In 1958, the school was rebuilt, and again in the 1990s when it transitioned from one to three classrooms serving fifty students with seven staff and faculty.[14]

A rather tall woman, who served as both the school's computer lab supervisor and math teacher, greeted us as we pulled up into the parking lot, which was becoming a familiar gesture here in rural America. "Welcome to Swan Meadow," she said enthusiastically as we got out of our cars.

In 2019, fifty students from the county attended the school in grades K-8. According to the Maryland Department of Education, for the 2018–19 academic year, the elementary portion of the school ranked in the 77th percentile and the middle school in the 96th percentile. Fifty three percent of students demonstrated proficiency in both math and reading.[15] In 2018, the school received the Sustainable Maryland Green Award for helping students facilitate better relationships with the environment.[16] Swan Meadow students were also involved in the Garrett County FIRST Robotics team that qualified for the world championship.[17]

Grinning proudly, the teacher shared, "We have an extensive robotics team here at the school and in the county. We have two students on the team who are building robots and going to national competitions. This all happens after school and with the technology that we have now."

The school, with only five classrooms, was composed of students mainly from Amish backgrounds, whose access to the internet at home is largely nonexistent. The "homework gap" was an obvious problem for this segment of religious students, whose parents prohibited access to digital platforms outside school. "Many of these students do not have technology at home due to their religion, so we use it here as a teaching tool," the teacher reminded me.

Here, educators respect the religious proclivities of their Amish and Mennonite students. Despite the school's integration of technology into the main curricula, they are careful not to offend family members who might not value such modernization. The reality is that most Amish students who graduate return to work in their family businesses of woodworking or textiles despite having a formal education.

"Most of our students will stay in the community. But it is my goal to make sure that they understand what's happening in the world around them," she said, as she looked down at me from her slightly taller frame and we made out our way up the short stairway into the school building.

Walking slowly through three of the five classrooms and then a common area in the building did not seem quick because every corner in each room was stacked with something, including a whiteboard, shelves, books, and supplies, among other things. The last space, she pointed out, is where she stores her iPads for teachers and students—all on a single cart.

"Prior to Barry coming in and helping us, we didn't have a quality broadband connection or devices," she admitted. "We bought laptops with the proceeds from our harvest sale, where we sell baked goods that are produced on local farms and other artisan items. But before Barry, we had no internet on the twenty-nine laptops that we have."

Only a couple of places in the community offered free or commercial Wi-Fi access, making the school building the most likely place for students to get online. "Learning and teaching experiences have been enhanced because of the school broadband connection. Kids work hard here at school, so they don't need the technology at home. We were pushing for it here," she shared, and pointed to the lack of viable transportation for the students to get to the public library.

DNG's NeuBeam service for this five-room school was enabled through a mounted antenna on the side of the school building, which protruded off the side of the small structure. Listening to the teacher summed up a slice of life growing up and learning in rural areas without internet access. But with some surprise, Swan Meadow School had nurtured a highly successful robotics team in a town with various religious proclivities and norms.

More Needs Than Services

I think it was the large geography that made the county feel sparse. Unlike the city, no one walked the curbs of the local community near the school, the farm, or the mechanic shop, until you made it to Oakland, which was the commercial district and hub of the county. It was the location of the county's government buildings, small businesses, and a huge replica of a railroad car in the center of downtown, which boasted its history as a main transportation corridor for the state.

I soon discovered when we pulled up to the county building that there was a lot more to the area than hard-pressed local farmers and business owners. Like other isolated and insulated rural communities, Garrett County had fallen victim to high rates of opioid addictions and dependencies.[18] The issues of prescription medication abuses garnered national attention from the Trump administration, whose political base during his run for presidency was largely rural.[19] The state of Maryland also had been in crisis due to the rising opioid epidemic and increasing numbers of overdoses before and during the pandemic. Garrett County was experiencing major difficulties tackling these crises—largely due to uncoordinated responses from public health officials, which was becoming more the norm than the exception in rural communities.

On our last stop with Barry, we visited the Garrett County Action Center, which had received one of several grants from a $1.1 million federal program in 2019 to address the opioid epidemic locally and support recovery efforts.[20] Maryland state lawmakers introduced several bills and new initiatives targeted at harm reduction, including shields against criminal prosecution when reporting overdoses and the immediate administration of Narcan to treat them.[21] But the uncontrollable spread of these drugs had fallen victim to the county's rugged and vast terrain, which exacerbated not only the poverty but also the lack of accessible communications infrastructure and services.

We came to meet Gregan Crawford, who was the executive director of the Action Center, which was the only social service agency in the county that served as a one-stop shop for residents by ensuring access to food, shelter, and other forms of public assistance. Gregan has lived in Garrett County since 1989, and in the last few years, has had been tasked with reaching and staying connected to those residents most in need. In his office was also Daphne Gooding, an older white woman in her late sixties or early seventies who volunteered at the Action Center and shared her experiences of being a former welfare recipient. She said that she swore on the power of technology, dating back to when she was a single parent and used the internet to apply for benefits and educational opportunities.

"I lived in subsidized housing," she recalled. "I know what it's like to be always trying to figure things out before I was exposed to computers and the internet."

I am not going to lie, but if I closed my eyes as Daphne spoke, she sounded like the Black women in Northwest Tower who were also in the computer lab applying for housing, jobs, and public benefits. She continued: "We need broadband so if you are a low-income mother with five kids, you can get help where you live. For people who are in poverty, they need office skills. The kids need computer skills. It's our job [here] to make that connection."

Like so many other mothers dealing with hard times, Daphne understood that without access to information in real time, the navigation through the social service system and community-based resources was tough and stifling—a fact that became even truer as women worked through COVID-19.

In Garrett County, the type of institution or business—social service agency, school, farm, or tire shop—really did not matter. Dependence on analog models was completely ineffective for them, especially since 12.8 percent of the residents were living at or below the poverty line, were primarily children, and were located more than *two hours* away from the nearest service provider.[22]

But the expansive terrain made it difficult for residents to get to Oakland to sign up for public assistance, and it restricted case workers from making regular visits to them. Gregan also pointed out that most county residents lacked reliable transportation to make it to Oakland or the Action Center. When I visited in 2019, no ride-sharing services operated in the county because poverty made it impossible for residents to own and maintain an operable vehicle. The distance between towns and within communities disincentivized individuals from becoming Uber or Lyft drivers. And without reliable and accessible high-speed broadband, it was impossible to receive notifications about a potential pickup.

"We have to send our people to them," Gregan pointed out, "[it] could be a two-hour drive in the most rural parts of the county." Even when his caseworkers made it to the client's house, Gregan continued that they would return to the office to input the client's case information, and it could be two weeks before they went back to the home to verify the data and check the status before starting the process over again. Gregan jabbed at D.C. lawmakers who prioritized the issue of addiction but failed to create programs that offer pragmatic solutions, like leveraging technology for client treatment and recovery.

But this rural county was not alone in its inefficiencies, and most social service providers remain dependent on "in line" or in-person service delivery versus "online" methods of administration, and use paper-based, tracking, other non-digital case management systems. In hopes of addressing this, the Action Center and county officials partnered with DNG and Barry to bring broadband access to subsidized housing in rural areas, which for a small monthly fee, allowed tenants to receive monthly service without being charged for equipment and other set-up fees. Funded by the Rural Maryland Council, the pilot was designed to accelerate connectivity for families in the most need of supportive services, whose members have a location of residence where the internet can be installed and accessed.[23] DNG was also piloting local kiosks throughout the county to better connect residents to services. It is betting on these public devices to benefit the members of the Amish and Mennonite communities, who tend to cluster with their own.

The limitations of the Action Center should incent opportunities for federal and state dollars to modernize analog and archaic service delivery systems for caseworkers to track, certify, and report on vulnerable families. Having residents with broadband access enables them to maintain steady contact with their case workers or relays the urgency for an office visit for rural residents. If broadband access for rural areas is primarily focused on addressing more common concerns—once again, based on a binary definition of the digital divide—millions of people in these geographically isolated communities will continue to succumb to the dispositions of poverty, social isolation, deteriorating mental health, and increasing drug use for no other reasons than the absence of other alternatives.

"We need technology that is right for our tool kit," Gregan asserted on these points. While Washington lawmakers have echoed similar calls to action for rural residents, it has not really heard their particular wants and needs.

Gregan summed it up this way: "In the end, it's all about the people. We need to build a sustainable plan for them to access broadband."

In my years working in community technology and exploring pertinent public policies, it does seem as if the people are often forgotten in the grandiose plans of policymakers to make broadband more universally available. Despite the emphasis on connecting their constituents, the channeling of extraordinarily expansive resources to areas that are the most difficult to activate does not generate the appropriate returns on investment—at least that what is said by large telecom incumbents, which before the COVID-19 pandemic found create ways to distribute 5G wireless services.

Why Is Closing the Rural Broadband Divide So Hard?

All the personal encounters with ordinary individuals struggling to connect in a digital world led me to wonder why closing the rural broadband divide is so challenging. Bruce Rieker represented the Nebraska Farm Bureau Federation at a 2018 roundtable that I attended in Lincoln, Nebraska. He said: "It's simple. A farmer can buy a million-dollar tractor with all the bells and whistles enabling it for broadband use. But without high-speed access, that farmer just bought another tractor."

Jon Yoder and his farm, the mechanic and the teacher in one of the five rooms at a local school, Gregan and Daphne, and the Action Center have all found Barry and DNG's television white spaces as their solution to the battles they face when it comes to digital access.

These shared experiences also show that rural America is not monolithic, and their varied problems cannot be resolved by a one-size, wholesale solution. Online connectivity—whatever the route for provisioning it—can help mitigate current social problems—not the other way around.

For Garrett County, TVWS was perhaps their short-term solution for deploying networks that made sense for daily activities of county residents; but in other rural communities, other choices like fiber, fixed wireless, and maybe satellite may be the most reasonable route. What was clear in this technology application to disseminate connectivity was that the farmer, the teacher, the business owner, the case manager, and the small ISP could all become more visible and effective in the digital ecosystem.

The Wholesaling of Rural Broadband

In 2017, the FCC reported that it would cost $40 billion to bring high-speed broadband access to 98 percent of the United States.[24] The proportion of investments allocated to expanding rural access is much greater, largely due to the large topographies and costs that make it more difficult to co-locate broadband assets alongside existing telecommunication facilities. During the Trump administration, in September 2019, FCC chairman Ajit Pai authorized $1.49 billion over the next ten years for the existing Connect America Fund, which has led the part of the country's universal service program that is charged with accelerating communication services to rural areas. This and other more recent Connect America Fund investments are projected to reach upward of 700,000 underserved rural households and businesses in a variety of midwestern and western states.[25] And these monies are complementary to other resources appropriated by the FCC, including an 2019 allotment of $4.9 billion that was awarded to 171 local wireless carriers over the next ten years to accelerate rural broadband deployment, and is expected to reach more than 455,000 homes and businesses that are in high-cost rural areas with limited proximity to telecommunications facilities.[26]

The FCC also has the $20.4 billion Rural Digital Opportunity Fund, to bring high-speed fixed broadband services to rural homes and small businesses. Two years after Pai's first announcement and into the later part of Trump's term, in November 2021, the Rural Digital Opportunity Fund program disbursed over $1.7 billion and also authorized spending $709 million on fifty providers serving 400,000 locations.[27]

During the pandemic, the FCC released additional monies to mitigate the lack of broadband access in rural America as part of the coronavirus stimulus program, which was funded by increased congressional relief for affected families and businesses. In addition to the $3.2 billion Emergency Broadband Benefit to make the internet more affordable for Americans in need and the $7.17 billion Emergency Connectivity Fund to help schools and libraries provide internet access to local communities, the FCC also created a Rural Telehealth Initiative and increased funding for Rural Health Care Program services, providing $802.7 million for the 2020 funding year.[28] In addition, the FCC granted providers additional spectrum to help reach rural communities.[29]

Even before Trump prioritized these areas, funding has always been significantly higher due to the more expensive infrastructure expectations when compared with those of urban areas. Yet despite the healthy streams of resources through multiple programs managed by the FCC and the U.S. Department of Agriculture, the digital divide in rural areas has remained constant and, in some instances, has had an impact on more residents than we are probably aware of.

But another factor resonates around the constant and consistent support for rural broadband in the United States: it has become a highly politicized issue, even more so during the COVID-19 pandemic. From campaign priorities to legislative directives, rural broadband has been an integral part of national conversations to close the digital divide. Policymakers have made these promises to bridge the rural connectivity gaps that affect farmers, small and large business owners, students, and other residents time and time again, while little has changed for them.

And It Does Not Stop Here

In 2019, former representative Antonio Delgado (D-NY), an alum from my college, Colgate University, who is now lieutenant governor under Kathy Hochul in New York State, led a bipartisan effort with colleagues Rodney Davis (R-IL), Abigail Spanberger (D-VA), and forty-six other House members to call for increased funding for the U.S. Department of Agriculture's Rural e-Connectivity Pilot Program (ReConnect), which supported partnerships for local officials interested in expanding high-speed broadband to their respective communities.[30] Introduced in 2020, the bill complemented efforts to increase support for the Farm Bill loan and grant program.[31] Delgado is from Schenectady, and our paths never crossed when we were both in the Upstate area.

The previous and future referenda on rural broadband should not come as a surprise from a legislator who understands what it means to live geographically isolated and for a country familiar with and nostalgic for the Rural Electrification Act in 1936 under the New Deal–era President Franklin D. Roosevelt. His efforts allowed the federal government to make low-cost loans to farmers who established nonprofit cooperatives to bring electricity into rural areas.[32]

Decades ago, Senator George Norris (R-NE) expressed concern for farmers or homesteaders from rural America who were not receiving their "fair chance" to participate in the economy due to the economic meltdowns precipitated by the

Great Depression.[33] Rural Americans were prematurely growing old and dying, due to the "great gap between their lives and the lives of those whom the accident of birth or choice placed them in these towns or cities."[34] Through the newly created Rural Electrification Administration by the federal government and the work of rural electric cooperatives, more than 80 percent of farms had electric service by the 1950s, revolutionizing these locations and how they provided their services.[35] Today, rural electric cooperatives continue to exist, providing service to more than 5.5 million rural customers. Over $34 billion has been invested in these types of cooperatives and projects from the U.S. Department of Agriculture since 2009, and the availability of electricity continues to support emerging use cases, including renewable energies and smart grid technologies.[36]

A *New York Times* opinion writer in 2019 called for the re-creation of a similar entity for rural broadband.[37] Congressman Jim Clyburn (D-SC) and Senator Amy Klobuchar (D-MN) made a similar case with legislation they introduced in 2020.[38] Citing market failures as the primary reason for government intervention, both legislators presented that a more coordinated approach to data collection and deployment would generate better outcomes for the rural poor and business-disadvantaged, whose circumstances have seen little change despite the decades of generous investments.

Rural broadband can be the sweet spot for most legislators, regardless of party line. Notably, in his 2016 presidential campaign, Trump made claims to rural populations as his prime constituents and allies. And the strategy paid off. Rural white men and women flocked to the polls to vote for him over former secretary of state Hillary Clinton due to their heightened anxieties around the economy, jobs, immigration, and the future for their children.[39] Getting broadband to their communities was one of the pillars of the Trump campaign, who vowed to accelerate 5G deployment, restrict Chinese telecom companies from entering U.S. markets, deregulate the industry, and implement infrastructure proposals during his four-year term.[40] Yet by the end of his presidency, Trump was unable to deliver on his infrastructure promises.[41]

During the 2020 presidential election, President Biden included rural broadband development in his campaign.[42] Once in office, he also put forth one of the most aggressive economy recovery plans, the Infrastructure Investment and Jobs Act, which I discussed throughout the book so far.[43]

But despite the efforts to make rural broadband a bullet on campaign flyers and in politicians' talking points, huge infusions of federal dollars and political leaning on this issue have changed little for the residents of Garrett County. Many of the federal proposals did not meet people where they were, and because of that, the policies were never going to solve the connectivity problem they had. People like Jon Yoder are technology-neutral, in the sense that they have no preference for fiber, cable, Wi-Fi, or even TVWS. They simply want an affordable solution that provides high-speed broadband access. Social service providers like Gregan and the now retired Daphne desire to leverage existing and emerging technologies to do a better job serving the residents who simply cannot avoid the consequences that come with living in a very geographically isolated town within a very large county. Efforts to depoliticize rural broadband, and approach it from a more hyperlocal circumstance, could alleviate the digital disparities experienced by thousands upon thousands of people who have lived in rural America for generations.

However, there are other dimensions of the problem that warrant attention. That is the fact that in my travels to Garrett County, I did not see anyone who looked like me. All the residents I encountered in this county were white. I was the only person of color during those eight hours—still identifiably Black, even as the white snowflakes fell thickly on my black, knit cap and face. Daphne mentioned that the county needs to do better with diversity, especially as it is one of the areas known to have a more active Ku Klux Klan affiliate. In 2020, a Middle Eastern family reported the sighting of a KKK member as they backed out of their vacation rental in Deep Creek, which was found unsubstantiated by the local police.[44] This incident, in the backdrop of the swollen racial polarization during the pandemic after the murder of George Floyd in 2020, sparked further condemnation of the Klan and the history of such activity in the county.

For me, this prompted a deeper inquiry into who lives in rural America and how communities of differing demographics handle the digital divide there. In my various travels, I discovered that there is, in fact, the tale of two communities within large cities and small towns—often divided by a railroad track that once represented the end of racism, discrimination, and thwarted economic opportunities.

This is why I also traveled to Staunton, Virginia, in hopes of learning more about the diversity of America's rural populations and how they leverage broadband for the quality of their lives. In the next chapter, I show how rural broadband is of interest not just to white farmers but also to others of differing backgrounds who seek to find jobs and gain the benefits of the digital economy. This was part of my quest to find more people than cows in rural areas.

Notes

1. U.S. Census Bureau, "QuickFacts: Garrett County, Maryland," https://www.census.gov/quickfacts/fact/table/garrettcountymaryland#.
2. Maryland Department of Labor, "Garrett County Major Employers Size Category," https://dllr.state.md.us/lmi/emplists/garrett.shtml.
3. Brad Smith and Carol Ann Browne, *Tools and Weapons: The Promise and the Peril of the Digital Age* (New York: Penguin, 2021).
4. Microsoft Airband Initiative, *Microsoft: Corporate Social Responsibility*, https://www.microsoft.com/en-us/corporate-responsibility/airband-initiative.
5. Garrett County Government, Maryland, "DNG Announces Launch of NeuBeam High Speed Internet: Technology," October 20, 2016, https://business.garrettcounty.org/2016/news/10.

6. Federal Communications Commission, "Amendment of Part 15 Rules for Unlicensed White Spaces Devices," March 20, 2019, https://www.fcc.gov/document/amendment-part-15-rules-unlicensed-white-spaces-devices.

7. Microsoft, "Declaration Networks Group and Microsoft Announce Agreement to Deliver Broadband Internet to Rural Communities in Virginia and Maryland," April 24, 2018, https://news.microsoft.com/2018/04/24/declaration-networks-group-and-microsoft-announce-agreement-to-deliver-broadband-internet-to-rural-communities-in-virginia-and-maryland/.

8. Microsoft.

9. "FCC Authorizes Nearly $2.9 Million for Broadband in Garrett County," *Cumberland Times-News*, August 13, 2019, https://www.times-news.com/news/local_news/fcc-authorizes-nearly-2-9-million-for-broadband-in-garrett-county/article_1389c72d-ecdc-577f-bc2a-20095c57e517.html.

10. John B. Horrigan, "Disconnected in Maryland," Abell Foundation, January 2021, https://abell.org/sites/default/files/files/2020_Abell_digital%20inclusion_full%20report_FINAL-web.pdf.

11. Horrigan.

12. Renée Shreve. "County Working with Broadband Companies to Expand Service," *Garrett County Republican*, January 16, 2020, https://www.wvnews.com/garrettrepublican/news/county-working-with-broadband-companies-to-expand-service/article_aad7a431-df41-5c4e-bd29-666ff0e1bb85.html; Columbia Telecommunications Corporation, "Broadband in Garrett County: A Strategy for Expansion and Adoption," May 1, 2012, https://www.garrettcounty.org/resources/broadband/pdf/Broadband-Feasibility-Study.pdf.

13. U.S. Department of Agriculture, Economic Research Service, "Farming and Farm Income," https://www.ers.usda.gov/data-products/ag-and-food-statistics-charting-the-essentials/farming-and-farm-income/.

14. U.S. Department of Agriculture, Economic Research Service; Garrett County Public Schools, "Garrett County Public Schools Annual Report and Education Superlatives: 2018–2019," https://go.boarddocs.com/mabe/garrett/Board.nsf/files/BMEL4M54C036/$file/GCPS%20Annual%20Report%20and%20Education%20Superlatives%202018-19.pdf.

15. Maryland State Department of Education, "Maryland Report Card," https://reportcard.msde.maryland.gov/Graphs/#/ReportCards/ReportCardSchool/1/E/1/11/1812/2019; Garrett County Public Schools, "School Improvement Plan 2021–2022 Swan Meadow," https://docs.google.com/document/d/1lXDVHACr3IAxGlMvoCxrOf2JgW5AjVtjN5SSF_diyJg/edit.

16. Garrett County Government, Maryland, "Swan Meadow School Receives 2018 Sustainable Maryland Green School Award: Education," April 30, 2018, https://business.garrettcounty.org/education/news/swan-meadow-school-receives-2018-sustainable-maryland-green-school-award.

17. Garrett County Public Schools, "FIRST Robotics Team 1629 Qualifies for World Championship: Public Information," April 6, 2018, https://www.garrettcountyschools.org/2018/news/04.

18. Beth Macy, *Dopesick: Dealers, Doctors, and the Drug Company That Addicted America* (Boston: Little, Brown, 2018).

19. Allan Coukell. "President Trump Signs Bipartisan Bill to Fight Opioid Crisis." Pew Charitable Trusts, October 24, 2018, https://pew.org/2CvSCaG.

20. "More Than $1.1 Million Awarded to 'Fight' Opioid Crisis in Garrett County," *Garrett County Republican*, August 23, 2019, https://www.wvnews.com/garrettrepublican/news/

more-than-1-1-million-awarded-to-fight-opioid-crisis-in-garrett-county/article_
e078799a-51f0-5536-a8b0-d8363e973729.html.

21. Before It's Too Late, "What You Need to Know About Naloxone," https://howtoadminister
naloxone.maryland.gov/en/drawer.html.

22. U.S. Census Bureau, "QuickFacts: Garrett County, Maryland," https://www.census.gov/
quickfacts/fact/table/garrettcountymaryland#.

23. "GCCAC and Rural Maryland Council Provide Declaration Networks Group with
Grant for Internet Adoption | Declaration Networks, Inc.," March 15, 2018, https://
declarationnetworks.com/press/gccac-and-rural-maryland-council-provide-declaration-
networks-group-with-grant-for-internet-adoption/.

24. Paul de Sa, "Improving the Nation's Digital Infrastructure," FCC Office of Strategic Planning and Policy Analysis, January 17, 2017, https://docs.fcc.gov/public/
attachments/DOC-343135A1.pdf. See also, https://docs.fcc.gov/public/attachments/
DOC-343135A1.pdf.

25. Broadband Breakfast, "Broadband Roundup: FCC Announces More Rural Funding,
Everyone On Expands Footprint, U.S. Telecom Gets Political," September 12, 2019,
https://broadbandbreakfast.com/2019/09/broadband-roundup-fcc-announces-more-
rural-funding-everyone-on-expands-footprint-us-telecom-gets-political/; Federal Communications Commission. "Connect America Fund Phase II FAQS," June 14, 2016,
https://www.fcc.gov/consumers/guides/connect-america-fund-phase-ii-faqs.

26. Federal Communications Commission, "FCC OKs $4.9 Billion to Maintain, Improve,
and Expand Rural Broadband," August 22, 2019, https://www.fcc.gov/document/fcc-
oks-49-billion-maintain-improve-and-expand-rural-broadband.

27. Federal Communications Commission, "FCC Announces Over $700 Million for Broad-
band in 26 States," November 10, 2021, https://www.fcc.gov/document/fcc-announces-
over-700-million-broadband-26states.

28. Federal Communications Commission, "Connecting Americans to Health Care," October 19, 2018, https://www.fcc.gov/connecting-americans-health-care; Federal Communications Commission, "FCC Announces Increase in Rural Health Care Program Funds
for FY 2020," June 30, 2020, https://www.fcc.gov/document/fcc-announces-increase-
rural-health-care-program-funds-fy-2020.

29. Federal Communications Commission, "Keep Americans Connected," March 17, 2020,
https://www.fcc.gov/keep-americans-connected.

30. Representative Antonio Delgado, "Rep. Delgado and USDA Under Secretary Torres Small
Announce $1.15 Billion Broadband Investment in Rural Communities," October 23,
2021, http://delgado.house.gov/media/press-releases/rep-delgado-and-usda-under-secretary-
torres-small-announce-115-billion.

31. U.S. Department of Agriculture, Rural Development, "Rural Broadband Access Loan
and Loan Guarantee," https://www.rd.usda.gov/programs-services/telecommunications-
programs/rural-broadband-access-loan-and-loan-guarantee.

32. National Park Service, "The Rural Electrification Act Provides a 'Fair Chance' to Rural
Americans: Homestead National Historical Park (U.S. National Park Service)," https://
www.nps.gov/home/learn/historyculture/ruralelect.htm.

33. National Park Service.

34. National Park Service.

35. Brandon McBride, "Celebrating the 80th Anniversary of the Rural Electrification Administration," U.S. Department of Agriculture, February 21, 2017, https://www.usda.gov/
media/blog/2016/05/20/celebrating-80th-anniversary-of-rural-electrification-administration.

36. McBride.

37. Christopher Ali, "Opinion: We Need a National Rural Broadband Plan," *New York Times*, February 7, 2019, https://www.nytimes.com/2019/02/06/opinion/rural-broadband-fcc.html.

38. Senator Amy Klobuchar, "Klobuchar, Clyburn Introduce Comprehensive Broadband Infrastructure Legislation to Expand Access to Affordable High-Speed Internet," March 11, 2021, https://www.klobuchar.senate.gov/public/index.cfm/2021/3/klobuchar-clyburn-introduce-comprehensive-broadband-infrastructure-legislation-to-expand-access-to-affordable-high-speed-internet.

39. Rich Morin, "Behind Trump's Win in Rural White America," Pew Research Center, November 17, 2016, https://www.pewresearch.org/fact-tank/2016/11/17/behind-trumps-win-in-rural-white-america-women-joined-men-in-backing-him/.

40. Todd Haselton, "President Trump Announces New 5G Initiatives: It's a Race 'America Must Win,'" CNBC, April 12, 2019, https://www.cnbc.com/2019/04/12/trump-on-5g-initiatives-a-race-america-must-win.html; Ellen Nakashima, "Trump Administration Moves against Chinese Telecom Firms Citing National Security," *Washington Post*, April 10, 2020, https://www.washingtonpost.com/national-security/trump-administration-moves-against-chinese-telecom-firms-citing-national-security/2020/04/10/33532492-7b24-11ea-9bee-c5bf9d2e3288_story.html; Annie Snider and Anthony Adragna, "Trump's Latest Strike against Regulations: His Infrastructure Plan," *Politico*, February 16, 2018, http://politi.co/2EtIVYo; *Washington Post*, "The Attack: Before, During and After," https://www.washingtonpost.com/politics/interactive/2021/jan-6-insurrection-capitol/.

41. John Hendel, "Democrats Torch Trump Failures on Rural Digital Divide," *Politico*, August 17, 2019, https://politico.pro/2z6zLjA.

42. Joe Biden for President: Official Campaign Website. "Joe Biden's Plan for Rural America: Joe Biden for President," https://joebiden.com/rural-plan/.

43. Ayesha Rascoe, "Harris' Broadband Push Could Be Political Windfall—or Pitfall," NPR, https://www.npr.org/2021/05/06/994017450/harris-broadband-push-could-be-political-windfall-or-pitfall.

44. "Family Claims Klan Encounter in Garrett County," *Garrett County Republican*, December 17, 2020, https://www.wvnews.com/garrettrepublican/news/family-claims-klan-encounter-in-garrett-county/article_10c6fd3b-c09b-5bb5-987f-7bd606712c42.html.

4

Rural Is Not Just White and Straight

On the way to Staunton, Virginia, it can be easy to let your mind wander: Corn farms pepper the edges of the highway, cows and farms replace shopping centers, and the smell of manure is hard to ignore if you roll your window down just a nudge. At one point on my journey there in 2019, the route veered farther away from the interstate. Cellular data were quickly waning as only one or two bars were showing up on my mobile phone.

"You have a signal?" I asked my colleague, who joined me again on this trip to photograph the interviews.

"I've got nothing, but we can't be far, so let's keep going," he replied.

Riding in rural areas without navigational assistance reminded me of a previous trip with my kids to summer camp. The first drop off was to the Boy Scouts campground in Goshen, Virginia, before heading to nearby Mount Airy for my daughter's summer adventure. Directions to the first stop were decent because the back roads were manageable and short. But traveling to drop off my daughter was scarier, largely due to the navigation directing us via the backroads with limited or no satellite signals. We were not OK when we first encountered a wide-eyed cow staring down the hood of the car after I took a wrong turn. The second shock was driving through the small town of Craigsville, Virginia, where residents used Confederate flags as curtains. This was around the time of the Trump campaign's feverish attempt to reclaim white, rural residents, and that was obvious with his huge, red signs that sat proudly next to large and round satellite dishes. As with many rural residents' experiences, Walmart would soon be our saving grace after my daughter and I received more than two bars on our phone, and this time, we took screenshots of the directions before getting back on the two-lane road.

When I encountered the same problem on our way to Staunton, the solution was to find a Walmart, pull into the parking lot, and take a photo of the directions. Fortunately, there was one a few miles ahead.

Staunton is divided by its railroad tracks. On one side, the town's green landscape blanketed with proud historical Confederate monuments becomes gray. Sidewalks are replaced by slabs of cracked concrete and a large vacant storefront. In this part of Staunton, historic statues were replaced by large, historic Black churches, whose white exteriors had faded over time. There were no houses immediately near the tracks in this part of town, just an abandoned store propped up on a concrete ledge at the top of the hill leading into the adjacent community.

Founded in 1747, Staunton sits at the crossroads of two interstates in Virginia, 81 and 64. The town was a vibrant transportation hub in the Shenandoah Valley during the Civil War. Back then, residents stood up against the Southern Confederacy until 1902, when the city gained its independence.[1] The town became a refuge for many people within the divided rural South, with freed African Americans migrating to the city for higher wages and better jobs.[2]

Many Black residents have deep roots in the town. After Reconstruction, African Americans migrated to Staunton for higher wages, and mainly found themselves living on the other side of the railroad tracks while working as general laborers and domestics.[3] In the words of the poet Langston Hughes, race relations were no crystal stair in the town, as issues of educational inequities plagued Black residents.[4] Until 1966, the city's public schools were segregated, some twelve years after the U.S. Supreme Court's ruling in *Brown v. Board of Education*.[5] Such is typical of other Black migration movements to flourishing towns after the abolishment of slavery.

Today, Staunton is one of Virginia's fastest growing cities, with a median income of nearly $52,611 and a per capita income slightly more than $30,166, according to 2015–19 U.S. Census data.[6] As of 2019, only 11.3 percent of the city's total population was African American, with non-Hispanic Whites accounting for 81.1 percent of the city's residents, and Hispanics, Asians, and indigenous populations constituting less than 5 percent.[7] Over 11 percent of the population in Staunton lives in poverty—a significant portion of whom are children and seniors over the age of sixty-five.[8]

On the day that I visited Staunton, I was with my friend Christopher Wood, an LGBTQ+ advocate who had recently moved here. While driving around, we spotted an older Black couple in their seventies sitting in front of a modest blue, vinyl siding home. The guardedness of the older couple softened as I introduced myself and disarmed them with my focus on the quality of their internet access. I quickly found out that they both grew up in Staunton and had four children, who were also raised there. When I started asking about their online access, the older woman adamantly shared that she does not go on "the Facebook" anymore, which she perceived as the entirety of the internet. They introduced me to their son, a twenty-something young man who introduced himself as Joseph. Less than a second after he stepped out, his fiancé, holding the hands of two small children, introduced herself as Kizzie.

Joseph and Kizzie shared with me the importance of having internet access, especially in their new roles as parents. She opined about why being connected was crucial to her children's upbringing.

"I went out and got my kids a tablet so they can play games and do educational activities. They need this right now. The world is different," she said, proudly admiring her two children under the age of five.

"You need to have the internet to find a job, go to school, and do just about everything," Joseph chimed in, with his fiancé nodding her head in agreement.

But despite their clear reasons for being connected, Joseph and Kizzie acknowledged the challenges of maintaining online subscriptions, which required them to juggle internet service with other critical expenses. One strategy for prolonging her mobile phone was to use the free Wi-Fi at her mother's house so she could "get on the internet a little longer."

Joseph shared similar tactics, but in his case, his mother did not have home broadband, and the closest coffee shops with public access were downtown, which did not help him much because he did not have a car. For him, the cost of being disconnected was that he had trouble finding and staying employed when his mobile service was interrupted.

"Usually, by the middle of the month, I've run out of minutes [on my phone], making it more difficult to do just about anything to help my fiancé and my children," he explained. "I can't even look for work. This [phone] just becomes a box."

In the middle of his sentence, Joseph's two adult brothers came out of the house to join us. Talking with three generations of brothers, I discovered a very different portrait of rural America than the one gained in Garrett County. There, the internet allowed business owners and farmers to thrive. But here in Staunton, for these young Black men, it was their way of finding and keeping employment. These guys were not farmers, small business owners, or white, but they experienced the same employment drawbacks related to their lack of online connections.

Don, who looked older than Joseph, started; "Here in Staunton, you realize that you're going to be here for a long time. You need some way to keep up with the world and that's through the internet." He had recently moved back home after a short stay out on the West Coast.

Like his brothers, Don relies on his smartphone to stay connected to the internet, much like the estimated 42 million people who lack access to broadband in the United States, according to 2021 data from the watchdog Broadband Now.[9] At least 17.6 million people living in rural areas lack fixed terrestrial broadband, making any type of wireless communications essential to complete basic functions, like searching for work, goods, and services.[10] Don worked in Charlottesville, Virginia, which is a good hour away by car, and described the importance of having a phone as he travels back and forth. The third brother also talked about his long commute to his factory job, and the importance of having his mobile phone, especially when working the night shift.

This tale of two cities reminded me of the complex differences that exist in rural areas—some of which are controllable and others that are not. On one side are people like Chris, who move to rural areas to improve their quality of life. They seek less congestion and the quiet reprieve that rural areas offer. But this is a very different experience from that of these brothers, who have lived here for generations and have virtually no way out. Despite this place being "home," life has become increasingly complicated, as the connected world outpaces the digitally disconnected and invisible.

In many ways, these young men are not too different from the people in Garrett County, Maryland, who benefit from the area's simplicity but remain stagnant when it comes to utilizing emerging innovation and advancement. But these three Black men were also very different from other rural people, because they are not the usual foci of policymakers desiring to advance rural broadband. Black populations were not even the targets of Trump's campaign promises, despite high numbers of Black, Hispanic, and tribal residents living in rural areas, especially in the South.

While wholesaling the deployment and adoption of high-speed broadband is not the solution for achieving universal service, strategies for rural broadband development must consider the wide range of diversity that exists among residents, instead of being zealots about the "most of rural is white" narrative. The three brothers, Kizzie, the mother who distrusted Facebook, and those two adorable children are also part of rural America who live without sufficient access to high-speed broadband and, more importantly, the social and economic opportunities that result from being online.

Further, being poor in Staunton is no different than the experiences of places like Garrett County. When the pandemic hit, physical social distancing prompted more online use, and the navigation of the perfunctory functions in life, including shopping, working, learning, and scheduling a vaccination appointment to avert the potentially fatal consequences of the public health crisis.

The combined effects of income and information poverty have resulted in decades of historical and systemic racism that brought free slaves to the rural areas post-Reconstruction and Amish farmers to the agrarian countryside in search of religious freedoms.[11] The effects of information poverty are more pervasive today, leading to less innovative and sustainable farming, declining job prospects, and other modern-day inefficiencies, like receiving real-time health care or applying for public benefits. Rural communities like Staunton, which were once known for their location near an interstate and railroad,[12] are quickly becoming both unserved and underserved by high-speed broadband, transforming this city and many more like it into invisible places with unrecognizable people.

Chris Wood, the Rural LGBTQ Advocate

On the other side of Staunton, life looks different, though the problems are like those of the people who reside on the other side of the railroad tracks. I came here thanks to my friend Chris, who stopped by my D.C. office as he waited out the traffic on his commute back home in the spring of 2019. Until that day, I did not realize that he lived in Staunton. From how often I saw him at meetings and social events in the city, I assumed that he lived nearby, or at least in the immediate Northern Virginia or Maryland areas. But after meeting his husband, who grew up here, he relocated and was building his third nonprofit, LGBT Technology Partnership, whose mission is to bridge the technology gap for all LGBTQ+ individuals by engaging in research, education, volunteerism, and providing technology resources, like smartphones, to disadvantaged members of the community. The organization primarily focuses on the technology needs of LGBTQ+ populations in rural communities as part of its efforts to bolster digital equity and inclusion.

Chris is no stranger to taking such risks. At twenty-five, he survived a tense hostage situation by the first U.S. suicide bomber when James Jae Lee came into the headquarters of Discovery Communications in Silver Spring, Maryland, on September 1, 2010. Chris was one of two hostages, and was instrumental in navigating their escape from Lee, who was eventually shot dead by the police. Chris's heroism landed him an invitation on the *Oprah Winfrey Show*, during which he recounted the experience: "As I was laying on the floor, I just said I am not ready to die," he shared with Oprah. "This is not the way I'm going to die. I have a lot more to do."[13] Back then, he was a marketing professional for Discovery's TLC network, and today, he is an out gay man, advocating for technology access for LGBTQ+ populations held hostage in rural communities.

During his visit, Chris quipped about having too many meetings, lunches, blah, blah, and blah, but he also dreamed out loud about his goals for LGBT Tech and the excitement of becoming a new dad to a young foster child, whom he described as a jewel, and the reason for taking the drive back home instead of crashing at his mother's, who lived nearby. Today, Chris and his husband are dads to four young boys and just recently moved to New York.

When I visited Staunton, I met Chris met in front of an old dairy building, which was being converted into Staunton's first tech incubator and co-working space. Called the Staunton Innovation Hub (iHub), LGBT Tech was planning to share office space with other local organizations and entrepreneurs. As soon as we approached him, he reminded me of Barry Toser with a wide-grinned smile, and pride that we had made it.

A young woman in her late twenties, the founder of iHub, stood next to him. Covered in colorful tattoos peeking from the collar of her shirt and running down her arms, she shared her vision for the redesigned dairy factory. A former resident of Richmond, and a graduate of Virginia Commonwealth University, she shared how she spent her professional career helping low-income women transition into entrepreneurship and how broadband access was going to be critical for residents who want to productively engage the new economy—now at this location in the middle of rural Staunton.

"Broadband is going to be the critical link for this space and the city to be successful," she said. "More people would come to this community if we had better access to high-speed broadband."

The iHub has other anchor organizations, including space for Mary Baldwin University, one of the oldest women's universities in Virginia. It supports individual co-working spaces for local artists, entrepreneurs, and business owners, which came in handy when the global pandemic hit. In an ideal world, the gold standard for high-speed broadband would be gigabyte service to drive improved economic opportunities for residents and small business owners. But that was a long while away—right now, the focus was on getting people who chose to live in rural Staunton what they needed to stay productive and self-sufficient.

Chris expressed his own enthusiasm as it related to his nonprofit. "Having access to technology gives LGBTQ+ youth and adults the ability to fend for themselves when it comes to finding social services like housing and food," he shared. "It's already tough being gay, but when you're LGBTQ in rural Staunton that's another story." Such assertions should not be taken lightly. In 2015, a group of researchers published on the higher rates of suicide among youth age ten to twenty-four in rural communities.[14] The authors also noted that such incidences were increasing over time, especially due to the lack of real-time and available resources.[15] The Trevor Project, a national LGBTQ advocacy organization, reported that rural youth reported feeling like their communities were unaccepting of their sexual orientation at double the rate of their suburban and urban counterparts.[16] This has devastating effects on youth. Overwhelming feelings of depression, suicide, or attempted suicide have followed rural youth, and in some instances, led to explicit discrimination, which makes Chris's work of offering smartphones and other technologies to the youth of Staunton and surrounding communities even more compelling. It also surfaces the digital invisibility of people based on their sexual orientation and preferences who have been unable to live out loud and openly in communities with fierce repudiation of their lifestyles.

That is why rural is not just the familiar political persuasion of white, heterosexual farmers, religious conservatives, and other stark ideologues who only voted for Trump. There is diversity on Main Street, which also requires online access to fully express their needs and their sense of belongingness.

Prioritizing Main Street

Every rural town always has an area designated as its main port of economic vibrancy for residents. It has the furniture store, the post office, and the store that has just about everything. All of them sit on Main Street, among a few jewelers and antique establishments. My friend Chris and his husband owned a store on Main Street, selling candles and modern décor. It turns out that his husband's grandparents were the owners of the city's first Burger King, putting the spirit of entrepreneurship in his genes. I could not resist buying one of their scented candles and could not help but smile when I saw that the store used a wireless-enabled device as their cash register. Since 2019, these online credit and debit processing units have become more widespread in the city and country.[17]

Before the pandemic, in-store sales were more regular, but Chris's husband forecasted the need to get his goods online long before the public health crisis affected their business. Now, he is glad they did that.

"We make so much more money from our online sales," he shared as we finished the transaction, "But without faster broadband, we find it hard to keep up with demand."

Talking to him, I realized—this time, in person—the source of Chris's joy. Minutes later, a young toddler ran into the store, hugged them both tightly and ran in a circle around this familiar place. He was the beautiful foster child who was now legally his son. He was the reason why he needed that one hour to wait out the traffic and stave off his exhaustion before making his way home for dinner. Their son even hugged me as he jumped from the top of a stairway leading to the upstairs of the store.

After leaving the store, we met another city resident, who owned the local barbershop. He was African American with a huge, welcoming smile—something that felt like a commonplace sight in these rural communities. He was also open about being formerly homeless in Richmond, going between local housing shelters before bringing his family to Staunton. Despite overcoming such economic hurdles, the barbershop had his own perceptions about the embeddedness of digital invisibility in a small, rural town—not only because he is Black but also because of the lack of internet access.

"The internet is so important today. What would we do without it?" he shared.

This barber also knew something that the nation apparently forgot when the pandemic hit—that twenty-first-century learning requires an internet connection. In late 2018, he installed a Wi-Fi hotspot in his tiny barbershop of one chair for local students to complete their homework, even if they were not waiting for a haircut.

"I want to make sure that these kids get an opportunity to see the outside world through the internet," he said emphatically, "I didn't have that chance and so it's important that they can do so at my shop, especially the kids that don't have internet at home."

After leaving the barbershop, we interacted with many more Main Street business owners who desired to be connected to the internet for the purpose of being able to live out similar quality that they experienced in larger cities. One of these folks was an executive sous-chef at the renowned Inn of Little Washington in nearby Washington, Virginia, who came to Staunton with his love for food from locally grown products.[18] But, according to him, the lack of reliable broadband access stifled his ability to order other products and services.

"I speak to our local broadband provider all the time, and they are pretty honest when they say it is expensive to bring better service to Staunton," he shared with me as I stood at the counter.

"And what do they say?" I asked.

"We do need more broadband. [Listen,] we want to do more to showcase our local crops, our products, and services. Without high-speed internet, you can't do everything possible for the residents and businesses of Staunton. If you go just 15 minutes outside of the city and live on a farm, you have nothing, unless you have satellite."

In many ways, his feedback mirrored that of Jon Yoder, who shared the impact of limited online resources, or the mechanic shop owner in Garrett County who badly needed to be online to enhance productivity. From farmers, merchants, and restauranters, the challenge of having less-than-desirable broadband resonates. Thwarted broadband access and digitization affects prospects for profitability. Less than two years after meeting the sous-chef, the pandemic forced the energetic businessman with decades of experience in hospitality to close the restaurant in late 2020 due to the lack of profit and the increasing need for broadband to transition to other business models.

In my mind, I kept thinking, "Do our lawmakers and other policymakers understand that this is not a matter of wishing, but of necessity, for connecting millions of rural Americans?"

America's Broken Lifeline to Broadband

To answer this question, one only needs to examine the concept of universal service in the United States. As described in the previous chapter, two programs of the Federal Communications Commission have been the primary drivers for rural broadband deployment and use: the Connect America Fund, which addresses rural infrastructure; and the Lifeline program, which confronts affordability.[19] The latter is critical in rural areas with an unequal distribution of income and wealth.

Lifeline, or America's solution to advance universal adoption, was established in 1984 under President Ronald Reagan. It was created for eligible families who lacked adequate and stable connections to communications, which were dial-up telephony at the time.[20] Since its inception, the program has undergone continuous scrutiny, largely by Republican legislators and regulators, who tout the perceived waste, fraud, and abuse.[21] From all my years studying this program, these are not relevant and justified concerns.

More than 2.3 million people were stripped of the $9.25 subsidy by the Trump Federal Communications Commission, after it undertook measures to curb duplicate accounts and instituted the National Eligibility Verifier, which is still a work in progress.[22] These measures created unnecessarily complicated hoops that those in need of the service were unable to jump through. Under Trump, the program also limited the number and type of participating service providers eligible to screen and allot payments for the Lifeline program, affecting the nation's largest telecom provider, TracFone, whose business model was primarily funded through Lifeline subscriptions.[23]

Despite how the program is perceived as a significant element in the fight to close digital disparities, in Staunton, Joseph, his fiancé, and his brothers knew nothing about it. Contrary to political complaints that the program has been abused by people who have applied for multiple accounts or smuggled the phones into prisons, it appears that many in need still are not reached by the program. It is worth pointing out that white rural residents are also Lifeline subscribers. According to 2021 National Lifeline Association study, 38 percent of polled Lifeline subscribers reported their race as white;[24] this compares with 20 percent of polled subscribers reporting their race as Black and 16.5 percent as Hispanic. While neither the study nor Universal Service Administrative Company data report the percentage of Lifeline subscribers in urban versus rural areas, an analysis of October 2021 county-level Lifeline subscriptions revealed that 814,000 Lifeline subscribers (12.75 percent) were in counties where most of the population lives in what the 2010 Census considered rural areas.[25]

We Are a Long Way from Closing the Rural Divide

The experiences in rural Garrett County and Staunton demonstrate that policymakers continue to employ the same models and solutions to rural broadband development but are not getting the needed results. While the people on the wrong side of digital opportunities tend to be low-income populations, they are also farmers, educators, social service providers, small business owners, and entrepreneurs who are affected by the speed at which broadband is being deployed. That is why one-size-fits-all strategies for rural broadband deployment are insufficient for closing the digital divide and addressing the challenges affecting the disconnected. In fact, the lack of connectivity is further deepening the consequences for these individuals and their communities over the pandemic, when being connected to jobs, health care, education, and more became even more important.

In Garrett County, the mechanic closed the doors of the tire shop because he could not transition to a fully online platform; much like the restaurant owner in Staunton. Gregan and Daphne saw an increase in opioid deaths during the pandemic and their ability to facilitate care and interventions worsened. The whereabouts of the barber are unknown at this point, much like the students who regularly came to his shop for haircuts as they became disconnected from learning.

In fact, I could not locate Joseph after my initial visit. I had written a short blog on my visit to Staunton in early 2020 for Brookings and received a note from a reader who wanted to donate a laptop to his family and pay for a year of internet service. On a trip to Roanoke later that year, I stopped by the family home to share the good news. This was almost six months after my initial visit. His mother once again came to the door. This time, she kept the door partly closed because I must have come at a bad time. But after she recalled my face, she let me know that she had not seen Joseph in a while, and that he had broken up with his fiancé. He also did not have his phone because of nonpayment and the only way that she could contact him was through his new girlfriend's cell phone. She dialed her, then handed me the phone.

This was before the pandemic spiraled into a global nightmare, when I reconnected with Joseph, through a partially opened screen door at his parents' home.

"Hi, it's Nicol. The lady that you met a few months ago," I shared over the phone. "I have good news. A person wants to give you a laptop and pay for your mobile service for at least a year. How does that sound?"

"Very nice, ma'am," he said, not clearly understanding the offer. "I'm interested, but right now, I can't give you all the details. Maybe, my momma can help out." The conversation ended with only two more sentences—one of which included a "thank you" before I handed the phone back to his mother.

"You know, they are not together anymore, so I'm not sure if the laptop will help," she chimed in. "But thanks, though." The door closed and I returned to my car, feeling somewhat as if I had not been able to reach the young men, but not sure why that had happened.

America has broken its social contract with rural communities and has failed to support their critical needs. And we continue to violate that trust because we idolize old remnants of what used to be in cities created by horrid histories. Instead, we should be leveraging the transformative power of technology and innovation to piece together the fragments of what is left. What is clear is that the number of digitally invisible people in rural areas is much more than counted or imagined.

Notes

1. City of Staunton, Virginia, "All About Stan-Ton," https://visitstaunton.com/feature/all-about-stan-ton/.

2. William G. Thomas, Richard G. Healey, and Ian Cottingham, "Reconstructing African American Mobility after Emancipation, 1865–67," *Social Science History* 41, no. 4 (2017): 673–704, https://doi.org/10.1017/ssh.2017.23.

3. Valley Project, "A Brief History of Staunton, Virginia," http://www2.iath.virginia.edu/staunton/history.html.

4. Langston Hughes. "Mother to Son," Poetry Foundation, November 22, 2021, https://www.poetryfoundation.org/poems/47559/mother-to-son.

5. Justia Law, "*Bell v. School Board of City of Staunton, Virginia*, 249 F. Supp. 249 (W.D. Va. 1966)," https://law.justia.com/cases/federal/district-courts/FSupp/249/249/1457633/.

6. U.S. Census Bureau. "QuickFacts: Staunton City, Virginia," https://www.census.gov/quickfacts/fact/table/stauntoncityvirginia/PST045219.

7. US Census Bureau.

8. US Census Bureau.

9. John Busby, Julia Tanberk, and Tyler Cooper, "BroadbandNow Estimates Availability for All 50 States; Confirms That More Than 42 Million Americans Do Not Have Access to Broadband," Broadband Now, May 5, 2021, https://broadbandnow.com/research/fcc-broadband-overreporting-by-state.

10. Busby, Tanberk, and Cooper.

11. Library of Congress. "Reconstruction and Its Aftermath: The African American Odyssey—A Quest for Full Citizenship," February 9, 1998, https://www.loc.gov/exhibits/african-american-odyssey/reconstruction.html.

12. Library of Congress, "Valley Railroad, Folly Mills Creek Viaduct, Interstate 81, Staunton, Staunton, VA," image, https://www.loc.gov/item/va0260/.

13. Library of Congress.

14. Cynthia A Fontanella, Danielle L Hiance-Steelesmith, Gary S Phillips, Jeffrey A Bridge, Natalie Lester, Helen Anne Sweeney, and John V Camp, "Widening Rural-Urban Disparities in Youth Suicides, United States, 1996–2010," *JAMA Pediatrics*, May, 2016, 466–73, https://pubmed.ncbi.nlm.nih.gov/25751611/.

15. Fontanella and others.

16. Trevor Project, "Research Brief: LGBTQ Youth in Small Towns and Rural Areas," November 2021, https://www.thetrevorproject.org/wp-content/uploads/2021/11/The-Trevor-Project_-Rural-LGBTQ-Youth-November-2021.pdf.

17. Julia Rittenberg, "Square vs. Clover for Businesses," *Forbes Advisor*, October 1, 2021, https://www.forbes.com/advisor/business/software/square-vs-clover/.

18. Susan Kiers. "Mike Lund FOOD," Oxeyevineyards, October 2, 2012, https://www.oxeyevineyards.com/post/mike-lund-food.

19. Federal Communications Commission, "Connect America Fund Phase II FAQS," June 14, 2016, https://www.fcc.gov/consumers/guides/connect-america-fund-phase-ii-faqs; Federal Communications Commission, "Lifeline Program for Low-Income Consumers," January 27, 2012, https://www.fcc.gov/general/lifeline-program-low-income-consumers.

20. "The Lifeline Program Through The Years: From Origins to the Present," CBS Miami, January 19, 2015, https://miami.cbslocal.com/2015/01/19/the-lifeline-program-through-the-years-from-origins-to-the-present/.

21. Brendan Sasso, "Republicans: 'Obamaphone' Program Is 'Everything That's Wrong with Washington,'" *The Hill*, October 11, 2013, https://thehill.com/policy/technology/328171-republicans-obamaphone-program-is-everything-thats-wrong-with-washington.

22. Jared Bennett and Ashley Wong, "Under Trump, Millions of Poor Lose Access to Cell-phone Service," *USA Today*, November 5, 2019, https://www.usatoday.com/story/news/investigations/2019/11/05/under-trump-millions-poor-lose-cellphone-service/2482112001/.

23. Ryan Barwick, "Millions Could Lose Low-Cost Phone Service under FCC Reforms," September 4, 2018, https://publicintegrity.org/inequality-poverty-opportunity/millions-could-lose-low-cost-phone-service-under-fcc-reforms/.
24. National Lifeline Association, "Summer 2021 NaLA Lifeline and EBB Subscriber Survey Results," https://ecfsapi.fcc.gov/file/1007003413241/NaLA%20Lifeline%20and%20EBB%20OCH%20Ex%20Parte%20(Oct%202021).pdf.
25. Universal Service Administrative Company, "Program Data," https://www.usac.org/lifeline/resources/program-data/.

PART **III**

Continued Urban Neglect

In this nation where you live matters. Your address determines almost everything about you—your chances of graduating from high school or college, getting arrested, net worth, income, ability to own a home, credit score and how long you will live. Your zip code is a better determinant of your health than your genetic code. Segregation creates a built inequitable environment where resources and opportunities get concentrated in predominately white communities and are sparsely located in communities of color."

—Testimony of Lisa Rice, president and CEO,
National Fair Housing Alliance, before the
U.S. Senate Committee on Banking,
Housing, and Urban Affairs, April 13, 2021

5

The Persistent Housing Crises

I n 1991, Alex Kotlowitz published the book *There Are No Children Here*, in which he documented the experiences of two young boys growing up in one of the many public housing developments in Chicago—the Henry Horner Homes.[1] Built in 1957 and named after the state's former governor, the development originally covered more than ten city blocks near the West Side. By the late 1990s and after multiple building additions, 1,897 residents lived in 1,580 units at Henry Horner, whose buildings stood desolate in the backdrop of Chicago's United Center, where the Bulls played championship basketball.

In 2015, Kotlowitz returned to Henry Horner Homes. By that time, the properties were slated for demolition as part of the larger urban removal campaign of Chicago's low-income Black residents. The city's "Plan for Transformation" was spearheaded by then Mayor Richard M. Daley, whose own father had created the disaster that generated the Chicago public housing crisis. Part of the plan included tearing down public housing developments that, over the years, had become more like industrial prison complexes to make way for 25,000 new and renovated mixed-income housing units. The Henry Horner Homes was on the list with pretty much all the existing housing stock. While designed to combat the decrepit living conditions of poorly managed housing and surrounding communities, the plan also turned out to be a sweeping attempt to erase any remnants of the city's beleaguered and racist public housing crisis. After his last visit to the Henry Horner Homes, Kotlowitz wrote these words in a *Chicago*

Reporter article that pretty much summed up life in America's public housing developments:

> They were neighborhoods of mostly African American families tucked away, out of sight, out of mind. To say that they were neglected feels too benign. They were abused. Their spirits were broken by decisions made by city's fathers, including the decision to build public housing, the bulk of which was erected in the late 1950s, on the edge of already existing ghettoes so that they served as a kind of bulwark to segregation. The sequestration, the concentration of the very poor, the construction of high-rises on the cheap led to a set of conditions that a presidential commission compared to "a concentration camp."[2]

I had just moved to Chicago at this time and was fully aware of the inhabitable conditions that confronted public housing residents. Before starting the Northwest Tower computer lab, I had seen the conditions at the Robert Taylor Homes, which were ironically named after an antipoverty activist who fought for equal access to housing, especially for Black populations migrating to Chicago post-Reconstruction. Within a few weeks of moving to the city for graduate school, I met a woman from Brooklyn at the Carter G. Woodson library on the South Side, who encouraged me to volunteer at Firman Community Services—a request that I also did not refuse because you probably figured out that I love volunteering. Firman was founded in 1872 as a local church's outreach mission and is still located on the same corner in the community today; it provided social services to Robert Taylor residents stuck in the crossroads of increasing community violence, drug trafficking, and high rates of addiction and unemployment. I spent time in the South Side for about a year, which was around the time I met Don, and, since life is circular, I returned to the South Side to open a new computer lab many years later after the mayor announced his new Plan for Transformation. My computer technology partners and I had won a bid to start a third computer lab in the Grand Boulevard community some would refer to as Bronzeville, where Firman was also located. The community was not only the hub of African American businesses and cultural artifacts in the early twentieth century but also the birthplace of many Black influential leaders like Gwendolyn Brooks, Richard Wright, Louis Armstrong, Bessie Coleman, and Ida B. Wells, among others. For the sociologists Drake and Cayton, Bronzeville was the Black Metropolis.[3]

In the middle 2000s, the community changed, as 50,000 of the predominately Black residents became unemployed, which worsened the already spiraling housing, economic, and social conditions of the community. The Black residents were segregated from the opulence and security of the city's downtown and wealthier white communities. Our newest computer lab was created in response to these conditions, after the Chicago Housing Authority (CHA) commissioned a request for proposals for not only a new lab but also related job training programs at the Charles A. Hayes Family Investment Center, as I mentioned earlier in the book. Hayes was also a well-known Black union leader and former congressmen. The intentions of the computer lab were deliberate, as the CHA had imposed new criteria on existing Robert Taylor residents to complete or be enrolled in qualified training programs for recertification of their housing eligibility in the future mixed-income developments—which had been half the size of their original community. Honestly, it was as if our lab was conspiring with the devil to aid and abet the further exclusion of Black residents who had already paid their dues for second-class residency. But this opportunity landed in our laps around the time of the Bush administration's reduction in spending, which made the new lab quite appealing, as well as the multi-million-dollar, multi-year grant agreement that came with the project. We were also surrounded by good people at the agency, Adrienne Bitoy Jackson was working alongside Cass Miller, who was the newly appointed facilities manager for the entire building.

We gave the same energy to the new lab on the South Side as we had given to the residents at the Northwest Tower and Homan Square. With a team of about eight people—including administrative staff, course designers, and instructors—we enrolled current and former public housing residents in a range of course offerings, including computer hardware and software skills like Microsoft Office, network and security certification, and just about any training curricula that I could get my hands on free or at a nominal cost. At one point, we partnered with CompTia and taught residents—some of whom did not have a GED, A+ certification, and fiber installation. I will never forget when two former CHA residents completed the security and refurbishment classes and returned as program instructors. One of them even moved out of public housing while working for us.

Throughout the various experiences establishing, managing, and operating the computer labs, I kept thinking about Don Samuelson, who talked about the importance of placing technology in the home or ensuring that the transformative connections made through technology be readily available to people wherever they lived. But the digital revolution was slow to reach the tens of thousands of people living in Chicago's public housing, and many people like them across the United States. For decades, policymakers have been busy carving out these boundaries between rich and poor communities and between Black and white populations, along with other attributes like language, age, and ability. And with very little coincidence, our digital history has merely replicated this, which is why I consider being connected to the internet another social determinant of one's quality of life.

The History of Housing and Community Redlining

That all or most urban areas with predominately low-income and nonwhite populations remain sorely underconnected should come as no surprise. And to understand how this came to be, we have to first look at the history of housing redlining and discrimination in America. The first public housing development in the United States, Atlanta's Techwood Homes, was created by President Franklin Delano Roosevelt as part of his New Deal programs in 1935.[4] Two years later, Roosevelt signed the Wagner-Steagall Housing Act, or the National Housing Act, which established the U.S. Housing Authority, which assumed the responsibilities of Roosevelt's previous Public Works Administration and allocated $500 million in loans for low-cost housing.[5] Roosevelt's successor, President Lyndon B. Johnson, expanded public housing in the late 1960s, and went on to institute the U.S. Department of Housing and Urban Development to provide rent subsidies for the elderly and disabled, expand low-income housing, and support other public works projects.[6] Johnson also signed the Civil Rights Act of 1968, which included the Fair Housing Act, which prohibited discrimination concerning the sale, rental, and financing of housing based on race, religion, national origin, sex, (and, as amended) disability, and familial status.[7]

A year later, U.S. senators Edward Brooke and Ted Kennedy of Massachusetts passed the Brooke Amendment to update the 1969 Housing and Urban Development Act, which required public housing authorities to only rent to people with very low to no resources, or to fix the out-of-pocket outlays at no more than 25 percent of one's household's income.[8] Senator Brooke was the first African American elected to the Senate since the Civil War, and while he had hoped that his legislation could help stabilize the living conditions of Blacks, it only made their circumstances worse over the years.[9]

However, some researchers and housing advocates argued that the Brooke Amendment was one of the many reasons why the perception of public housing as temporary housing changed dramatically. Stalled rents and incentives to invest in the maintenance of properties led to slum landlords and horrible (and, in some instances, inhabitable) living conditions for public housing residents. In other words, the Brooke Amendment starved, rather than fed, the operational costs of public housing developments, leading to unresolved and persistent maintenance and building issues.[10] And that reality is still with us today. In 2021, public housing faces more than $70 billion in needed repairs to restore and maintain human sanctity.[11]

Starting in the late 1960s and early 1970s, other noneconomic factors became part of the eligibility screening for public housing. During that time, President Johnson commissioned a report on the topic led by the sociologist and former labor secretary Daniel Patrick Moynihan, who called himself reporting on the deviances and deficits of Black lives, including households purportedly led by Black women and children abandoned by their Black fathers.[12] The report's presumptive findings later defined social welfare programs for President Richard Nixon during a time when Moynihan was a senator and trusted senior adviser to him.[13] Thus, in addition to the disparate income formulas applied for public housing eligibility, other factors had equal weight in housing determinations, including one's employability, drug use, and even personal character.

As a little girl, I frequently watched the 1970s movie *Claudine*, largely due to its constant reruns on television and because it starred the beautiful Brown actress Diahann Carroll, who lived in public housing. Her beau, who was played by the actor James Earl Jones, had to sneak gifts and other belongings into her home to avoid running into the family's case worker. She feared an immediate cancellation of her public benefits and other social supports, as well as a roof over the heads of her six to seven children. In other words, the definition of the Black family was and continues to be unfairly scrutinized as part of the historic repudiation of their human and civil rights—a point that was to be repackaged during the Black Lives Matters movements decades later. Behaviors were also eerily reminiscent of what low-income residents experienced after the Clinton administration dismantled the social welfare system.

President Nixon tried to carry forth the intent of federally assisted housing options for the poor. He appointed George Romney, former Michigan governor, as the first of secretary for housing and urban development, and later Samuel Simmons as the first assistant secretary for equal housing opportunity.[14] But racism and discrimination are great forces in the United States, and more cases of unfair practices in housing continued to emerge back then and continue to exist today.

It is no surprise that housing options have never been readily available and accessible for Black Americans. When legislative action on housing issues was happening, the nation was in extreme turmoil around civil rights for Black people. The late Reverend Dr. Martin Luther King Jr., known for his nonviolent approaches to racial protests, made fair housing one of his priorities. His pivot to housing came as the rent strikes in the 1960s intensified throughout big cities like New York, Chicago, and Detroit, as tenants and community leaders decried the ongoing neglect of buildings by both public and private owners, and the substandard conditions that made them ripe for rats and other inhabitable conditions for renters.[15]

From the late 1970s to today, public housing has proven inadequate for the people living there. Black people and other vulnerable populations were, and continue to be, redlined out of communities when it comes to housing options, and the scarcity of these housing choices has resulted in greater living instabilities among working-class and low-income populations.[16] Being eligible for low-income housing is no longer the sole issue. It is about finding neighborhoods that will accept Section 8, housing vouchers, or being on long-term waiting lists for existing public housing units in cities with limited housing options. Historical trends and public policies have played significant roles in thwarting such opportunities for African Americans. Millions of Black households are unable to qualify for or are outrightly denied home mortgages that would enable them to graduate from being renters to owners, opening doors to other avenues of wealth building, including credit, assets, and housing stability.[17] Meanwhile, low-income Black renters often cannot afford market rent units in urban areas with rapidly increasing values, a sign of forthcoming gentrification in places that they previously lived.[18] The lack of immediate access to homeownership, the inability to afford rent due to rising urban gentrification, and the persistent presence of racism have made public housing the only option for poor and transient households—despite years of economic disinvestment in public housing communities. Rural areas are equally affected by the limited and suitable housing options for their residents, resulting in more obvious sightings of poverty as people scramble to live wherever they can—whether with family and friends, in motels, or in predatorily financed double-wide trailers.

Municipal efforts to reel in efforts for greater urban renewal in large metropolitan areas like New York City have served to mask the struggles of the poor, and allowed for rapid gentrification, which brings a host of other problems, including the removal of settled populations in these places. Back then in Chicago, the Plan for Transformation was, at best, a more politically correct way to describe the fate of hundreds of thousands of families and individuals gated in discriminatory public housing communities. Despite the conditions, many residents considered these places as "home." In my early years of volunteering at the Robert Taylor Homes, there was the same sense of community although the place and spaces were highly segregated by race and class.

In the end, the exacting of housing redlining, and the future communities where many displaced residents found themselves, were pretty much the same. In Chicago, public housing residents who could no longer live in their deliberately dysfunctional communities were asked to relocate to similarly situated places—only this time in adjacent cities and states with high concentrations of poverty as well. Some researchers have argued that the late 1980s to the 1990s was more about housing security than qualifying Black Americans for housing. Matthew Desmond's bestselling book *Evicted* points out the glaring and disproportionate number of evictions waged on the poor and people of color in communities, continuing housing fragilities for Blacks and other people of color in the United States.[19] The moral of this chapter is that where and how one lives are critical determinants of socioeconomic stability and mobility in the United States. A fact that is evident in the lives of public housing residents, who to this day struggle, because they are fenced into communities that are victimized by what Kotlowitz defined as abused and broken spirits. And now being unable to be fully integrated into the digital economy and digital transformation comes as costs to their future livelihoods.

Public Housing Is Still Stood Up by Congress

But despite what we know and have seen about public housing, legislators today are still pushing for its construction. Today, 1.2 million people live in "public housing" in the United States, which includes federally assisted, scattered-site, Federal Housing Administration (FHA)–backed or insured, and low-income, senior residences.[20] Across the country, 3,300 housing authorities manage these properties.[21] But over the years, and largely due to systemic racism and discrimination, places where public housing exists have been intentionally redlined on the other side of expressways, acting as dividers like the railroad tracks in rural Staunton. The consequences of such redlining have resulted in concentrated poverty, disinvestment, and the invisibility of whole populations to city governments of middle-class and sometimes working-class people who rarely interact with them. Today, local governments are now addressing neighborhood redlining and other housing disparities due to land shortages in downtown areas, invoked guilt from bad press, or other related deviances like violence in these poor communities over the years.[22]

In 2019, Democratic Congresswoman Ilhan Omar (D-MN) put forth legislation calling for 9.5 million new public housing units across the United States, at a cost of $800 billion over ten years.[23] Alongside her were other progressive Democrats, who called out the abysmal failure of the private sector to provide ample, affordable housing for low-income populations and the poor, despite the persistent and ongoing erosion of existing conditions and the related violence occurring on and within close proximity to these units.[24]

Housing Redlining

Housing redlining refers to services withheld from communities deemed "hazardous" to economic investments. The term was codified under President Roosevelt, when maps used by the federal government were literally "color-coded by the first Home Owners' Loan Corp. and then the . . . FHA . . . and then adopted by the Veterans Administration to designate where it was safe to insure mortgages."[25] Such actions were explicitly discriminatory, preying upon people of color who have been concentrated into communities with people who look like them and who have been denied the same opportunities as them. Rothstein's *The Color of Law* explores redlining's history, which started when the FHA refused to insure mortgages in or near Black neighborhoods—despite the massive overbuild of entire subdivisions for white families.[26] The practice of redlining historically justified housing discrimination based on race and income, and affected the property values of homes purchased by Black families, which in turn affected local infrastructure, including the quality of schools and libraries, as well as proximities of businesses, hospitals, and other necessary social supports.

Whereas history has demonstrated the persistence of housing redlining, not much research exists on the correlation with noncompetitive and unavailable broadband networks. For example, one of Los Angeles' public housing developments, the Imperial Courts, was not served by any internet service provider when it came to broadband access, which became a larger problem in 2020 and 2021, when the pandemic hit.[27] Households without internet connections face obstacles in accessing critical resources and tools in our twenty-first-century economy. Without the internet, public housing residents cannot do what others do online, such as apply for jobs, utilize distance learning, and access health care.

In addition to experiencing societal and individual paralysis, less competitive and available broadband service, along with the lack of affordability among low-income residents, impedes the progress of these communities and feeds into traditional narratives of urban poverty. In urban areas, large telecommunications companies—especially cable—report more than 85 percent penetration rates, meaning that broadband service is readily and easily available to city residents.[28] But for those living in transient, rental communities on fixed incomes, broadband access can be dicey, especially if the choice of discretionary expense that month is between broadband and a week of groceries.

So far, there has been no legislative attempt to ensure that every public housing unit is connected to quality broadband (let alone every unit of affordable housing), which would enable the online capabilities for families who cannot wait in line to recertify housing vouchers or apply for new public benefits. From this history, the obvious physical and now digital redlines in public housing in America had chilling effects on marginalized populations, whose housing has not only dictated their life chances but has also left them with substandard communications infrastructure. That is another reason why I argue that being on the wrong side of digital opportunity is symptomatic of poverty and geographic isolation—an experience that I witnessed first hand visiting Syracuse.

The City of Syracuse

In 2019, the city of Syracuse was listed as one of the worst cities for Black Americans to live, according to an index that assessed race/income gaps across the United States.[29] Researchers have long found systemic disparities for Black and Latino populations in housing, employment, and educational opportunities. The lack of broadband access is a notable mark on the city's care of its marginalized communities. In 2019, one out of every four homes in the city did not have internet access, making it the tenth-worst city in the United States when it came to home broadband connections, despite being home to a large public university.[30]

That same year, top city officials announced plans for redevelopment that placed a senior-assisted public housing development on the demolition list. This was part of a 2016 plan to erase some of the city's oldest public housing developments—like the oldest state public housing community, Pioneer Homes—and replace them with new mixed-income housing that city officials referred to as the "real Mecca," or another political move to absolve the city of concentrated urban poverty. Built in 1938, Pioneer Homes was one of New York State's first public housing developments, and was under the authority of the Syracuse Housing Authority (SHA), which made the federal agency one of the first of five such agencies in the United States to build and manage public housing.[31]

In 2019, Syracuse's population was about 149,000, which made it the fifth most populous area in Upstate New York. With a median age of thirty two, just over 50 percent of its residents were non-Hispanic white, while 30 percent were Black and 10 percent were Hispanic, making it barely a majority-white city.[32] Nineteen percent of its residents spoke a language other than English at home, just under the national average of 22 percent.[33] Of its residents age twenty five and over, 17 percent did not not have a high school degree; 71 percent did not have a bachelor's degree, which was 6 percentage points, or 20 percent, less than the rate in New York State overall.[34] According to the 2019 U.S. Census, median household annual income for the city was $38,000, with an overall poverty rate of 31 percent and a childhood poverty rate of 50 percent—more than double the rate of poverty elsewhere in the state.[35] In 2019, Syracuse had a 5.5 percent unemployment rate, slightly above the national average.[36]

Before the COVID-19 pandemic, internet access was unequally distributed and available; 75 percent of households in Syracuse had a broadband internet subscription in 2019, and 65 percent of households had cell phone data; 20 percent of these households used this as their sole way to access the internet.[37] While the FCC's 2019 Form 477 data indicated that Onondaga County—the county in which Syracuse sits—had fixed broadband available in over 99.9 percent of the county, Microsoft broadband usage data indicated that 35 percent of the 475,000 residents in Onondaga County did not use the internet at acceptable broadband speeds. Microsoft data also suggested that 30 percent of students in households—22,000 children—also did not have acceptable broadband speeds.[38] It was no coincidence that the Census Bureau also reported that 18 percent of households in Syracuse did not have access to the internet at all.[39]

My Drive across the Expressway

The city's 42 low-income, housing apartment complexes are managed by the SHA, whose website landing page features four Black kids spinning around in hula hoops as if life has always been good for them there.[40] As I pulled into the community, all that I saw were vacant storefronts that looked like they closed decades ago and a mix of stoic high- and low-rise buildings consumed the neighborhood that I entered. There were no children playing and laughing, replaced instead by familiar faces of Black men and women waiting for the time to pass in front of their homes. Now, these low-income housing units did not compare with Chicago's Robert Taylor Homes. But they were close in the sense that the social and geographic isolation of these communities revealed the earnest truth about poverty in America's urban cities, including in Upstate New York.

People walked in and out of the high-rise building for seniors, which sat alone on the corner of this neighborhood, facing a fenced-in area at the very front. To the side of the building were more closed storefronts that looked like they had been there since the 1960s, as if an old Pepsi sign propped up in the window was any indication. To the far left of the parking lot were older homes—some in pristine condition, others ready for demolition. But judging from the foot traffic on the street and near the high-rise building, people still lived in them.

When I got to the entrance, I rang the buzzer, announced myself to the property manager, a young woman, who greeted me with a semiclosed smile. She was part of the property management group appointed by the SHA and quickly went into detail on the building's units, households, and the history of the community. There was a plaque plastered into the concrete of the building, denoting a launch date in the 1960s. The building was solemnly quiet, with very few people walking or standing around. After she showed me the plaque, we walked down another long hall until we took a sharp left into a small, cinderblock room.

Debra, a woman in her late sixties, sat on the ledge of one of the windows in the computer lab, looking out at the adjacent highway and downtown area. When we entered, she greeted us with her medium frame and wide-rimmed, black glasses. She introduced herself as a tenant and the computer lab assistant and instructor. I immediately felt an affinity given my own history with community technology earlier in my life. It was as if I was looking at an older version of myself who had I stayed in Chicago.

Debra's Computer Lab

"Welcome to our computer lab," she shared, with a tight-lipped smile. "We have a couple of computers, printer, paper, and the internet for the people that need to access them." You could tell that she enjoyed this role. The room was impeccably neat, and signs—some of them typed and others handwritten—were taped to the walls with information on the lab rules and hours.

Debra let me know that, in her role, she helped residents set up their email accounts that they needed for jobs and government benefits. She acknowledged how outdated the computers were—they were old and large units, like the big 386 CPUs—but assured me that they worked. She also had an assistant in the lab. Monetary support from a local foundation provided for an Americorps VISTA volunteer, just like my lab at Northwest Tower Apartments in the 2000s.

Walking into Debra's space took me back to almost thirty years ago in the startup computer lab with a couple of computers and the multiplicity of dreams that I had for my residents. But Debra's lab was sorely out of date: This was 2019 in the age of rapid sophistication in emerging technologies and related apps. Debra continued, "you see, there are some things that I am good at, like email or searching the internet or YouTube. Other things, I need my grandchildren to do, or my volunteer to show me, which is why I like the help in my space."

Debra took full charge of her responsibilities in the small computer lab, despite it not being a competitively paid position or the best of technical resources. At the senior housing complex, she killed time during the day in the lab, and sitting there, among the couple run-down computers and bookshelves. It gave her a good excuse to avoid small talk with residents at the front of the building she shared. But it also offered her a chance to better her community: She felt that she was making a difference with her neighbors who visited the lab by giving them opportunities to work on job applications or communicate with others via email.

"I try to remain open as much as I can to help people with their online job applications," she stated as if she bore the official title of job coach for her peers. "I show them how to get to the site and schedule online appointments, too."

It would take a whole other book to talk about why Black people over sixty-five are still in the workforce, but at least, the residents here understood that job listings had migrated online from hard copy newsprints.

Still stuck in a personal déjà vu, the property manager quickly snapped me out of it as she spoke of the vulnerability of the lab. The small grant that supported Debra had expired last month. Debra spoke about the problems maintaining materials, like paper and ink, but she did not seem to care too much, given that she had nothing but time to kill living in this building and community.

"Being here is sometimes better than being in the house," she laughed with a slight undertone of seriousness.

In the mid-2000s, community tech centers in affordable housing communities were widely available—a point made earlier in the book. The Clinton administration appropriated monetary and in-kind resources to expand Neighborhood Networks across all fifty states in 1995, allowing public housing and FHA-assisted and insured developments to build computer labs for residents.[41] With the same intentions, the more updated goal of the program was to offer open, on-site, multiservice technology centers that would provide residents with access to the internet and digital literacy training, as well as General Education Development (GED) preparation, and English as a Second Language (ESL) courses, among other things. Youth programs focused on afterschool and mentoring activities were also taught at the center, along with senior digital literacy training to facilitate better connections with family and friends, and medical providers.

Sounding like she was reading from the earlier versions of the Neighborhood Networks playbook, the property manager shared how her company forged partnerships with philanthropic institutions and businesses to bring technology to their residents. That is how she was able to give Debra a small stipend to make sure the computer lab was always open. Despite the building making available subscription-based home cable and broadband services from an incumbent internet service provider, the basic broadband service was priced at $14 to $15 per month, and in some instances, still too costly for seniors on fixed incomes.

Debra explained that because of that some residents were entirely dependent on their mobile phones to get online. In other cases, the phone may be more outdated as she noted that "Most people have phones in the building and sometimes, it is a flip phone because of cost."

Older populations are also less likely to enable the capabilities of the internet, given their limited ownership of devices like smartphones, tablets, laptops, or home personal computers. Some older populations are also outright fearful of what modern technologies entail for them and future generations. Of course, Debra opined on the negative effects of what she called "too much technology."

"My kids in South Carolina, their kids have that newer phone," she said, sounding like a doting grandmother. "But there is so much more that happens with this new stuff, like bullying. I call [my grandkids] though if I want to do something or need help. It's just used for so many more things with the kids."

Debra was partly right. In 2020, former Facebook employee and whistleblower Frances Haugen confirmed before Congress that Facebook's Instagram product was promoting negative body images among young teenage girls and promoting bullying.[42] It is, of course, an enormous issue that has still not been resolved. But it does not change the other realities of the building's residents. Debra spoke about the limitations of data caps on mobile devices—a similar concern of Joseph in Staunton, whose minutes kept running out and restricting him from staying in touch with employers.

While the building had open Wi-Fi here in the property's communal areas, I can only imagine that many chose not to browse in poorly lit hallways, or even share their data openly over such networks—a feeling that was confirmed as I met others on my way to the car. But even the property manager was enthusiastic about the transformative power of technology, evangelizing what she saw in her building when it came to community connections:

> I see a place [here] where people have smartphones, tablets, laptops, or PCs. Where there is open Wi-Fi and applications for applying for benefits, like social security or jobs. It's important to have a place like this too in the building. People can't apply for jobs on their smartphones, or even a flip phone. We really need budgets within affordable housing to create these types of spaces for our residents with classes, equipment, and access.

On the day of my visit in May 2019, Senator Chuck Schumer (D-NY) was in Syracuse to promote a bill that he was cosponsoring with senators Ed Markey (D-MA) and John Thune (R-SD) called the Telephone Robocall Abuse Criminal Enforcement and Deterrence (TRACED) Act.[43] The bill was a response to many Upstate residents, especially older populations, who were bombarded daily by telemarketers and other fraudsters who inadvertently preyed on seniors and the poor. During his press conference, Senator Schumer bragged about having a flip phone to avoid robocalls, but later retracted that statement because, of course, his flip phone did not protect him from robocalls. While the annoyance of staggering robocalls is real among consumers and citizens whoever you are, the poor and older populations often become victims of these phone scams. They also still rely upon outdated technologies with limited privacy: Flip phones lack the security

Figure 5-1. *Smartphone Ownership and Social Media Use Continue to Grow among Older Adults*

Percentage of U.S. Adults Who Say They . . .

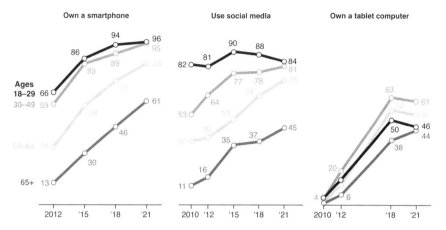

Source: Pew Research Center, "Share of Those 65 and Older Who Are Tech Users Have Grown in the Past Decade," survey of U.S. adults, January, 25–February 8, 2021, https://www.pewresearch.org/fact-tank/2022/01/13/share-of-those-65-and-older-who-are-tech-users-has-grown-in-the-past-decade. Used by permission.
Note: Respondents who did not give an answer are not shown.

features to fully block and outsmart these robocall fiends, putting seniors with these devices at an even higher risk of being scammed. Of course, these experiences will worsen as the forthcoming election faces greater exploitation due to more capable and advanced technologies, like generative artificial intelligence. Compared with identity security, many of these seniors may be subjected to deceptive advertising, and the extraction of familiar voices and images to dissuade or intimidate them from voting.

Broadband among Older Populations

For decades, older populations have become the hardest to serve when it comes to broadband service and internet adoption in the United States, largely due to the cost of service and their lack of familiarity with digital hardware. The pandemic led to a positive uptick in broadband adoption among existing older tech users, whose smartphone ownership and social media use skyrocketed in the last decade.[44] Figure 5-1 presents recent data from the Pew Research Center (2021), which found significant jumps among individuals sixty-five years of age and up. But according to the same research, older populations were not likely to be constantly online; 8 percent compared with 48 percent, when compared with those eighteen to twenty-nine years of age, which suggests that some still teeter between analog and digital functions.[45] As the pandemic essentially forced remote medical care through telehealth, this wavering use of broadband suggests that seniors have a longer way to go when it comes to broadband adoption and use.

For older rural residents not connected to the internet, regular communications with family members and other caregivers, especially in places like very remote Garrett County, made wellness checks or routine care more difficult before the pandemic. At its peak and in the months to follow, the social isolation of rural seniors during the pandemic further exacerbated social and geographic isolation, subjecting them to greater levels of infections, the likelihood of death due to poor access to screenings and vaccinations, and outright loneliness. Older populations experienced similar challenges, and further scrutinized the trustworthiness of being online for private activities, like speaking with one's doctor. My almost eighty-year-old mother, recently widowed after my father died, sat in her condo alone for most of the pandemic, figuring how out to turn her camera's video screen to see her doctor during telehealth visits. With the looming variants, only my sister, who lives in Brooklyn, had been able to put eyes on her face beyond our regular Facetime and voice calls, and daily family text chats.

The internet is equally debilitating for Hispanics in the city, who are even more marginalized due to language issues; people with disabilities, who are challenged by the accessibility of many webpages and apps; and people with an intersection of all these factors. Taken together, traditionally invisible people fall lower on the totem pole when it comes to online access. According to the website of the American Association of People with Disabilities, 54 percent of adults living with a disability use the internet, compared with 81 percent without; 41 percent of people with a disability have broadband at home, compared with 69 percent without.[46]

The persistent broadband challenges experienced by older Americans and people living with disabilities often blend into the backgrounds of nationally dominated conversations on broadband supply or infrastructure. Their focus becomes bylines, rather than subtitles in national plans to accelerate access. A rational and more universal path for facilitating digital equity in the United States is necessary, and one that I revisit later in the book.

Just as I was prepared to wrap up my conversation with Debra, she shared something unprovoked. "The city is preparing to tear down Pioneer Homes across the way," she shared, staring out the only window in the computer room. "We are concerned because no one has really come to talk with us about it. We hear that we are also on their list."

Everything Is About to Change Here

In 2016, Syracuse's leadership announced a plan to entice middle-income residents to communities that had become areas of concentrated poverty and poor housing options. Pioneer Homes, along with the high-rise senior building, sit in what some have called the "shadows" of downtown, due to I-81 creating redlines between communities. Like other metropolitan areas, the city of Syracuse has a history of redlining complaints. It has been found to rank first among others in the concentrated poverty of Blacks and Latinos, which trail behind the increasing presence of poverty in the broader Onondaga County.[47] More than 70 percent of residents of the Pioneer Homes were living in poverty at the time of the plan's announcement, a statistic that is only a reflection of the egregious handling of housing for poor and low-income people in the United States throughout history.[48]

Redlining is alive and well in Syracuse and other large metropolitan areas across the United States. The SHA has 1,400 of its 2,340 public housing units in a twenty-seven-block area of the city center, which has created boundaries for the residents. In Syracuse, this boundary is the highway across from Pioneer Homes.[49] Built in the late 1950s, the interstate piled Black people into the Fifteenth Ward and deepened divides in an already polarized communities.[50] On top of that, the construction forced Black people who were previously homeowners into what was thought to be temporary public housing.

During press conferences announcing the 2016 plan, the SHA director touted the redevelopment of these communities as positive for the residents, whose coalescing with middle-income neighbors would lead to increased economic development opportunities, like jobs and commercial ventures, along with an assumption about behavioral shifts in terms of violence and aspirations. The plan also included wider streets for pedestrians and bicyclists, more stores, and better schools for residents. The leadership driving the plan pontificated that the community, once redeveloped, could be a "real mecca" for residents of all incomes.[51]

But Debra did not think so. I could see the lingering pain in her eyes as her mouth grew even more tight, her eyes locked on whatever she was watching beyond the window.

"They said something about a library, computer lab, grocery stores, laundromat, and improved streets," she stated, regurgitating what she had heard or seen on the television. "They don't know what to do with the highway, whether to keep it or tear it down. It's right there and it's been here all my life."

What will soon become part of the reality for Debra and her neighbors will be skyrocketing rents, relocations and dislocations, family and friends separated at the time of construction, and sooner rather than later, a revitalized part of the city with a Starbucks, retail shops, grocery stores, and "Yield to Bicycles" signs. This is the same scene that we saw a few years ago in Washington, New York, Chicago, Detroit, and other large metropolitan areas, whose code word, "redevelopment," signals "gentrification."

And gentrification is much like the abuse that Kotlowitz shared in his 2015 *Chicago Reporter* article. The actions imposed by federal, state, and local legislators seem ill placed because they pile on top of the persistent redlining of these communities. Yet, changes are needed because people deserve not just housing but also communities that offer greener spaces, healthier food choices, and safer communities—free from random bullets hitting babies who play on what are supposed to be safe street corners and playgrounds. But these reforms do not consider the voices and needs of the Black and Brown people who came to these places for better lives than what they experienced just a couple of decades ago on plantations as sharecroppers or indebted servants to generations of slaveowners who demanded that they continue to pay their debts.

In the city of Syracuse, the poor conditions of Black and Latino populations were widely known, and poor housing options, along with a range of other injustices faced by these groups, were growing. In 2017, the city was named the worst place for Black Americans due to its residential segregation and inequalities in infrastructure.[52] The lack of access to high-speed broadband is the newest inequality experienced by residents in the city's public housing, and the case for its use will become even more pressing because, one year after this visit, our world shut down.

I knew that these concerns about being excised from her community were keeping Debra up at night, and probably the property manager, whose "I have a dream" speech minutes before was hinging on the destiny of her residents. But like the other communities I visited, I had to surrender the hope that having access to broadband and internet-enabled devices was going to solve the problems before us, because it likely would not.

In fact, the conversation about the lab, the I-81 redevelopment, the obvious sadness about what would become of this neighborhood just reminded me that the people most affected by digital invisibility are the same ones constantly fighting for their voices, their land, and their retribution for promises never kept by systems put in place to fence off their dreams and aspirations. In his research, Nall compared the development of federal highways and expressways as demarcations of the suppressive effects of voting disenfranchisement, and other barriers to civic participation by groups on the other side of flourishing downtown areas.[53]

It was time for me to leave, as the conversation with Debra reminded me of more than three decades of unrealized progress toward closing the digital divide. As I walked back to the car, I stopped to speak with an older man to have a conversation about the community. Without missing a beat, he said, "I have everything in my house, home internet access, a tablet, a computer, and a phone." But in the middle of his excitement, he revealed, "But my phone is off until the end of the month because I ran out of minutes. But I have everything, though."

Then, a second guy jumped in and shared: "I had internet in my house until I started getting all those scams, you know the ones that they try to fraud the seniors. The robocalls. That happens a lot in this area."

He kept going, "Listen, I don't trust the internet. People have stolen my identity and as an old man, it's hard to understand what is happening to you now. I leave that thing alone." The TRACED Act will hopefully protect people like him and even others that have some resistance to internet use, providing federal agencies with more tools and authority to trace, prosecute, and enforce fines on robocall scammers.

Then, finally, another man who was with them interjected. He stood up, and with his bright white teeth set against his dark brown skin and with a huge smile on his face, said that he was almost seventy in age, and he, too, had opinions about the internet.

"Listen, I go on the internet," he started. "Yes, I do. I buy things, get on the Facebook, and most important, I go on the internet to look at pornography. Yes, I said it and my wife knows that I do that too." Almost instantaneously, the four of us burst out laughing because we knew that he was telling the truth.

Referring to the space that I had just left, which Debra managed so diligently, he continued: "They have a computer lab in there, but sometimes you like to do things at home—in your place."

And while his comment might be primarily related to the privacy he wants while watching porn, the issue that he is pointing to is much larger. Certain segments of populations are used to being surveilled in all walks of their lives, and when we try to promote open access and connections to digital literacy in public spaces—as at libraries, community centers, clinics, and computer labs—those spaces can feel like just another excuse to survey the community's every move.

I was almost to the rental car when two Black women who knew that I was a stranger to the community called me over. Their names were Dolly and Edna. After getting their permission to interview and photograph them, I asked about their internet use, much as I did with the fellas at the previous bench.

Dolly started, "You know, I get online because I like to go onto Amazon. Even though I had my credit card information stolen a couple of weeks ago, I can't help it. They have so much stuff."

"Yea, she can't get enough of those wigs that they sell at Amazon," Edna quipped. "You better tell the truth, Dolly."

"You're right. Sometimes the prices online at Amazon are cheaper than the beauty supply store down the street, and I like it when the boxes come right to my house," Dolly continued. Edna caved in and admitted that she shopped at Amazon too.

"Listen, I like going on Amazon, but you have to read the fine print. I tell Dolly all the time, what does the return policy say and things like that," Edna said authoritatively. "Too many people don't understand that and sign their lives away."

"Are you both impacted by robocalls or online scammers?" I asked.

Dolly jumped in, "They are out there—all over. Like Edna said, you just must know what you're getting into. That's all."

It was clear on that visit to the senior public housing development that the protection of their personal data online was a more commonly considered threat among residents. Then there is algorithmic discrimination, where markets track the actual and inferential purchasing and other online behaviors to make determinations about one's creditworthiness, or suitability for employment and housing. What some are suggesting is the next digital divide.

As I slid into my car, I stared at a vacant building in front of me with the barely hanging Pepsi-Cola sign. Its memories were now reduced to a lonely sign in a closed storefront with weeds overtaking the sidewalk at the front entrance. It was time for me to leave this community to make it back to the airport, and I wanted to ride around the community and by the Pioneer Homes before they too became distant memories.

For a moment before pulling out of the parking space, I started to imagine the plans for redevelopment and what the community would look like upon completion. My guess is that there will be no Debra, Dolly, Edna, or the fellas counting down the hours of daylight in front of a place they call home. They will be gone, along with generations of families that called public housing complexes home.

COVID-19 in Syracuse

Fast forward to one year after meeting Debra, and New York State was the first to be hit hard by the pandemic. And Syracuse was one of the first cities to feel the impact of it. The city's death toll among Black Americans and other people of color exceeded any other part of the state; it not only led in infections but also deaths related to COVID-19.[54] Housing poverty often correlates with health disparities. According to county statistics, Black people were more likely to experience a range of health issues and other co-morbidities, including risk of cancer, heart disease, diabetes, and obesity, especially the elderly.[55] When the pandemic reared its ugly head, the residents of the city who lacked access to quality health care suffered. With two-thirds of Black residents in Syracuse living in high-poverty areas, quick infections were likely, and death was often imminent. In one zip code in the city, which is majority Black, 20 of every 1,000 residents had COVID-19 within three to four months of the 2020 outbreak.[56]

Technology was very much a part of mitigation strategies during this time, from online alerts on public health numbers to scheduling of doctors' visits via telehealth. But communities like this one and the other ones that I visited as part of my tour were positioned for failure. Public housing developments were on the wrong side of the interstate, and for dealing with the systemic consequences of housing discrimination.

Since I visited Syracuse in 2019, more news articles have emerged about the need for increased funding for the SHA to complete the renovation, the efforts to maintain residents' homes during and after the transition, and housing non-profits coming to the aid of the SHA to execute its plans.[57] But everything was suspended in 2020, when the pandemic started.

Instead, Black and Latino city residents experienced massive job layoffs. Moving around the city became unsafe, especially for vulnerable populations.

The historical and ongoing health disparities in the city's most segregated housing communities took a toll on the hospitals, families, and individuals highly susceptible to the virus.

This is life in one of America's urban centers; it encompasses the tales of what it means to be redlined into public housing and the negative impact on social life, communications, and economic opportunities. From what I have heard and learned over the years; you make it work. And the people of Syracuse are not alone. Cleveland faces similar issues to those of Syracuse, but despite efforts to identify and quell digital discrimination there, the city is still stumped by the lack of economic investments in its most vulnerable residents and their communities.

Notes

Part III epigraph: Statement of Lisa Rice, National Fair Housing Alliance, "Separate and Unequal: The Legacy of Racial Discrimination in Housing," before the U.S. Senate Committee on Banking, Housing, and Urban Affairs, 117th Cong., 2021.

1. Alex Kotlowitz, *There Are No Children Here* (New York: Liveright Press, 1991).
2. Alex Kotlowitz, "Revisiting the Hornets," *Chicago Reporter*, March 13, 2015, https://www.chicagoreporter.com/revisiting-the-hornets/.
3. St. Clair Drake and Horace R. Clayton, *Black Metropolis: A Study of Negro Life in a Northern City*, reprint (New York: Harcourt, Brace, 1945).
4. Irene V. Holliman, "Techwood Homes," *New Georgia Encyclopedia* (blog), June 20, 2008, https://www.georgiaencyclopedia.org/articles/arts-culture/techwood-homes/.
5. FDR Library & Museum, "FDR and Housing Legislation: FDR Presidential Library & Museum," https://www.fdrlibrary.org/housing.
6. FDR Library & Museum.
7. U.S. Department of Housing and Urban Development, "Fair Housing Is 50," https://www.hud.gov/fairhousingis50.
8. Howard Husock, "How Brooke Helped Destroy Public Housing," *Forbes*, January 8, 2015, https://www.forbes.com/sites/howardhusock/2015/01/08/how-senator-brooke-helped-destroy-public-housing/.
9. Husock.
10. Husock.
11. National Association of Housing and Redevelopment Officials, "Capital Fund Backlog," https://www.nahro.org/wp-content/uploads/2020/04/CAPITAL_FUND_BACKLOG_One-Pager.pdf.
12. Daniel Geary, "The Moynihan Report," *Atlantic*, September 15, 2015, https://www.theatlantic.com/politics/archive/2015/09/the-moynihan-report-an-annotated-edition/404632/.
13. Stephen Hess, *The Professor and the President: Daniel Patrick Moynihan in the Nixon White House* (Brookings, 2014).
14. Nikole Hannah-Jones. "Living Apart: How the Government Betrayed a Landmark Civil Rights Law," ProPublica, June 25, 2015, https://www.propublica.org/article/living-apart-how-the-government-betrayed-a-landmark-civil-rights-law?token=gTxcPWjXmZYvtzVTlrsurtrCPbPuyFPR.
15. Joel Schwartz, "The New York City Rent Strikes of 1963–1964," *Social Service Review* 57, no. 4 (1983): 545–64.

16. Gene Demby, "50 Years Ago: President Johnson Signed the Fair Housing Act," NPR, April 11, 2018, https://www.npr.org/2018/04/11/601419987/50-years-ago-president-johnson-signed-the-fair-housing-act.

17. Diana Olick, "A Troubling Tale of a Black Man Trying to Refinance His Mortgage," CNBC, August 19, 2020, https://www.cnbc.com/2020/08/19/lenders-deny-mortgages-for-blacks-at-a-rate-80percent-higher-than-whites.html.

18. Jacquelynn Kerubo, "What Gentrification Means for Black Homeowners," *New York Times*, August 17, 2021, sec. Real Estate, https://www.nytimes.com/2021/08/17/realestate/black-homeowners-gentrification.html.

19. Matthew Desmond, *Evicted: Poverty and Profit in the American City* (New York: Crown, 2016).

20. U.S. Department of Housing and Urban Development, "Public Housing," https://www.hud.gov/program_offices/public_indian_housing/programs/ph.

21. U.S. Department of Housing and Urban Development.

22. Tracy Jan, "Redlining Was Banned 50 Years Ago; It's Still Hurting Minorities Today," *Washington Post*, March 28, 2018, https://www.washingtonpost.com/news/wonk/wp/2018/03/28/redlining-was-banned-50-years-ago-its-still-hurting-minorities-today/.

23. Representative Ilhan Omar, "Rep. Ilhan Omar Introduces Homes for All Act, a New 21st Century Public Housing Vision," November 20, 2019, https://omar.house.gov/media/press-releases/rep-ilhan-omar-introduces-homes-all-act-new-21st-century-public-housing-vision.

24. Howard Husock, "Public Housing Becomes the Latest Progressive Fantasy," *Atlantic*, November 25, 2019, https://www.theatlantic.com/ideas/archive/2019/11/public-housing-fundamentally-flawed/602515/.

25. Terry Gross, "A 'Forgotten History' of How the U.S. Government Segregated America," NPR, May 3, 2017, https://www.npr.org/2017/05/03/526655831/a-forgotten-history-of-how-the-u-s-government-segregated-america.

26. Gross.

27. Shara Tibken, "The Broadband Gap's Dirty Secret: Redlining Still Exists in Digital Form," CNET, June 28, 2021, https://www.cnet.com/features/the-broadband-gaps-dirty-secret-redlining-still-exists-in-digital-form/.

28. U.S. Federal Communications Commission, *2020 Communications Marketplace Report*, FCC-20-188 [36 FCC Rcd 2945 (6)], December 31, 2020, https://www.fcc.gov/document/fcc-releases-2020-communications-marketplace-report.

29. Evan Comen, and Michael B. Sauter, "The Worst Cities for Black Americans," 24/7 Wall St. (blog), November 3, 2017, https://247wallst.com/special-report/2019/11/05/the-worst-cities-for-black-americans-5/.

30. Chris Baker, "Syracuse's Digital Crisis: 1 out of 4 Homes Doesn't Have Internet," Syracuse.com, April 4, 2019, https://www.syracuse.com/news/2019/04/syracuses-digital-crisis-1-out-of-4-homes-doesnt-have-internet.html.

31. Syracuse.com, "1938: Pioneer Homes Gives Syracuse Families a Chance at a 'Decent' Place to Live," https://www.syracuse.com/living/2021/05/1938-pioneer-homes-gives-syracuse-families-a-chance-at-a-decent-place-to-live.html; Kenneth Londono, "Pioneer Homes, First Public Housing Complex in New York, Provides Living Space and Hope for a Place of Their Own One Day," My Housing Matters (blog), May 6, 2015, http://myhousingmatters.com/pioneer-homes-first-public-housing-complex-in-new-york-provides-living-space-and-hope-for-a-place-of-their-own-one-day/.

32. U.S. Census Bureau, "QuickFacts: Syracuse City, New York," https://www.census.gov/quickfacts/fact/table/syracusecitynewyork/PST045221.

33. U.S. Census Bureau, "Why We Ask About . . . Language Spoken at Home," https://www.census.gov/acs/www/about/why-we-ask-each-question/language/.

34. Census Reporter, "Census Profile: Syracuse, NY," http://censusreporter.org/profiles/16000US3673000-syracuse-ny/.

35. U.S. Census Bureau, "QuickFacts: Syracuse City, New York," https://www.census.gov/quickfacts/fact/table/syracusecitynewyork/PST045221; Census Reporter, "Census Profile: Syracuse, NY," http://censusreporter.org/profiles/16000US3673000-syracuse-ny/.

36. Census Reporter, "Census Profile: Syracuse, NY," http://censusreporter.org/profiles/16000US3673000-syracuse-ny/.

37. U.S. Census Bureau, 2019, "Presence and Types of Internet Subscriptions in Household American Community Survey 1-year estimates," https://censusreporter.org/data/table/?table=B28002&geo_ids=16000US3673000&primary_geo_id=16000US3673000.

38. Federal Communications Commission, "FCC Fixed Broadband Deployment," https://broadbandmap.fcc.gov/; "Microsoft Airband Initiative," https://app.powerbi.com/view?r=eyJrIjoiYzlhZWIyNWEtMDlkOS00MWJkLWExZGYtOWQ3NTNjNzJiNDIwIiwidCI6ImMxMzZlZWMwLWZlOTItNDVlMC1iZWFlLTQ2OTg0OTczZTIzMiIsImMiOjF9.

39. U.S. Census Bureau, 2019, "Presence and Types of Internet Subscriptions."

40. Syracuse Housing Authority, "Syracuse Housing Authority: Building Neighborhoods. Growing Dreams," https://syracusehousing.org/.

41. U.S. Department of Housing and Urban Development, "About Neighborhood Networks," https://www.hud.gov/program_offices/public_indian_housing/programs/ph/nnw/nnwaboutnn.

42. "The Facebook Files," *Wall Street Journal*, October 1, 2021, https://www.wsj.com/articles/the-facebook-files-11631713039.

43. Andrew Donovan, "Hearing from People Bombarded by Robocalls, Sen. Schumer Co-Sponsors Bill That 'Will Stop It,'" WSYR-TV, May 6, 2019, https://www.localsyr.com/news/local-news/hearing-from-people-bombarded-by-robocalls-sen-schumer-co-sponsors-bill-that-will-stop-it/.

44. Pew Research Center, "Share of Those 65 and Older Who Are Tech Users Have Grown in the Past Decade," January 13, 2022, https://www.pewresearch.org/fact-tank/2022/01/13/share-of-those-65-and-older-who-are-tech-users-has-grown-in-the-past-decade.

45. Pew Research Center.

46. American People with Disabilities, https://www.aapd.com/advocacy/technology.

47. Central New York Community Foundation, "How the History of Redlining and I-81 Contributed to Syracuse Poverty | CNY Vitals," May 18, 2018, https://cnyvitals.org/how-the-history-of-redlining-and-i-81-contributed-to-syracuse-poverty/.

48. Patrick Lohmann, "Syracuse Housing Authority Plan Uses I-81 Project to Resurrect City Center, Combat Poverty," Syracuse.Com, December 27, 2016, https://www.syracuse.com/news/2016/12/syracuse_housing_authority_plan_uses_i-81_project_to_resurrect_city_center.html.

49. Lohmann, "Syracuse Housing Authority Plan Uses I-81 Project."

50. Lohmann.

51. Lohmann.

52. Geoff Herbert. "Syracuse Named One of the 'Worst Cities for Black Americans,'" Syracuse.Com, November 28, 2017, https://www.syracuse.com/news/2017/11/syracuse_worst_cities_black_americans.html.

53. Clayton Nall, *The Road to Inequality: How the Federal Highway Program Polarized America and Undermined Cities* (New York: Cambridge University Press, 2018).

54. Tim Knauss, "How a Pandemic Laid Bare CNY's Health Crisis," Syracuse.Com,
    August 13, 2020, https://www.syracuse.com/coronavirus/2020/08/how-a-pandemic-laid-
    bare-cnys-health-crisis.html.
55. Knauss.
56. Knauss.
57. "Syracuse Announces $800 Million Housing Project Renovation Plan," WSYR-TV,
    January 20, 2022, https://www.localsyr.com/news/local-news/syracuse-announces-800-
    million-housing-project-renovation-plan/; Michelle Breidenbach, "Syracuse Embarks on
    $800 Million Plan to End Public Housing as We Know It," Syracuse.Com, January 18, 2022,
    https://www.syracuse.com/news/2022/01/syracuse-embarks-on-800-million-plan-to-
    end-public-housing-as-we-know-it.html; Teri Weaver, "I-81 Construction Could Force
    Hundreds of Syracuse Public Housing Residents to Move, Director Says," Syracuse.Com,
    July 16, 2014, https://www.syracuse.com/news/2014/07/i-81_construction_could_displace_
    hundreds_of_syracuse_public_housing_residents_d.html.

6

The Beginnings of Digital Redlining

I n January 2023, City National Bank, headquartered in Los Angeles, settled
with the U.S. Justice Department on allegations of racial discrimination and
was assessed a fine of $31 million.[1] The bank, which is the largest in the city, was
accused of avoiding loans to homebuyers in Black and Latino neighborhoods. The
city's population was 49 percent Latino and 9 percent Black, and yet their white
counterparts were averaging six times more loan applications within these same
communities.[2] Although the settlement was not an admission of guilt, the company vowed to invest $29.5 million in home loan subsidies, including down pay-
ment assistance and interest rate cuts to Black and Latino borrowers.[3] The bank
also committed support to multicultural advertising, financial literacy programs,
and the opening of a new branch in a majority Black or Latino community.

City National Bank is not the first large financial institution to settle with the
Justice Department after alleged violations of federal fair lending laws. In 2022,
one of the largest lenders of federally backed mortgages, Fannie Mae, agreed to a
settlement of $53 million with the Justice Department over allegations that the
company better marketed and maintained foreclosed homes in predominantly
white neighborhoods, compared with the explicit disregard for those in Black
and Latino communities.[4] The landmark action set a precedent in fair housing
that mandates the upkeep of foreclosed lender properties, whatever the location.
The discovery came after the National Fair Housing Alliance found that homes
in cities and counties like Chicago, New Orleans, Las Vegas, and Prince George's
County (Maryland), among other predominantly Black and Latino communities,
were being overlooked, and, in many cases, subjected to discriminatory appraisals.

Housing discrimination has a long history in American society, beginning under President Franklin Delano Roosevelt, whose administration enacted the National Housing Act of 1934 as the United States crawled out of the Great Depression. Millions of existing homeowners were experiencing some type of foreclosure or missed payments at that time, and in 1933, the Home Owners' Loan Corporation (HOLC) was established to provide emergency relief through forbearance and refinancing options. Between 1933 and 1936, the HOLC approved more than 1 million loans, many of which were among the riskiest and most delinquent. In 1934, the Federal Housing Authority, which later became the Office of Housing in the U.S. Department of Housing and Urban Development (HUD), was instituted to protect lenders from these high-risk loans, and commissioned the HOLC to complete a survey of neighborhoods in 239 cities to measure and attest to their security and desirability for lending.

The results were the formal ranking of cities with grades from "A" to "D" and associated color codes on physical maps that put in motion the first wave of explicit redlining and racially polarized neighborhoods. Green-coded "A-ratings" suggested the high desirability of the neighborhood, while "D-ratings" were coded as red, and therefore were flagged as less desirable, riskier investments for home lenders.

Black populations were the hardest hit by the effects of the Great Depression and were scrutinized under the color-coded housing maps to qualify for mortgages both within and outside their red-zoned communities. In Los Angeles, redlining by race began as early as 1939, when the maps substantiated lending decisions and resulted in the polarization seen today in the housing market (see figure 6-1).

City National Bank was accused of being one of the more recent perpetrators of the discriminatory practice of redlining, which has manifested in a multiplicity of other ways in the United States. The rejection of rental housing applications based on race and other federally protected characteristics, unfair and often racist housing appraisals, and evasive mortgage and credit decisions all stifle home-ownership and wealth building for people of color.

In 1968, President Lyndon B. Johnson secured passage of the Fair Housing Act as an extension of his broader civil rights legislation, after an intense partisan battle. The enacted legislation made it illegal to ban the sale, rental, and financing of housing based on race, religion, national origin, sex—and, later, special ability and family status.

But the wounds of housing discrimination have not entirely healed since the 1930s, and new instances of redlining show up in more explicit ways when city officials choose to build large, urban public housing developments on the outskirts of vibrant commercial districts, as in Syracuse, or when people of color find themselves trapped in neighborhoods that sit on the opposite side of railroad tracks, including four generations of Joseph's family in Staunton, Virginia. Modern-day "reverse redlining" practices are also at play when banks engage in predatory

Figure 6-1. *1939 Housing Redlining Map in Los Angeles County, California*

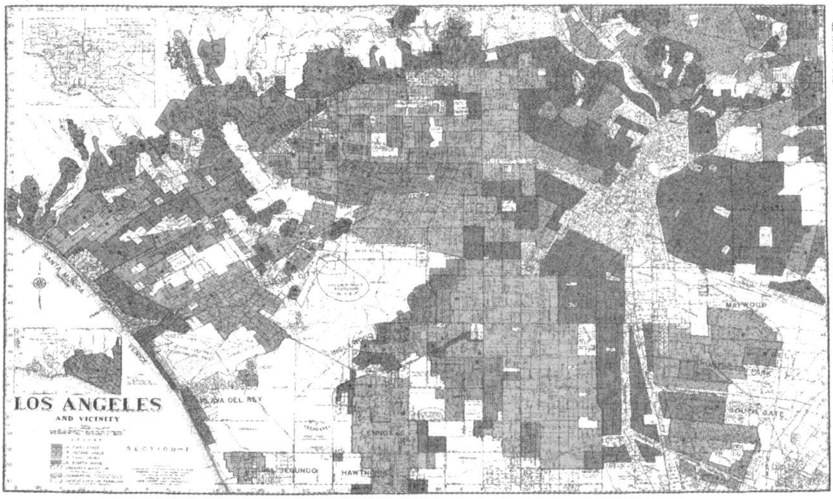

Source: Robert K. Nelson, LaDale Winling, Richard Marciano, Nathan Connolly, et al., "Mapping Inequality," in *American Panorama,* ed. Robert K. Nelson and Edward L. Ayers, htps://s3.amazonaws.com/holc/tiles/CA/LosAngeles1/1939/holc-scan.jpg.

lending practices that place credit-challenged and economically vulnerable populations in subprime loans, including "no doc" and balloon payment loans that lead to high foreclosure rates among low-income borrowers. And even when physical buildings are forcefully demolished with the attempt to reconstruct communities, the accrued experiences of living in poverty and social isolation maintain the invisibility of populations affected by decades of systemic inequality.

In 2021, the Biden Justice Department instituted a formal initiative to combat redlining under Attorney General Merrick Garland. The Combating Redlining Initiative is said to be the agency's most aggressive coordination and rigorous pursuit of housing discrimination, whose goal is to reinforce the nation's fair lending laws. City National Bank was one of the many banks prosecuted under the program, joining Trustmark National Bank in Tennessee, Cadence Bank in Houston, and Trident Bank that originated loans in Philadelphia, among others that been accused of restrictive race-based lending choices and settled for millions for their actions.

Yet it may be too late to fully improve equal access to housing in the United States. The redlines of housing inequality also have bled into other areas of economic and social mobilities that influence full participation in our society, including the ability to connect and compete in the twenty-first-century digital economy. It is no coincidence that communities across the country that lack affordable, good-quality, high-speed broadband service are redlined, housing communities—partly due to the origins of the problem, and partly due to the concentrated poverty that comes along with such discrimination.

The city of Cleveland provides a compelling illustration of what happens with the mix of such depravities, and it is also demonstrated the complexity of viewing the lack of broadband access in certain communities outside of the settled history of housing redlining, which makes internet service providers (ISPs) rather than government the culprits for engaging in quite intentional digital redlining, and as recently described as digital discrimination—a concept developed under the Biden administration.

The Historic Redlining of Cleveland

Some may wonder what life looks like within redlined housing communities. There are food deserts, or pockets within neighborhoods without grocery stores or any type of healthy food options that ultimately exacerbate poor health and lifestyle outcomes for residents. Redeveloped housing lots exist in redlined communities, most prominently considered as brownfields, or environmentally distressed lands, which have been known to incubate a series of chronic and potentially fatal diseases, like asthma and cancer. There are few children playing outside because playground equipment is often rusted and old, and litter may flow freely as the wind takes it in communities of invisible gates.

When I was in Chicago in the 1990s, this was the scene of the Robert Taylor Homes, to which I previously referred. Solid yet cracked concrete overwhelmed the community on buildings, sidewalks, parks, and streets. It was a community of public housing that was essentially forgotten through disinvestment and the racist policies of the mayor, who was committed to racial segregation in concept and theory.

Historically, redlined communities have been described by their physical scarcity of resources, but public health experts also consider housing segregation as a major contributor to existing and emerging health disparities, including mental health deterioration for residents who live in such conditions. It is the dearth of resources, coupled with the disincentive on the part of government and private industry to bring more to these communities that keep the cycle of poverty and isolation going. And to be redlined by discriminatory housing policies does not mean that one has to live in extreme poverty. Modern-day gentrification is proving to be another way to limit who gets to live in communities with wealth as a major indicator.

The lack of access to high-speed broadband is expected in redlined communities that have essentially been neglected without considerations given to the people who live in isolated urban areas, and rural communities where trailers or scattered sites of affordable housing instead of high-rise buildings contain people in redlined communities.

In this book, I keep returning to the conceptual frame of race, place, and space, either taken together or analyzed separately. The sad reality is that digital deserts thrive in places where there is no rhetorical water for residents who are thirsty to obtain social and economic mobility, and the material gains of our twenty-first-century economy. In redlined communities, the lack of online access presents itself as another factor of housing segregation. Every city and rural town that I visited during my tour had some form of housing redlining that correlated with inaccessibility to viable commercial broadband options, either due to less competitive options for affordable services or nonexistent networks resulting from difficult topographical deployments. The residents living in the most rural parts of Garrett County were unable to maintain contact with their case managers or area health clinicians. For the seniors who lived in Syracuse's public housing, they lived in uncertainty as the city government caught wind that their residential conditions and outlook were grim after years of disregard and neglect— making way for urban dislocation and the dismantling of Debra's last community asset: the computer lab.

Digital deserts are the results of life within communities established by intentional public policies to support housing discrimination, which reduce viable and affordable options for many Americans facing economic challenges.

That is why policymakers and advocates must start interrogating the digital divide as it relates to other systems of oppression and understand that many of the issues that we see are exploited from the tragedies of housing inequities and insecurities, which are much greater concerns than getting low-income residents shiny laptops or tablets, and a wired connection. Do not get me wrong that the interim investments and programming invested in digital inclusion and equity are very worthy of consideration for the accelerated access to populations living in redlined and geographically isolated communities. But unsettled debates over what came first—the chicken of housing discrimination or the egg, which is the lack of broadband—will serve to minimize greater inquiries and strategies for developing public policies that attack both housing and digital inequities at the same time.

My visit to Cleveland revealed the how these challenges and the debates over them play out in real life. Before city advocates worked to sue AT&T, there had always been a battle between civil society against ISPs, which focused on the former's accusations of intentional discrimination due to where broadband services were being deployed. Among ISPs, the concerns were market related and primarily linked to the return on investment from communities with less stable subscriberships for their services.

Cleveland ranks in the top five most segregated cities in the United States and has a long history of housing discrimination and redlining that has bled into its digital ecosystem. In 2012, the city's population was 367,991 and the median household income was around $34,000. Almost a quarter of the residents are under twenty-one years of age. The city is 47 percent Black, and that is quickly outpacing whites, who comprise 39 percent of the population. Thirty percent of city residents live in poverty. In terms of broadband access, 85 percent of households had a computer in 2021, and 75 percent had a home broadband connection.

Like other metropolitan areas, Cleveland's redlining was largely precipitated by the federal government's mapping and unfair housing practices. Starting in 1914, real estate deeds prohibited the sale or lease of housing to "colored people, Jews, and foreigners generally."[5] In 1926, the U.S. Supreme Court heard the case *Euclid, Ohio v. Ambler Realty Co.*, which pointed out discriminatory zoning practices in the city that violated the Fourteenth Amendment and other equal protection laws by regulating land use and neighborhood composition.[6] This case and others started the more ingrained housing redlining *before* the Federal Housing Authority maps that kept Black renters and owners out, as well as predatory subprime mortgages that deepened such discrimination.[7] This process evolved throughout the 1930s.

It was not until the 1960s that more than 100,000 Black Americans migrated to Cleveland for prospective manufacturing jobs and family stability. During the same period, over 170,000 whites left the city for the suburbs. There was even a forceful effort at that time to oppose public housing in these white, middle-class areas, forcing most Black Cleveland residents to fend for themselves in communities that rapidly deteriorated in the critical areas of education, health care, and commercial economic development.

To be clear, the now more segregated city of Cleveland was not always that way. During the early nineteenth and twentieth centuries, European immigrants came in droves to the city for new manufacturing jobs, but their numbers declined after World War I, in response to more restrictive immigration laws. Many Black populations saw opportunities to fill many of the vacant production and manufacturing jobs throughout the Midwest after World War II and moved to places like Cleveland, Chicago, and Detroit. In the 1920s, the city had a Black population of about 35,000, which grew to 85,000 in the late 1940s. By the time the First and Second Migrations of Black populations from the South to the North and Midwest ended, more than 4.3 million Black Americans had settled in the Cleveland area in the 1970s.

During the Civil Rights Movement, Blacks also held different views on the explicit segregation being experienced, making this a hotbed for leaders like Dr. Martin Luther King Jr. Some households in Cleveland that witnessed "white flight" to the suburbs favored the integrationist approach to secure their spot in the social strata, and within those same communities. Other Black residents preferred to stay racially isolated, focusing on the development of Black institutions like schools, businesses, barber and beauty shops, and churches. Back then, social justice leaders from the National Association for the Advancement of Colored People (NAACP) and the National Urban League organized themselves as the "New Negroes" of Cleveland, positioning formidable and vocal responses to increasing racial segregation.

In the 1960s and 1970s, Carl Stokes, who grew up in redlined public housing, was elected the first Black mayor of Cleveland. In 1968, his brother, Louis,
was elected to Congress. The late 1980s saw Cleveland's second Black mayor
elected and initiated the beginning of Black flight from the city itself. By 2010,
the city lost more than 30,000 Black residents to the suburbs because of increased
predatory practices for those remaining in the metropolitan vicinity, including
predatory evictions like bank foreclosures or subprime mortgages. As soon as
many of the Cleveland suburbs—like Euclid and Garfield Heights, among other
areas—became predominantly Black, some whites fled again—only this time,
farther out.[8]

The massive Black exodus exacerbated the resegregation of the city. This time,
it was primarily economic, with low-income populations designated to certain
areas. Despite having some of the nation's best quality health care resources
within the boundaries of less wealthy communities, including the famous Cleveland
Clinic, many residents in these resegregated areas suffered, particularly the city's
Black women, who to this day experience the nation's worst health outcomes,
according to Bloomberg CityLab rankings.[9]

In a city wrought with public equity concerns, it is not a coincidence that these
same quality-of-life concerns have made parts of the city less attractive to the private sector, especially for investments in high-speed broadband infrastructure.
But, in 2017, the National Digital Inclusion Alliance (NDIA) and Connect Your
Community (CYC) accused the incumbent AT&T of redlining certain areas
in Cleveland that were denied access to similar consumer broadband services
offered to other communities. NDIA and CYC used public information in Federal
Communications Commission Form 477 between 2008 and 2014 to allege discrimination in the deployment of AT&T's fiber-to-the-home (FTTH) product in
predominantly Black Cleveland neighborhoods that included Hough, Glenville,
Central, Fairfax, South Collinwood, Saint Clair–Superior, Detroit-Shoreway, and
Stockyards. Despite AT&T upgrading its infrastructure and slowly rolling it out
in certain markets, it was believed that the communities bypassed for new service
upgrades were not already able to qualify for AT&T's Access discount rate program, largely due to their inability to connect at 3 megabits per second (Mbps)
download speed. Instead, white and wealthier neighborhoods were provided immediate FTTH service options with download speeds above 24 Mbps, along with the
ability to access internet protocol video cable subscriptions, which were not available
or offered to these predominantly Black communities, which, by the way, were still
largely dependent on copper-only networks, which do not qualify as high-speed
broadband.

In response, a high-profile civil rights attorney, Daryl Parks, who was a former
partner in the Florida-based Parks & Crump legal firm before venturing on his
own, filed a formal complaint that AT&T had engaged in digital redlining by
unfairly rolling out infrastructure upgrades in lower-income communities

at unreasonable costs. This suit was submitted to the FCC on behalf of three Cleveland AT&T customers—JoAnne Elkins, Hattie Lanfair, and Rachelle Lee, whose justification was that the company had violated the provisions of the Communications Act of 1934, which prohibits unjust and unreasonable discrimination in communications services. In this case, "digital redlining" was in the appearance that AT&T had overlooked several Cleveland neighborhoods, like Glenville and Hough, in its rollout of its U-Verse technology.[10]

The case was never formally litigated outside the FCC, but it triggered a Notice of Inquiry by the agency around the practice of digital redlining in low-income areas, especially after residents in Toledo, and later Detroit, made similar claims. The 2020 Notice of Inquiry sought to gather additional input on the potential practice of digital redlining and defined it as intertwined with the agency's universal service obligations: "low-income areas experiencing less facilities deployment when compared to other areas, and that low-income consumers in those areas may experience increased difficulty obtaining affordable, robust communications services. We seek comment on how the Commission can address this issue with the Lifeline program." Reading between the lines, the commission made the issue of digital redlining about the affordability of services, and not the actual physical expansion of high-speed networks.

Cleveland would then become the national poster child for digital redlining, despite allegations accusing other ISPs of similar behavior. In 2017, before the Cleveland complaint, Google was also under the radar for digital redlining in its broadband rollout in Kansas City, Nashville, and Atlanta. The company was accused of rolling out its Google Fiber project in more affluent and downtown neighborhoods first, and applying exorbitant one-time installation fees that many low-income households could not afford.[11] A *Philadelphia Tribune* journalist accused the Google Fiber project of passing over communities of color, a claim that was bolstered by, among many other factors, its dismal track record in employee diversity worldwide.

Verizon was also accused of digital redlining in its inaugural optical fiber-to-the-protocol product (FTTP), or FIOS, which was not readily available in low-income neighborhoods at the onset due to capital infrastructure costs. In 2005, FIOS offered the fastest speeds among competitors at the time. But despite lofty goals to bring FIOS across the United States, efforts stalled in 2010 after Verizon experienced higher-than-expected build and delivery costs. In 2015, before the Cleveland allegations, former New York mayor Bill DeBlasio audited Verizon's FIOS offerings in the city and found that it had only passed 2.2 million of the projected 3.1 million households. DeBlasio then sued the company in 2017 for violating its coverage agreement. His argument was that the company had promised, as part of the agreement, to have "fiber up and down each street and avenue in the city."[12] Verizon later settled and agreed to bring FIOS to another 500,000 NYC households by the summer of 2023 after vehemently denying any practice of digital redlining.[13] That commitment would increase the number of households to 3.2 million from 2.7 million households in 2019.[14]

Google, Verizon, and AT&T, and some other ISPs, have publicly denied any form of digital redlining. Instead, they have countered that investment decisions for expanding their networks have been dictated by capital access and the long-term viability of the targeted markets. For example, from the start of the allegations in Cleveland, AT&T maintained that the company's network decisions were based on projected returns on investments, thereby suggesting that there has never been intentional redlining in Cleveland or anywhere else. Between 2012 and 2016, the company announced the investment of $135 billion in wireless and wired networks, as well as capital infrastructure costs and other wireless spectrum acquisitions. Of these dollars, a company spokesperson shared that $325 million was allocated to the city of Cleveland.[15] In 2021, another AT&T spokesperson updated its FTTH actual rollouts and projections and stated that the company's FTTH product has covered more than 14.5 million customer locations in over ninety areas, with deployments projected to double by 2025.[16]

But again with the history of housing discrimination in Cleveland running so deep that even with the flush of cash into new internet networks, there would still be a racial digital divide.[17] Three years after the dust settled on NDIA's report, new research found that the broadband adoption rate among the city's majority-white neighborhoods was 81.2 percent, compared with just 63 percent in Black-majority neighborhoods.[18]

I met with one of the more vocal critics of digital redlining and one of the leaders at NDIA who advanced the lawsuit, Bill Callahan. We have known each other since the late 2000s when I was working for an international nonprofit, One Economy. Back then, Bill was a leader at the Ohio-based nonprofit called One Community and they were our competition. Like One Economy, his organization was leveraging the funds appropriated from Obama's Recovery Act to expand community technology centers and digital literacy training. One Community was also helping low-income families in Northeast Ohio find affordable refurbished computers, and it established the CYC Corps, which was a spinoff of the community service programs managed by the Corporation for National Service.

Bill had brought along another well-respected technology leader, Leon Wilson, who is the chief of digital innovation and chief information officer at the Cleveland Foundation, and someone else who was no stranger to me. It was no coincidence that we all met that day at Digital Cs, which is an incubator founded in the early 2000s to offer open connections to broadband, digital literacy training, and available space for the community to rent or use for free. The founder, who had since moved to Phoenix to work for Arizona State University, was another digital advocate and friend, Lev Gonick. It really is a separation degree of three in the community technology space, especially after government flushed the economy with resources to support our activities.

As soon as we all sat down to start the discussion, Bill began with his own version of the redlining allegations against ISPs. "Someone made the decision," he shared, with his medium-sized build, "AT&T did it with U-Verse, and Verizon with FIOS. They didn't turn the fiber on in these communities here in Cleveland." Not certain of who the "somebody" was, we continued the discussion, with Leon jumping in.

With over twenty-five years of experience working on digital access, Leon offered his own thoughts on how a city like Cleveland got to this point where affordable and available broadband was not more ubiquitous. "In Cleveland, there are many people here who are digitally stuck and challenged," he stated, before delving deeper into the circumstances of being digitally stuck:

> I have a smartphone, but I am paying as I go. I run out of minutes or data for two weeks. I'm not living off Wi-Fi for the other half of the month. On Panera Bread's free network for Wi-Fi. Or maybe, I have a phone, but not a physical device like a PC. I don't realize that I need the latter to do certain things online. I don't know what else I need to even know what to do.

What he was really describing was the lifestyle of being connected in digital deserts—something similar was mentioned by Kizzie from Staunton, who constantly made choices about going to her mother's home to jump on her Wi-Fi to save her wireless minutes. But the most profound commentary that Leon shared was this: "We are a broadband cemetery here in Cleveland. We are at the same point today that we were with electricity."

Cemeteries are where we bury our dead—above or below ground depending on where you grew up. In the beginning, we visit our loved ones more frequently; and as times roll by, the graveside visits become less frequent and we, unfortunately, become less apologetic about it. We never forget the names of the departed, and their legacies. It is just that our acknowledgment of their presence becomes less important as our everyday routines take over. I know about this; despite my father being one of the most important people in my life, I rarely return to the cemetery where he is buried, and it has been almost eight years since he died.

Places like Cleveland have been left to die—socially, economically, and sometimes politically, which I think was Leon's point. He continued:

> The east side of Cleveland, which is predominantly African American, has three neighborhoods—Hough, Glendale, and Fairfax, that are struggling. They don't have internet, but more importantly, they are unequal in terms of educational access and housing. They lost more affluent Black residents. They used to be like a Black Metropolis, and today, they would also tell you that their internet is not great.

But who is responsible for ensuring equitable access across the United States, and especially in cities like Cleveland? How has housing inequality more or less buried the proverbial dead who have been forgotten in urban areas like this?

Advocates like Bill believe that ISPs have been the named Lucifers, who have created and widened the digital divide, choosing profits over morality. "Everybody is an object of the process, and others who participate are the subject," Bill opined. "What has changed in the last twenty years, fundamentally, is we have shifted from paper to digital for the convenience, not knowing that not everyone has caught up."

However, these shifts from analog to digital realities have been happening for quite some time and often were welcomed first by policymakers from both sides of the aisles. The migration of civil service jobs to the internet after 9/11 is a good example of this when Northwest Tower residents began to feel their erasure with the technology. Along the lines of how the FCC rationalized the mitigation of digital redlining, Bill shared these last words: "Anything that doesn't get people access to the internet and more reasonably priced services will not solve the digital divide."

It has been this sentiment, combined with other telecom debates, that has stirred the pot on this fundamental question of whether broadband service should be considered a new utility. This has been a dogmatic issue, to say it politely, that has dominated discussions in tech regulation for decades, and some might argue, have diverted the oxygen away from ways to redress digital inclusion and equity.

Leon seemed to think that we should reclassify broadband along the lines of his electricity statement, and the correct approach would be to treat it like former rotary telephone systems, where it becomes more of a public good for users than a luxury subscription. He also shared that some technologies have become more ubiquitous among consumers than others, particularly smartphones. More than 90 percent of Black and Latino subscribers have access to a mobile device; and, in many instances, that device is the primary gateway to the internet for them. Over the course of the pandemic, mobile broadband evolved into 5G access that reduced the latency of mobile data transfers and became more affordable for income-prohibitive subscribers.

Talking about 5G, Leon said: "Whether it's 5G or Wi-Fi 6 [cable], or something else. . . . We need broadband in whatever form, the same way that we need water. And when you build it, you should be required to be extended to everyone."

Leon also pointed out the importance of connecting students to these online resources: "We live in a very important time. We can have it all like 5G or Wi-Fi 6, but what's more important to us. What do we envision in the next five years? Do we have people that are more employable and connected? What about seniors or those K-12 students? How are we going to help them navigate their lives without the internet?"

Less than six months after his poignant observations, the world fell victim to the pandemic, and those K-12 students—more than 50 million of them— were left on their own to transition to distance learning. Many of them were left without home broadband or a device, and in some instances, they were forced to make do with a smartphone as their classroom. Before the pandemic, the Cleveland Foundation gave away more than 1,000 computers to students with some of them wireless hot spots under Leon's leadership. They partnered with the PCs for People program, a nationwide initiative led by the digital activist Casey Sorenson to provide reasonably priced, refurbished computers to residents of affordable and public housing. I would later visit his facility, which was quite impressive with their refurbishment turnaround time after donations, and customer service. Digital Cs where we met was another Cleveland Foundation grantee and was also doing its part to close the digital divide before the pandemic by offering residents open access to Wi-Fi, entrepreneur training, and digital literacy courses. Once the pandemic hit, the foundation stepped up these efforts to ensure the greater utility and sustainability of their community investments.

Having local, digital infrastructure was a clear message in discussions with both Bill and Leon because place matters when it comes to where it is provisioned. Or as stated by Lisa Rice of the National Fair Housing Alliance, where you live matters. On top of the supply of online services is also the demand for them, which requires an internet-enabled device and some type of training. That is why the Federal Communications Commission's arc on digital redlining as something more so related to affordability was a fact, but not the entire reality for people without competitive broadband services, including in rural areas.

The Start of Net Neutrality

To understand how Cleveland got into this problem, we do need to understand internet governance policies that started with President Clinton. In the early days of the internet, regulators adopted a largely hands-off policy on the new technology. In the 1990s, Clinton's FCC chairman, William Kennard, encouraged a deregulatory environment to motivate private investments in emerging networks and innovation. His hands-off policies gave rise to the diffusion of high-speed broadband, which dismissed and later squashed telephony-based connectivity. In the late 1990s and into the early 2000s, the commission referred to broadband as anything more advanced than plain old telephone service, including digital subscriber lines, cable, fiber-optics, wireless, satellite, and broadband over powerline. Between 2002 and 2007, these and other classifications codified broadband as an "information service" due to the dynamic and interactive nature of information flowing over these networks, subjecting it to Title I of the Communications Act of 1934, which never really anticipated the rapid evolution of more traditional communications infrastructure. Basic telephone service was under the regulatory guidance of Title II, and was considered a "common carrier service," which subjected it to various interstate commerce rules like stringent rate regulation for local and long distancing calling. The business models for the latter were on the verge of extinction as technologies that converted voice into digital signals became more prevalent, and cheaper—removing the public switched telephone network from the data transmission.

When Michael Powell took office as chair after Kennard, in addition to leading the digital TV transition, he, too, encouraged the deregulation of advanced communications. While in office, the Republican FCC chair became known for his policy doctrine, called the "Powell Principles," which became part of a binding FCC Policy Statement in 2015, a decade after his term ended. The Powell Principles outlined several consumer entitlements to this emerging communications infrastructure, including the entitlement to lawful content, applications and services of their choice, connections to devices that avoid harm to the network, and competition among network, application, service, and content providers. While the Powell Principles were never legally binding or enforceable, they influenced the future cadence of the internet's design and encouraged the conception of new industries—some that would challenge status quo policies, like new applications riding over existing and evolving broadband infrastructure.

So, here you have it. Two former FCC chairs from different sides of the aisle put in motion the foundational elements of the internet—the same one that survived through during a global pandemic. After their leadership tenures came tumultuous times, as others in government, the private sector, and civil society inserted their own ideas and values into the future of the internet, like whether broadband should be reclassified under common carrier regulations or Title II. Such conversations at the end of Powell's tenure at the commission emblazoned the existing debates and differences on the need for net neutrality, and the future reclassification of broadband services as common carriers, as dictated by Title II regulations. The internet's status as an information service exempted it from the same common carrier regulations as telephones, and thereby it averted being subjected to a series of related rate regulations around its use. In other words, the cost of the private service was not subjected to regulation.

In 2006, after leaving the FCC years prior, Kennard penned a telling *New York Times* op-ed about the spirited debates happening around internet freedom and ISPs, which were at the time more likely to be seen as the gatekeepers of the internet. He scrutinized the growing monopolies of big telecom giants like Comcast, AT&T, and Verizon, which were accused of charging more for faster bandwidth. Kennard equally chastised the net neutrality proponents, including Google and Amazon, which were the beneficiaries of the internet's two-sided market of service and content. At this time, these latter companies had no interest in supporting the expansion of the network's infrastructure.

"Any serious discussion of the internet should start with a basic fact: broadband is transforming every facet of communications, from entertainment and telephone services to delivery of vital services like health care," Kennard wrote a week after Google acquired YouTube for $1.65 billion.[19] In his 2006 op-ed, he also wrote: "But this also means that the digital divide, once defined as the chasm separating those who had access to narrowband dial-up Internet and those who didn't, has become a broadband digital divide."[20] Kennard scoffed at the primary focus of telecommunications services still being on competitive monopolies and not on the growing narrowband divide, which alienated those still on dial-up, keeping them apart from the burgeoning digital economy. Little did he know that the net neutrality debate would arise again in 2015, almost ten years later, when the internet had reached its adolescence and carved out a more distinguishable identity in the nation's communications infrastructure.

Net Neutrality in 2015

During the second term of the Obama administration, the new FCC chairman, Tom Wheeler, was appointed after acting chairwoman Mignon Clyburn, the first Black woman in that role, returned to being an FCC commissioner. Wheeler took a divergent stance from his predecessors and prompted a conversation on access and internet speeds, suggesting that the agency update the minimum thresholds for download speeds from the previous 4 megabits per second (Mbps) to 25 Mbps, and increase the 1 Mbps on upload to 3 Mbps. Wheeler also proposed that some of these changes be adopted by incumbent internet service providers seeking federal funds from the agency for broadband deployment— though these proposals were not favorably viewed. The somewhat dormant debates on net neutrality remerged in 2015, and, with a public declaration from President Obama on a YouTube channel, were rekindled when some say that the former president realized that an internet with gatekeepers would restrict his digital divide program, which was focused on getting 99 percent of the nation's schools connected to broadband. Once Obama launched that public YouTube campaign, Wheeler changed his moderate tone on net neutrality and obliged his boss by quickly appealing a previously struck-down District of Columbia Court of Appeals ruling that deemed the FCC had limited authority to strictly regulate the internet over everyone else.

Around this time, there were advocates who viewed internet openness as fundamental to civil liberties and free speech. At Harvard during this time, Tim Wu's inaugural definition of net neutrality provoked the removal of big telecom gatekeepers from the scene. The camp of people believed him then and still do today, that the government must ensure that the internet is free from content and pricing discrimination, allowing all types of information to flow over broadband networks without exception by large companies like Comcast, Verizon, and AT&T. In fact, President Biden brought Wu back to the White House after his election to rekindle these conversations under the guise of antitrust policy platforms.

Industry and promarket supporters argued to the contrary on the need for net neutrality by suggesting that too much government intervention defiled the intent of Kennard and Powell in the creation of free online markets, and the results of such a rule of law would stifle innovation, network investment, and competition. But their views, though supported by expensive lobbying, did not stop the other side from waging political and public smear campaigns in favor of the reclassification of broadband under Title II and arguing that the legal framework alone could end digital redlining, pricing, and deployment discrimination. But just like a group of young people playing tug-o-war, the rope was pulled by industry and free market experts, who refused to give up, and desired to maintain the hands-off the internet so it could flourish and lead to other economic opportunities, much as it did with the conception of the smartphone in 2009.

Wheeler's years as FCC chair were consumed by the net neutrality debate, and he ultimately succeeded when the High Court did not rule out the agency's jurisdiction over reclassification—an opinion that was quickly enacted. But the reinstatement of net neutrality rules was short-lived. When Republicans took over the White House, President Donald J. Trump appointed the thirty-second FCC chair, Ajit Pai. Acting in his party's interest, Pai immediately reversed by administrative authority, or a loophole, the existing net neutrality rules within the first thirty days of Trump's presidency. In 2019, a new D.C. court ruling upheld the repeal, but did not bar individual states from enacting their own net neutrality rules. In 2020, California was the first state to do so. California and other states—including Vermont, Washington, and Oregon—quickly responded to this repeal by establishing their own net neutrality regimes. In the 2021 state legislatures, nine other states introduced similar bills. During the early years of the Biden-Harris administration, officials toyed around with resurfacing the net neutrality debate, especially with Tim Wu, who started this whole thing, at the White House. In 2023, the FCC chairwoman took her shot at the debate by reopening the net neutrality debate, and with very similar language, requested the reinstatement of the Wheeler rules that had been overturned by the Trump administration. In an election year, this could very well become an important campaign issue.

During the early months of the COVID-19 pandemic, Tom Wheeler penned a blog post for Brookings that argued the internet was prepared for the resiliency of the urgent demands of physical social distancing, especially as internet usage among consumers now cooped up in the four walls of their homes soared around, from basic to more complex online activities. In his remembrance of how far the nation's communications infrastructure has come, he wrote: "In the days of analog telephone service, the network was designed with enough capacity to handle the surge in calls that happened on Mother's Day and other holidays." He continued: "For residential internet service, the equivalent of Mother's Day has been Netflix and other online video services. Typically, peak demand for online video is between 8:00 pm and 11:00 pm. Just like the old telephone company, internet service providers built their capacity to meet such peak demand. . . . Then came COVID-19. . . . [Because] of Mother's Day-like planning, network capacity was sitting there waiting for workday usage."

What this could be is his quiet admission that the internet did not break over the pandemic, and it probably still will not, due to the originating principles of the permissionless innovation led by two party chairs. And because of network resiliencies, the nation operated on business as usual—so it was surprising that Rosenworcel would restart the clock on the debate once again.

Industry Has Long Known About the Digital Divide

I bring up the issue of net neutrality in the same spirit that I referenced the digital TV transition. American broadband companies—whether invested in wireline or wireless—have consistently invested in resilient broadband networks, internet-enabled applications, and devices. Granted that over the years, some of the decisions of incumbent telecom have exacerbated existing housing segregation, leading to digital redlining and inequity. But just as the government created public policies that facilitated housing disparities, ISPs were handed the same permissions to build and to operate broadband services in accordance with free market values. While this does not make it right, it also does not make it wrong, and particularly when companies are subjected to dinosaur rules designed for the early telegraph.

There are many residents in cities like Cleveland, Syracuse, Hartford, and other economically challenged urban (and even rural) areas that experience the consequences of being digitally redlined. In a recent study that I conducted on rural access in predominantly Black and Latino communities in the country's Deep South, people in places like Mississippi and Arkansas would like to work from home, but the lack of high-speed broadband makes it impossible.[21] Because many of these same communities also do not have flexible local employment options, they are stuck and trapped, as Leon described, to stay within the boundaries of digital deserts unless they choose to relocate their families to places where the broadband services are better. But that move is also dependent on whether they qualify for rental or homeownership assistance, which is another aspect of the vicious cycle of living in poverty, and among others with such scarcities.

Bill Callahan referred to this as one segment of the broader digital divide: "If you are still in the world of the old rules around work, you are disadvantaged. The first rule is that some people can't play in the digital world. You cannot get prepared to work in the new digital economy without access." His hypothesis was not entirely wrong. A few months into the pandemic, those households and communities without broadband joined the list of other digital deserts across the United States.

In addition to housing depravities, limited internet access also contends with the lack of available workforce readiness and jobs. K-12 students who are left offline in digital deserts also suffer the consequences of being confined to analog learning environments that make it harder for them to envision themselves as coders, computer technicians, and data scientists. Those who are stricken with a range of chronic disease, or constrained by a disability, are unable to receive the best treatment or care—even if done remotely, simply because they lack broadband access or are disadvantaged by the plethora of internet-enabled activities, including the ability to catch a rideshare to a doctor's appointment or to send emails or voice messages to caregivers about the state of their health or mobility.

Bill pointed out the young people on the stoops of McDonald's parking lots before the pandemic revealed such normal use: "A great deal of what's happened in the world is that we have closed the doors on people. These are people locked out of normal life. The fact that some students have to sit in parking lots to do what has to be done is sickening. It is the other side of the divide that we have to worry about." It is the part of the digital divide that was largely invisible to a whole lot of policymakers and other concerned advocates who strongly believed, then and now, that closing the digital divide is about reclassifying broadband as an information service or private industry but who do not realize that everyday people are constantly choosing between having broadband or bread on their tables.

My mother used to say to my sisters and me, "It takes a good education to get out of poverty and have a better life." She is a living testament to this. She is the first in her family of fifteen siblings to receive a master's degree, which she earned in special education while working as a front-desk secretary for one of the offices in the school district—which at one point in time forbade Blacks from having front office jobs. As a new social and economic determinant, it is also the case that when left without the internet and related devices, one cannot break the trajectory of poverty and social isolation because these twenty-first-century tools are defining factors for personal and professional productivity in our new economy.

Digital Discrimination

As part of the Bipartisan Infrastructure Law, President Biden charged FCC chairwoman Rosenworcel to develop laws that facilitate equal access to high-speed broadband networks and avert practices of "digital discrimination" by ISPs that violate the rights of individual consumers on the bases of race, income, gender, ability, and other federally protected characteristics.[22] In addition to rules, the agency also had to establish infrastructure, like a complaint center, to identify and resolve any perceived violations or allegations. Early on in Rosenworcel's new role, she chartered the newly revamped Communications Equity and Diversity Council (CEDC) to develop model policies for states and localities benefiting from Broadband Equity, Access, and Deployment (BEAD) funds.[23] It was under the new federal infrastructure program that Biden wanted the rules to be established in order to ensure that no community would be left behind due to outright denial of services. As one of the vice chairs of the CEDC at the time, this was no easy task for an advisory with professionals from ISPs, who were essentially being told to tell on themselves, and civil society advocates who welcomed that shaming. When our work concluded, the FCC opened a Notice of Inquiry in March 2022 and established an internal Task Force to Prevent Digital Discrimination to explore equal access. Since its inception, the task force conducted a public listening sessions in large cities—one in Baltimore and the other in Los Angeles, at the time of this writing.[24] By November 2023, the agency is expected to deliver (1) a definition of "digital discrimination of access"; (2) a revised commission informal consumer complaint process to accept concerns of digital discrimination of access; and (3) the adoption of model policies and best practices for states and localities combating digital discrimination.[25] Before attendees at an event of the United Church of Christ, Chairwoman Rosenworcel suggested that she would be leaning toward a definition of digital discrimination that policed both intentional and unintentional denials of service, and that the agency would be ramping up its ability to capture such complaints from consumers. As suggested by the statute requesting this work, she also suggested in her speech that her agency had the bandwidth to take this on, which some would argue might be overly optimistic, given the plethora of other prescribed obligations the agency handles, including spectrum management and auctions, affordability programs, media ownership, emergency communications services, connectivity to schools and rural hospitals, intermodal connections, satellite, broadband service programs other than BEAD, and so many other things.

Her speech essentially detailed how the FCC responded to President Biden's charge and will likely be challenged by disappointed ISPs. If history is a marker, whoever becomes the next president in 2024 will stand up or overturn her actions.

Because such guidance on promoting universal access is critical to the success of the largest federal appropriation toward high-speed broadband, the application to just ISPs may be too narrow. The legacies of many states and localities are often responsible for the origins of residential segregation.

Digital discrimination is clearly symptomatic of larger and more systemic racism and structural discrimination. The housing developments on the other side of the railroad tracks and asphalt expressways in places like Syracuse, Cleveland, Chicago, Hartford, and Staunton, Virginia, are the outcomes of harmful housing policies that prompted and sustained racial segregation. Further, without comprehensive and accurate national broadband maps, which detail inequalities at the most granular level, it is hard to argue if broadband assets have ever been evenly distributed across the United States. Having more updated national broadband maps could have helped to identify redlined communities, but the monies released under Biden have been distributed without these assurances. The exclusion of wireless will definitely skew any hopeful view into digital equity because the current BEAD program does not fund it, and avoids hefty investments in urban areas where infrastructure may be already available, despite quickly eroding or scantily dispersed due to aged and relatively thick concrete buildings that are unable to accommodate the speedier transmissions of newer technologies.

Traditionally, complaints of digital redlining have been largely associated with physical infrastructure and services. But the Infrastructure Investment and Jobs Act's focus on fiber-only constitutes its own form of digital discrimination, especially if some urban communities have the least competition when it comes to that type of high-speed broadband access. Other technologies like mobile (especially 5G), satellite, TV white spaces, municipal networks, and other alternative technologies may be less expensive to roll out than fiber, but are not eligible in the current appropriations strategy. While the premise is true that all technologies propagate from fiber at some point, such inconsistencies in technology utilization will likely surface complaints of digital discrimination, especially among more urban wireless customers. An even greater offense in the presumption that internet service providers will always be the one breaking the law is the exemption of states and municipalities of similar accusations. In earlier work that I did at the Joint Center in the mid-2000s, my coauthors and I found that the location of broadband assets correlated closely with the economic development plans of cities and states.

My point is that in the symbolic gesture to ensure that we are boldly standing up nondiscrimination in the access and use of federal dollars, we should be prepared for levels of cronyism from government and repeated patterns of loyalties to constituents. As more Republican states are geared up to receive their large share of BEAD funds, we will need to watch if the investments are made around votes or the desperate needs of some communities where not having clean, running water runs parallel to the absence of updated communications infrastructure. I would assume that given the average allocation of federal dollars to states, the wiring of such communities alone would eat up all the resources this time around.

My point is that even when networks are fully available and accessible, will they be universally available, especially among marginalized populations who face myriad other socioeconomic concerns? And if not, who is to blame when the money dries up, or we have underestimated the same problem of digital access based on traditional formulas and paradigms?

These questions will be partly addressed by any final ruling on digital discrimination, but they will not explain why cities like Cleveland are unable to stop the bleeding of local economic resources and general infrastructure decades after the historic effects of housing redlining. That is why massive federal investments in the supply of broadband services must be about the provisioning of universal service to partake in the nation's communications infrastructure—that is becoming more advanced. Without a thorough inquiry, and one that I will suggest as part of my proposed recommendations toward more just digital access, stale Universal Service Fund programs started under the 1996 Telecommunications Act will merely produce the same outcomes for people without broadband and operationalize strategies that lean toward one-size-fitting-all, instead of grasping the needs and aspirations of residents and their communities, as well as the multiple modalities and use cases of different technologies.

In many respects, the historic challenges of a range of redlined activities, from housing to banking and now broadband, have put the invisible people and their communities deeper into their bunkered lives, including small farm owners, who struggle to stay profitable against more agricultural enterprises that are engaged in precision technologies to save money and facilitate greater productivity. Or returning to students who live in communities where they will not have the same attachments to an increasingly global workforce as they struggle to make it online, and in person, in our nation's schools.

If the Biden-Harris administration established parallels between these realities and the focus on racial equities, for example, we could have been more headstrong in challenging policies and practices that limit opportunities and restrict global competitiveness.

Bill Callahan nailed this point when he shared, "We need to stop worrying about what will happen when people are connected to the internet." He noted that "people have agency over their own lives." People can also become producers in new technology without physical barriers, or in places that show up as physically gated in person but can be imagined as much more online.

That is where any policy that is focused on eliminating digital redlining, discrimination, or both must raise awareness among residents who do not clearly understand what they are missing without internet access. For example, it can help people to recertify their public benefits, complete their homework, or visit more regularly with doctors. It can enable new entrepreneurial ventures. It can also expose incarcerated populations to new workforce development programs as they prepare for reentry. We must address universal access and the opportunities it offers so more people can consume more public goods, especially those that are important to them.

As the Federal Communications Commission shifts its focus from more known cases of digital redlining to greater policing of digital discrimination, the rules must apply to all parts of the broadband ecosystem, and they must carefully assess what came first to make more coherent and situational judgments on possible complaints. Groups like the National Urban League have recently suggested that perhaps the FCC institute a new Office of Civil Rights, which may not be a bad idea to follow the outcomes of broadband deployment and also the challenges associated with unequal access to media ownership, which has also been dismal for Black, Latino, and indigenous owners of broadcast media stations. Unless we deal with these underlying inequities, any proceeding, ruling, or reversal of what explains the unequal access to high-speed broadband will address it from the starting place of providing more—whether networks, money, devices, or training—despite the larger problem: that we have allowed our nation's institutions and communities to evolve into bastions of multilayered and intersectional inequalities. Thus, even tough guidance on antidiscrimination will never fully address its origins in housing and in what I talk about in the next chapter: our nation's schools.

Notes

1. Michael Finnegan, "City National Bank Accused of Racial Bias in LA Home Loans," *Los Angeles Times*, January 12, 2023, https://www.latimes.com/california/story/2023-01-12/city-national-bank-redlining-settlement.
2. Finnegan.
3. Finnegan.
4. Hassan Kanu, "Landmark Housing Discrimination Settlement with Fannie Mae Sets Key Precedent," February 11, 2022, Reuters, https://www.reuters.com/legal/government/landmark-housing-discrimination-settlement-with-fannie-mae-sets-key-precedent-2022-02-11/.
5. William Wayne Giffin, *African Americans and the Color Line in Ohio, 1915–1930* (Ohio State University Press, 2005).
6. Cleveland Public Library, "Cleveland's Legacy of Housing Discrimination: The Great Migration," June 7, 2018, https://cpl.org/clevelands-legacy-of-housing-discrimination-the-great-migration/.
7. Cleveland Public Library.
8. "Census Data Reveals New Migration Patterns as Black Families Leave Cleveland," March 28, 2011, https://www.cleveland.com/metro/2011/03/census_data_reveals_new_migrat.html.
9. Bloomberg, "What 'Livability' Looks Like for Black Women," January 9, 2020, https://www.bloomberg.com/news/articles/2020-01-09/the-best-and-worst-cities-for-black-women.
10. John Eggerton, "AT&T Accused of Digital Redlining in Cleveland," *NextTV*, March 10, 2017, https://www.nexttv.com/news/att-accused-digital-redlining-cleveland-163973.
11. Khalil Abdullah, "Google's Broadband War Redlining Black Communities," *Philadelphia Tribune*, January 6, 2017, https://www.phillytrib.com/commentary/googles-broadband-war-redlining-black-communities/article_78510d50-d377-59ef-8032-2db568d647c4.html.
12. David Rosen, "Confronting the Digital Divide: New York City vs. Verizon," *CounterPunch*, February 24, 2021, https://www.counterpunch.org/2021/02/24/confronting-the-digital-divide-new-york-city-vs-verizon/.
13. Jon Brodkin, "Verizon Wiring Up 500k Homes with FiOS to Settle Years-Long Fight with NYC," *ArsTechnica*, November 30, 2020, https://arstechnica.com/tech-policy/2020/11/verizon-wiring-up-500k-homes-with-fios-to-settle-years-long-fight-with-nyc/.
14. Brodkin.
15. Brodkin.
16. Shara Tibken, "The Broadband Gap's Dirty Secret: Redlining Still Exists in Digital Form," CNET, June 28, 2021, https://www.cnet.com/home/internet/features/the-broadband-gaps-dirty-secret-redlining-still-exists-in-digital-form/.

17. Lara Fishbane and Adie Tomer, "How Cleveland Is Bridging Both Digital and Racial Divides," Brookings, March 9, 2020. https://www.brookings.edu/articles/how-cleveland-is-bridging-both-digital-and-racial-divides/.

18. Fishbane and Tomer.

19. William Kennard, "Spreading the Broadband Revolution," op-ed., *New York Times*, October 21, 2006, https://www.nytimes.com/2006/10/21/opinion/21kennard.html.

20. Kennard.

21. Nicol Turner Lee, James Seddon, Brooke Tanner, and Samantha Lai, "Why the Federal Government Needs to Step Up Efforts to Close the Rural Broadband Divide," Brookings, October 4, 2022, https://www.brookings.edu/articles/why-the-federal-government-needs-to-step-up-their-efforts-to-close-the-rural-broadband-divide/.

22. Federal Communications Commission, "Implementing the Infrastructure Investment and Jobs Act: Prevention and Elimination of Digital Discrimination," *Federal Register*, January 20, 2023, https://www.federalregister.gov/documents/2023/01/20/2023-00551/implementing-the-infrastructure-investment-and-jobs-act-prevention-and-elimination-of-digital.

23. CEDC Working Groups, "Recommendations and Best Practices to Prevent Digital Discrimination and Promote Digital Equity," November 7, 2022, https://www.fcc.gov/sites/default/files/cedc-digital-discrimination-report-110722.pdf.

24. The listening sessions were recorded and are available on the Federal Communications Commission's website.

25. Federal Communications Commission, "Notice of Proposed Rulemaking in the Matter of Implementing the Infrastructure Investment and Jobs Act: Prevention and Elimination of Digital Discrimination," GN Docket No. 22-69, December 22, 2022. Available at https://docs.fcc.gov/public/attachments/FCC-22-98A1.pdf

IV

Schools in Crises

The good news is that by identifying the Homework Gap as a problem we can get started on developing solutions. But like any good homework problem, it's complex. There is no one single answer or quick fix. Still, there are things we can do right now to help bridge this gap and close this divide.

—Remarks by Jessica Rosenworcel,
then–commissioner of the Federal Communications Commission,
at the Aspen Ideas Festival in 2016

7

Online Dilemmas in Education

At the start of the COVID-19 pandemic, more than 53 million students had their classes cancelled. My own children were restricted to our home as part of the national call for physical social distancing, and for weeks literally did nothing as teachers struggled to transition their coursework and instruction to the web.

Soon many school districts realized that the rush to replace face-to-face interaction with distance learning had two large problems: the lack of equitable access to broadband connectivity and devices for certain students, and the inequity in electronic resources for educators.

I remember watching Betsy DeVos, Trump's controversial secretary of education, take the podium to discuss how schools would respond to the crisis in the spring of 2020. She stood beside then–president Trump and delivered her prepared remarks updating parents and guardians of school-age students, as well as college students who were equally affected by closures of private and public institutions.

"Education will continue for all students," she shared, when referencing the challenges caused by the coronavirus. "Learning should not be stopped or denied because schools fear regulators or doing something different," she continued.

She closed her remarks by saying that "distance learning is going to happen," before announcing microgrant awards to students and educators to temporarily cover broadband service, equipment, and other digital resources.

Secretary DeVos's remarks lasted less than 5 minutes, and her answers to press questions were even shorter, potentially flagging that her agency had not yet come up with a robust plan for educational connectivity. As expected, Trump offered his two cents as soon as she left the podium. A reporter asked his opinion on how the country was going to tackle these immediate school closures and online transitions, and his reply was directed to any student possibly watching the broadcast as he looked directly into the camera: "Take advantage of being at home because you live in the greatest and strongest country of all."

Two days after the White House briefing, Congress passed the Coronavirus Aid, Relief, and Economic Security (CARES) Act, which included $30 billion for schools. The resources were divided between funding for institutions and students. The institutional fund of $12.56 billon was earmarked for programs focused on K-12, colleges, and universities. A portion of this amount was also allocated to students with emergency financial aid grants to cover expenses related to the coronavirus disruption. But what did not make it into the 2020 act were proposals led by Democratic senators Ed Markey (MA), Michael Bennett (CO), and Brian Schatz (HA), who requested the temporary use of E-Rate program funding for Wi-Fi hotspots or devices with Wi-Fi capability for students without internet access. Markey created the E-Rate program as part of the 1996 Telecommunications Act. It is one of the oldest and largest funding mechanisms for in-school connectivity. Since its inception, the program has provided more than $50 billion in funding to connect schools and libraries to the internet, as well as ensure access to eligible low-income students and their families.

At the time of the request from Markey and his cosponsors, E-Rate was capped at $4 billion each year, and $2 million were still available in the fund, making the request for more funding less likely among the competing interests of other lawmakers. Despite the lack of additional funding for E-Rate in 2020, schools still received hearty resources to quickly address the disparities showing up among their student populations, like student laptops, broadband installations, and, in some instances, the ability to transmit Wi-Fi to the parking lots on school grounds.

However, taxpayers should be somewhat irate that universal access for schools and libraries was not sufficiently addressed long before the pandemic, particularly since the Obama administration had pledged resources to the ConnectEd initiative in 2013, which sought to address online disparities for students in public schools, with a specific focus on the unreliable and slow internet that prevented teachers from effectively using technology in the classroom.[1]

In a White House press announcement back then, the explicit goals of the ConnectEd program were to:

—connect more than 99 percent of students to the internet in their schools and libraries at speeds of no less than 100 megabits per second per 1,000 students at a targeted speed of 1 gigabit per second by 2018;

—create partnerships with the private sector and nonprofit organizations to make affordable devices available to students; and

—train teachers to incorporate technology into the classroom.

One year after its announcement in 2014, Apple, Microsoft, Verizon, AT&T, and the former Sprint Corporation joined the administration's effort. Apple provided one of the largest investments in the program by awarding $100 million in in-kind donations to eligible communities, including hardware, software, and necessary infrastructure upgrades. The experiences of principals from two participating school districts are brought up in this chapter and how they leveraged ConnectEd funds before the pandemic hit.

To be clear, before our public health crisis, there was a "homework gap" that limited school-age children without home broadband access to complete their assignments. In 2018, after the start of Obama's federal program, FCC commissioner Jessica Rosenworcel visited New Mexico, where she toured a Wi-Fi enabled school bus that was part of Google's Rolling Study Halls project, which enabled students with long commutes to complete homework while in route to either school or home.[2] The FCC knew that students had disparate access and so did the federal government. Given this intervention and many others to get students online, one has to wonder what went wrong when the the pandemic hit and sent millions of students home without sufficient internet access.

That is, three presidential administrations after the 1996 telecommunications legislation and heightened awareness of the digital divide, the United States issued embarrassing responses to the educational digital divide and panicked as school buildings and their educators faced an immediate, herculean task to shift learning online. The main difference between today and the previous attempts was that the online depravity for some of these students had worsened. The pandemic made it more difficult for students who not only lacked internet access but also food, housing, and other critical needs implicated by physical social distancing.

Earlier in the book, I mentioned a news interview I did around the start of school closures. I was interviewed for an NBC News segment that profiled a family from South Bend, Indiana. The mother of four shared that every morning, she drove to one or two Wi-Fi-enabled school buses provided by the city for students for her children to do their class lessons and homework. She also picked up the free breakfast and lunch for her children when it was soon discovered that children eligible for free or reduced price lunch were struggling during school closures. At the time, I, like Rosenworcel, was a proponent of these wired school buses—I even wrote an op-ed about them in *The Hill*—and my comments focused on the need to do something for families like this mother who were navigating the stresses of not being connected and finding themselves sitting in the parking lots of retail and fast-food establishments. But after the months turned into years, I reflected back on that family—only to realize how the process of getting an education for her children reeked of educational discrimination. In the news segment, her compact car was full of children, boxed food, and persistent hope to keep her family functioning.

What Happened to School Resources?

An analysis of internet use by school-age youth in 2015, five years before school closings, found that an estimated 15 percent of U.S. students lacked access to an internet-enabled device and the numbers were worse for those from lower income households.[3] The combined gap in available high-speed broadband networks, access to devices, teacher readiness, and limited resources earmarked to expand digital proficiencies all exacerbate the lack of readiness among U.S. students when compared with those in China, South Korea, and Singapore.[4]

What further complicates these gaps are that schools have historically been the prime beneficiaries of government resources and have received a range of other support from the private and philanthropic sectors. Funding has been primarily directed at in-school internet connectivity and a wide range of related activities, including teacher professional development, e-books, and on-site computer labs. One of the largest government funding programs for technology in schools is the 21st Century Community Learning Centers program, whose grants are distributed by the U.S. Department of Education and funding primarily procures equipment and software. Combined with E-Rate, these federal programs have allocated nearly $86 billion in the last twenty-three years, in addition to numerous investments from philanthropic organizations and corporations.

However, even with the monetary and programmatic resources, this support was not enough. We have many helpful federal programs, but they do not always target the right things and therefore cannot improve the social inequalities that persist in America. A problem that unfolded during the pandemic was that community organizations, especially the ones that assisted schools with social service concerns or tended to the needs of families before the pandemic, were disconnected—even those that were located right next to schools. The tragic isolation provoked by COVID-19 amplified the digital crisis among U.S. educational institutions and local communities, largely because the schools and communities needed each other to effectively transition from analog to virtual classrooms. The impact of the global pandemic on school-age children also revealed that the country is just not doing enough to invest in local, digital infrastructure—a former focus by Clinton when he invested in HUD Neighborhood Networks and community technology centers.

Almost three months after the DeVos press conference, broadband was *still* not available to hundreds of thousands of students across the United States, especially those in marginalized communities and vulnerable households. Thirty-five percent of the school-age children in the United States had the worst rates of home broadband access, a statistic that even surprised me, given the high rates of mobile phone use among lower-income and older populations.

Getting internet to schools was just one piece of the puzzle in addressing the consequences of the pandemic and the growing digital divide.[5] But even in communities with exceptional broadband in their schools, student experiences with distance learning and a host of security problems dampened the trustworthiness of the resources online.

Ironically, the challenges faced by schools during the pandemic were like the ones dating back to my interactions with Kiahna at the Northwest Tower computer lab. Or better yet, they were like some of the unattainable outcomes of the ConnectEd initiative that started strong, but whose partners soon realized how hard accelerating broadband access to more distressed and isolated communities could be.

I visited two ConnectEd schools, which were able to deploy a one-to-one iPad solution for their respective schools in Marion, Alabama, and West Phoenix, Arizona. These visits were complimented by another trip to Hartford, where students had reportedly been sitting on stoops in a parking lot to complete assignments for years, long before the pandemic and media popularized these phenomena.

Marion, Alabama

In August 2019, I visited a local school in Marion, Alabama. The closest airport was a solid 2 hours from the small, Black rural town. On the drive in, the two-lane road was flooded with colorful marketing signs advertising cheap internet offers. And as I got closer, my cellular service weakened, prompting me to pull into a motel looking for internet service to pull down the email with the school's address and other logistics of my meeting. Entering the lobby, I was greeted by the front desk clerk.

"Hello," she shared, "Welcome to Marion, how can I help you?"

Somewhat embarrassed because I wasn't checking in, I asked her permission to access the hotel's Wi-Fi. As she searched for the password, I looked around the empty lobby that reeked of cleaning solutions. The memories of visiting my aunt and uncle in North Carolina over sporadic summers as a child came to mind, and the trip to Marion also reminded me of my family's roots in the South: Clarksdale, Mississippi (that was far off when Marion), and was the birthplace for my father's mother. My mother's father was from Charleston, South Carolina—a place where I visited with her as a teenager.

After the motel clerk slowly emerged from the back with the password written on a small piece of paper, I quickly entered the code into my phone. Soon enough, I was online and taking screen shots of the directions to the Francis Marion School, where I was scheduled to meet the principal. After thanking the woman for her help in this still quiet lobby, I pulled out of the parking lot and headed to the school where I was greeted by a broken-down, yellow school bus that sat parked out front of the large school building. After parking, I opened the metal door of the school and announced myself to the receptionist, who asked me to take a seat while she found the principal. I forgot about the waiting that often happened in the south versus the city as people here took their time, and didn't fall victim to the often chaotic rush.

Minutes later, a petite, brown-skinned woman extended her hands to set up a friendly hug as I stood up.

"Hello, Nicol, I'm Cathy Trimble," she said, in a welcome that one could only get here. We walked into her office. Her desk was stacked with papers, and a couple of red reusable bags filled with canned goods sat on the left side. That was the food pantry.

Dr. Trimble was born in Marion and had lived here for nearly thirty years. Before becoming principal, she left the city once for college and then graduate school but soon returned after her now-husband became the school's physical education teacher. Dr. Trimble came back to serve as a substitute teacher in the Perry County school system, and over the last three decades worked her way into the role of the school's top administrator.

Going fully digital in each of her classrooms was Cathy's long-term goal for the teachers and students in the Francis Marion School.

"What we have now is a prelude to what is to come," she predicted. "I see us progressing to a mobile music program where the band director can help students learn how to play instruments from mobile devices. Marching bands are popular here in Alabama that would be such a complement to what the kids can do now."

Dr. Trimble was so close to achieving full connectivity because in 2016, the school received seven hundred iPads as part of the Obama administration's ConnectED initiative, and through a partnership with an incumbent internet service provider (ISP), she was able to include free internet service to each of them.

When I visited the school, all seven hundred tablets were distributed to students, who could take them home at the end of the school day. Dr. Trimble was adamant that devices went home with her students each day: "Before the program, I would come to the school on the weekends and see parents pulled up in their vehicles using the school's Wi-Fi. When we first got the iPads without the broadband package, kids would still be sitting on the ground or on the stoop, doing their homework or studying."

With some ingenuity, she brokered a partnership with AT&T, ensuring that her students had access to Wi-Fi during the school year. "Because we are African American, people thought that [the students] were going to sell or lose their iPads," she shared. "But, in one year, we may have lost two or three and one of them, someone [in the community] called and told me [the location of one of these iPads]."

The state of Alabama has been mired with long-standing educational inequities, especially around race, which prompted her statement. Fifty-nine percent of the state's students are white, 33 percent are African American, and the remaining percentages are other racial and ethnic groups.[6] Of all students in Alabama public schools, 52 percent are poor. The year I visited, it ranked forty-seventh or below on reading and math scores for the National Assessment of Educational Progress.[7] The state's Department of Education shows reading, math, and science proficiencies generally fall slightly below 50 percent for all categories. Though the graduation rate is roughly 90 percent, only about 75 percent of students are ready for college, according to state standards.

Francis Marion School, one of two schools in the Perry County School District, is a consolidated pre-K through twelfth grade school with 694 students, 99 percent of whom are African American at the time of my visit.[8] More than 70 percent of the students are poor. The students' performance in core studies, including reading, math, and science, are at 23 percent, 19 percent, and 15 percent respectively, ranking near the bottom of Alabama schools on standardized test scores in 2019. Despite these low scores, 92 percent of Perry County students graduate, with a little over 50 percent ready for college.

The county overall is highly rural and has a long history of racial segregation. In 1966, the school district was part of a landmark state desegregation case due to the noticeable concentration of Black students in public schools.[9] In fact, Francis Marion School used to be a high school, but after failing state review, it risked closure. Perry County school leaders immediately consolidated pre-K to high school grades in response.

Broadband access in Perry County is expectedly low: Only 39.8 percent of households are connected to the internet, according to U.S. Census Bureau data from 2013 to 2017. Alabama ranks forty-first in the nation in broadband connectivity and download speeds.[10]

Despite these statistical realities, students, teachers, and parents remain optimistic about the use of technology in their school. When the bell rang, I watched many students as they exited the building with the school iPad under one arm and a mobile phone in the other. One of the fifth-grade teachers standing by the door confirmed that "[the school] starts early to give these students the right values around the use of technology. Most of the students have phones, but we want to show them what the world will be like with forthcoming virtual and augmented realities. We are not stopping."

Creating Digital Norms in Schools

Effective school leadership at all levels is crucial to supporting the adoption and implementation of new technologies.[11] Teachers, principals, and county school board leaders drive the vision for how technology is used in schools, and they can energize participation by amplifying the critical importance of digital resources. And within school buildings, principals are critical actors, often pushing teachers to change how they plan and administer instruction. Dr. Trimble found herself constantly encouraging her teachers, students, and parents to use the technology, and to develop new teaching methods, which was very uncomfortable at first but eventually became part of her day-to-day routine.

Researchers Tyler-Wood, Cockerham, and Johnson confirm the difficulties that new technology presents in rural schools: less-equipped teachers and other disparate physical resources make technology integration more difficult in rural schools, layered on top of insufficient funding.[12] Francis Marion is no exception. When gaining buy-in from her parents, Dr. Trimble found herself identifying and solving their online needs so they could help their kids. After hearing more from parents, Dr. Trimble launched an onsite computer lab where adults could fill out job applications or conduct other online business. She empowered students to manage the lab and work with teachers to secure the school's computer equipment against viruses. These "baby steps" helped teachers, students, and parents gain what she called "the basics of the basics" after realizing their low levels of digital proficiencies.

Still, teacher buy-in was difficult. Some of them did not have internet access at home, not to mention that one of the biggest challenges of U.S. public schools is the lack of professional development for teachers. Unlike the private sector, public institutions often do not engage in organizational realignments to accommodate such changes; nor do they provide space for teachers to learn and try new things, which can be debilitating for technology use and adoption. The inability to hire staff focused on innovation can also affect how quickly digital learning environments are deployed. At Francis Marion School, one of the science teachers in the elementary school was assigned the joint role of the in-house technology and media lab coordinator—primarily supporting Dr. Trimble's integration plan. As to how she adjusted to this dual assignment that also came without additional compensation, she shared: "Students already know some of this stuff because they have cell phones. Dr. Trimble has just made it mandatory to bring technology into our lesson plans. There are some challenges with us, teachers. We had to figure out a way to put a lesson into our regular curricula and use some of the available online content on the iPads." The teacher was also looking beyond the more technical subjects, like math and science, to the arts, music, and writing areas that are usually less technical—an aspiration of Principal Trimble.

"Our students are coding, learning robotics, and also engaging the arts," Dr. Trimble shared as we returned to her office once most of the students left the building. "Sometimes, it's not uncommon for the students to even lead the teachers on ideas of what to cover."

Some of the students at the school were also being exposed to more advanced technology applications in after school clubs, such as designing QR codes for research projects and using iMovie for storytelling.

But without the iPads, none of these creative applications for students would have been possible. This is, in part, because African Americans have been found to primarily access the internet via their mobile devices at a much higher percentage compared with white individuals.[13] Moreover, these populations who tend to be more "smartphone dependent" rely on their mobile device as a gateway to the internet. While such access can be promising, it is difficult to use your phone to type out long essays, research projects, and perform the basic functions of being a student in the twenty-first century. Further, fluctuations in monthly costs for data can lead to more service interruptions for this population, resulting in less consistent access for lower-income households.[14] This was the case with Joseph from Staunton, who was unable to stay connected to the labor force due to monthly bill payment constraints.

Before the pandemic, Dr. Trimble knew that having such access mattered for student retention, too. According to a 2008 study from the Board of Governors of the Federal Reserve System, teenagers who had access to home computers are 6–8 percent were more likely to graduate from high school than teenagers without home computers.[15]

The ConnectEd program offered hope to forward thinking, educational leaders like Dr. Cathy Trimble, who shared her plans for sustaining the momentum of her technology plan after the formal partnership with Apple eventually ended in the summer of 2019:

> Next school year [2019–20] will be the first time without Apple and their program. The students will still have their tablets and we have now built the technology into lesson plans. Going forward, we have teachers who are ready to further customize the curricula to the different grade levels. When we gave the tablet to the high school students, they saw it as a new way to get on social media, but now, we are pushing it toward college applications. Last year, 100% of our graduates went to college. So, we have to keep going.

But Tech Is Not the New Normal Here

As I listened to Dr. Trimble, it was clear that technology access within the Francis Marion School was a game changer that forced a new level of digital engagement and responsibility among students and faculty. Such enthusiasm ran up against another challenge: resident exodus. Dr. Trimble shared how more of her students were beginning to leave the immediate community after graduation.

"We are doing such a good job [at the school] that many of these students are deciding not to return home," Dr. Trimble shared. The increasing relocation of families from Marion resembled new migration or reshuffling of Black Americans in the South, especially given the downward turn in the local economy.

"Believe it or not, this town used to be thriving," Dr. Trimble recalled. "The plant for Mercedes Benz [in nearby Tuscaloosa] used to be a reliable source for jobs before it closed. Now, some students are traveling within the South and even above the Mason-Dixon Line to attend college. In some cases, students are leaving school early to go with their parents who are finding work outside of the city." By happenstance, a parent stopped by her office while we were chatting to let the principal know that she had accepted a job in Selma, Alabama, and was moving immediately with her children, just a month into the school year.

"I'm going to miss this school and Dr. Trimble," the parent shared, with her eyes swelled with tears. "You know that my son was not doing well last year, then he got an iPad and he was able to get his grades up because he got more interested in school. I remember telling myself, the principal has taken my child from me because he always wants to be at school."

The parent also continued to praise Dr. Trimble on her own technology use: "I already know some things, but the program here has helped me to do things like apply for jobs, send my references, and track my application." But the lack of access to livable-wage jobs in Marion makes it impossible for single parents to survive—a fact that was exacerbated when the pandemic hit, and remote work opportunities were not even options for workers here.

Still, technology by itself is not transformative when systemic and structural disparities exist. For example, Francis Marion is still on Alabama's failing school list despite having access to robust digital resources and cultivating increased student engagement.

"We have successfully changed the culture of the school, but our test scores don't reflect this," she shared.

It is common for large states like Alabama to rely on traditional learning metrics and assessments to rank district schools, particularly test scores. Even when technology programs appear to have increased student engagement, research continues to conclude that it is not a catalyst for improved test scores, or at least not immediately.[16]

Alabama also published a state report card on a school's progress in student attainment. Francis Marion is at the bottom of that list. Race factors into their distinction from other schools. Jim Crow laws established a legacy of historically segregated schools in the South, which explains the high ratio of African American students at Francis Marion. While explicit educational discrimination was outlawed in Alabama, the new segregation is driven by income and wealth inequalities, causing communities like Marion to have more concentrated populations of lower-income students.[17] Further, more affluent white families in the town sent their children to the local private school, which is less than a few miles from Francis Marion.

Educational champions, like Dr. Trimble, understood that having access is part of breaking the cycle of other systemic inequalities, which is why I continue to refer to digital access as a social determinant throughout the book.

"I feed these children when they are hungry. I cry with them and their families when they are going through something. I used to complain about them to the teachers. But, somehow, God just won't release me from here," Dr. Trimble shared as we prepared to wrap up the visit.

But she should not be alone in her journey. In addition to state and federal legislators that need to be investing digital resources into schools, let us not forget the importance of surrounding communities and the local organizations that can help build local capacities and create shifts in acceptable digital norms and practices, including churches, small businesses, libraries, and community-based organizations.

Three months out of the school year, or during summer break, Francis Marion students are without their iPads. In a small rural town where students have few places to go, limited transportation, and even fewer locations with free Wi-Fi access, this leaves some students completely disconnected from the digital world for a quarter of the year.

A few miles away, there is a bustling commercial district where local businesses sit across the street from City Hall and the local library.

When it is open, the main library, which is also downtown, has computers that patrons can access. Still, transportation barriers or an unavailable parent or guardian for a ride stymie students' use of the library, during its set hours.

Across the street from the library was The Social, a newly opened ice cream parlor founded by a Black woman from Bridgeport, Connecticut, who moved to the area after her daughter secured a job at Francis Marion. The business blended into the row of antique stores and sat right next to a Southern cuisine restaurant. Dr. Trimble told me about The Social during our discussion and described it a place for ice cream and board games, but also internet access. It turned out that that owner wanted students to complete their homework and other assignments, while finding a safe space for eating and socializing with one another.

While grabbing my own scoop of ice cream, I briefly chatted with the owner who shared how she landed up in Perry County: "I came to visit [my daughter] and loved the community so much that I moved." "Local people didn't think that we would last, but we are still here." The Social offered breakfast to local kids on their way to school as early as 6:30 a.m., and a range of other fun activities after school and on weekends.

But without transportation, the students from Francis Marion School could not get there. "We sometimes have more white people here [at The Social] than [Black] students because they have no transportation," she pointed out. "I really wish that I could figure that problem out because we are here to offer a safe space for the kids to do their homework."

Less than a year after my visit, the venue closed after the social distancing demands of the pandemic made it impossible to operate. And despite the robust iPad program, the pandemic transitioned Marion, Alabama, to an even worse digital desert, lacking both the infrastructure and support services to get students and their families online. When the schools closed, so did access to the tablets, which Cathy more about in an email to me noted in the next chapter. The pandemic had blown out the fire that I experienced during my visit, and it was still hard to determine for how long as things worsened across the country.

Phoenix

Marion, Alabama, was not alone with regards to its own homework gap. I was able to go to Phoenix a few weeks later to visit a local elementary school, which was also a beneficiary of the ConnectEd program. The Pendergast Elementary School is in the westernmost part of metropolitan Phoenix. Of the 813 students at the school, 95 percent are Latino, majority low-income, and largely composed of children from undocumented families. In state math assessments, only 29 percent of Pendergast students in grades three to eight scored "proficient" or "highly proficient." In science, only 39 percent of students "meet" or "exceed" state requirements.

The predominantly Latino elementary school sits in controversial Maricopa County, which has an embattled history of villainizing immigrants under the leadership of former sheriff Joseph Arpaio, who was notorious for racially profiling and detaining Latinos in the Phoenix area.[18] After twenty-four years in office, he was unseated and sentenced to prison for his unfair and unconstitutional treatment of Latino residents, many of which were not legal residents at the time.

The entire county district has thirteen schools that enroll pre-K to eighth grade students at the time of my visit. There are 9,753 students and 500 full-time equivalent teachers, creating a student-to-teacher ratio of 19.5. In 2018, the per student spending in the district was $7,438, compared with $8,269 statewide. Even that number is low; average spending per student in Arizona was the fourth lowest in the United States.

Settled below the Arizona mountains, Pendergast Elementary School has extensive technology access, including smart boards and 3D printers. As in Marion, Alabama, students also received iPads for all students in 2016 from Apple's ConnectED program, along with three years of professional development training from the company. But unlike Francis Marion, these students were unable take their iPads off school grounds.

As soon as I walked into the school, the receptionist with the nameplate "Like a boss" greeted me and advised Principal Michael Woolsey of my arrival. Sitting there, I watched students in laundered and pressed school uniforms appear to respect her title as they started any request for help with salutations of "excuse me" and ending "thank you" respects. Arizona state law bans the use of bilingual education. So every student despite being of obvious Hispanic descent spoke in the English language to the "boss," before resuming Spanish in conversation with their friends on their way to class.

Principal Mike Woolsey—white, tall, and middle-aged—was also a "lifer" in the educational system, like Dr. Trimble. He was principal at the school for decades, and he had been a longtime Phoenix resident. Like his counterpart from the rural South, he sought to leverage technology access to help his students thrive and not just survive in the new digital economy.

"I wanted our kids to have options [so] that they are not stuck, unless they want to be," he asserted. "Many of their parents didn't finish school. I want my students to thrive instead of surviving in this world," he continued.

When Principal Woolsey wrote his grant to the Apple and ConnectED initiative, he started with the assumption that most of the students had smartphones because his teachers were already depending on these devices to assist their students with homework.

"We don't send a lot of homework home," Principal Woolsey shared. "But what I have done is to enable applications on smartphones since most students have them." Generally, Hispanic populations have heavy reliance on smartphones; approximately 25 percent of them are "smartphone dependent" and use their mobile device as their only gateway to the internet.[19] But like Francis Marion, students with only smartphone connectivity may be challenged in completing research papers or other extensive assignments.

Since the school received the Apple grant in 2016, the iPads have been cushions between students' smartphone use and their lack of home PC access. I also learned from him that mobile access is particularly important to this community because many of his students and their parents were undocumented. On this point, Principal Woolsey shared how discrimination against immigrants has affected his students:

> First, some of my parents are afraid to drive their kids to school. They drive with their passports in hand because of the fear. Maricopa County had a bad reputation because our neighborhoods were targeted by coyote people ten years ago and had to pay ransoms. Most of the students and their families have mobile phones for safety. Our parents are afraid to leave the house. Here, a phone is about safety and staying in contact with that child.

Like Francis Marion Elementary School, Pendergast undertook several steps to design and implement its one-to-one technology solution, starting with a formal plan. "You have to plan for the technology with an implementation plan that you can revise," continued Principal Woolsey. "You shouldn't put in place a plan of tech to just substitute paper."

At the time of the interview, only students in certain classes could take home their devices, like those enrolled in STEM classes. The principal asserted that the policy had nothing to do with the theft of the iPads.

"We have had these iPads for three years and had zero theft," the principal shared. "There will always be fears versus benefits. In my opinion, the benefits outweigh the fears."

Not all students had broadband access at home. This was despite the fact that Cox Cable, the local ISP, had a low-cost broadband offer before the pandemic; in addition, various local ISPs had affordable pricing. According to the school's lab assistant who met the principal and me as we walked and talked, many parents did not subscribe to home internet; only 79.6 percent of the households in the school district have broadband subscriptions, despite the city of Phoenix being among the most connected cities in Arizona.[20]

"Every year, we have a hard time getting the parents to complete the required paperwork for free or reduced-price lunch, which is a qualification for the offer," the media assistant shared. "Households with home broadband were probably signed up on a pay-as-you-go basis, especially given the limited incomes of residents."

Overall, being part of the ConnectEd program has helped the school to reach some of its technology goals, including equipment and software donations, as well as professional development. Reflecting on his school's experience in setting up the program, Principal Woolsey stated: "We were able to upgrade our network. There was so much to do, but each time we got better at it."

The teachers at Pendergast also underwent a paradigm shift related to the use of technology in the classroom, largely due to the principal gaining buy-in from them, and then working to phase in aspects of the new applications, software, and hardware. The school also implemented a new role for the media assistant who worked with the school's librarian to create computer policies and monitor related infrastructure, including a mobile iPad cart that transported a set number of them to each classroom.

Principal Woolsey also placed a teacher in charge of parents' engagement to address their fears about technology. This particular teacher worked with students to teach their parents about online tools, making it more comfortable for the parents to accept and understand the innovations happening inside and outside the classroom. In her research, Katz found that while media experiences have primarily benefited more affluent communities, they can generate more trust within immigrant communities when young people serve as brokers to online information.[21] In a survey of parents and children in an immigrant community in Los Angeles, her findings demonstrated that children's use of traditional and newer forms of media helped in the settlement of their families.[22] During my visit, the teacher enrolled several students as technology helpers in her classroom, who worked with the media assistant to gather the devices at the end of the day.

Teachers at the school also leveraged the technology for cultural storytelling, like a fifth-grade teacher who had the students use their iPads to identify and write about women of color in the community. While his students could not take their devices home, they used the time in school to engage in cultural and ethnic studies research. Once the project was completed, they shared their presentations with the local leaders who were the subjects of their research, and the parents who showed up. Despite being focused on engaging the parents, they often didn't make it to school for these and other presentations or school meetings.

Tech Exposure and Test Scores Are Not Aligned

But just like Francis Marion School, Pendergast is a low-performing school, in test scores and overall academic achievement, at least by state standards. While interviews here and in Marion suggest the benefits of more strategic and collaborative approaches to technology integration, their students still lag others in performance by regular metrics.

Principal Woolsey experienced the same type of disbelief around how local schools are assessed under rigid state standards—despite huge investments in new digital resources. "Our states still seem to see these things as black and white," he commented. "We are teaching our kids how to thrive and not survive in the new economy, yet when it comes to testing, they can't compete with other schools and other districts. For some of my students, this is their first experience in a formal school setting."

With a large immigrant population, this phenomenon is not unfamiliar among schools in low-income areas whose achievement gaps are already well documented. Moreover, educational research suggests very little correlation between technology access and test scores. In 2019, a report by the Reboot Foundation found that test scores declined for fourth graders who used tablets in "all or most" of their classes.[23] However, some variance appeared among students when the technology was used for research, for problem-solving, or complemented some other critical thinking skill.[24] A 2019 Gallup study on student creativity found that teachers who leveraged technology to assign "creative, project-based activities" experienced more positive responses from students, including higher self-confidence, and improved critical thinking and problem-solving skills.[25] While more research needs to be done on whether technology can be a catalyst for improved test scores, both principals identified an increase in student engagement and motivation, which were interesting correlates often omitted measure in educational achievement.

Principal Woolsey understood the importance of these factors when he shared: "We want to push our kids to do more extended things that go way beyond their personal experiences."

When the Community Is a Desert

Driving a few miles away from the school, it was apparent that the area around it was really a desert: a land desert, food desert, health desert, and commercial desert.

More than a half-dozen pawn shops, liquor stores, used-tire establishments line the main streets around the school, as well as coldly constructed health clinics, convenience stores, and lots of fast food restaurants. Given the school's location, a car or sufficient public transportation is needed to get around. Now it made sense what the school receptionist, or "the boss" had shared with me as I waited for the principal: "Students' households lack adequate transportation and because of the climate, they do not walk. It's too hot. And when they have internet access at home, most of the students go on[line] for entertainment." I didn't see a library, gym, or any type of social center within blocks away from the school.

Two local libraries are near the school if you consider approximately 5 miles on either side nearby. I drove to the Desert Sage Library, which took me about 15 minutes to get to by car. Like schools, libraries have also been recipients of grants to bring more access to communities. In this library, more than twenty computers were lined between the books and the walls. People were actively logged in and the location was extra quiet as patrons maintained their focus on their screens. When I was there, an African American woman was trying to renew a library card but was told that she had to go online.

After following her outside of the building, I learned that she had just moved to Phoenix to escape the cold weather in the northeast as we sat on an available bench outside in the dry heat. She was recently separated from her spouse and patiently waiting for her son to finish playing a game at one of the library stations. When asked how she would ultimately obtain her card, she shared that going online would be her best bet, but she would have to wait to use her son's phone. She gave it to him for emergencies at school.

"You can't do nothing without being online," Frances said. "Social services prefer that you go online and now the library. If you want to apply for a job, go online. Everything is digital and a lot of older people don't even know how to do it."

In many ways, Frances spoke to the challenges that the local teachers shared, and to the issues of the parents they were trying to engage. She also amplified the often-obscured digital divide within local communities that restrict the full use of new technologies by parents and other adults. In their cases, they learn as they go, or as Frances put it, "I need to rely on my son to help me get things that I need online."

Frances also shared the challenges of doing everything over a mobile phone in terms of cost. "If you do it, like internet surfing, on your phone, it's a cost [in terms of data] and I'm not working right now, so this all adds up." She knew of the low-cost broadband program available through Cox, but it was still more than she can afford. Her son is in high school, which did not have the iPad program. Instead, he had a Google Chromebook provided by the school district to which she directed some reservations; she was not sure if he is using it for homework or gaming.

I soon learned—despite starting to feel a bit dehydrated—that being connected to the internet mattered for Frances. In 2019, she was given an advanced stage cancer diagnosis, and learned about it after the doctor called her son's phone, leading to immediate hospital admittance. "My doctor also put all of my records online, through something like My Chart that I read on my phone," she recalled with half of a smile. "And here I am today getting treatment."

The story of Frances screams out that the United States needs to deploy more intergenerational support of technology. While deploying technology between schools and communities must be realized, the creation of connections within families is equally important to create a multiplier effect that not only amplifies what happens inside schools but also builds the individual and community capacities necessary to thrive in an increasingly digital economy. In the mid-2000s, I helped to deploy what we called the Digital Connectors program at the global nonprofit, One Economy Corporation, where young people from the community trained their neighbors, and refurbished computers, while learning necessary leadership and workforce development skills. With thousands of young people enrolled across the United States, I'd like to say we made a tremendous difference that led to Comcast eventually adopting a version of the program as part of their digital inclusion efforts.

The stories of Marion, Alabama, and West Phoenix, demonstrate the importance of resourcing educational institutions to facilitate the necessary interventions to close the digital divide, while addressing the wholeness of communities like health care, immigration, employment, and other such pressing needs.

In the city of Hartford, I saw what happens when schools remain as "schools" and do not center their resources outside of their traditional focus areas. Here, the students were not so lucky to have their own iPads, because the Trump administration abruptly ended the program. Because of this growing digital divide, two very different people in terms of race, background, and expertise got together to make a difference.

Hartford

A year before the pandemic, I met Elin Swanson Katz for lunch at Dupont Circle in Washington. We were introduced by a friend via email and agreed to meet the next time she was in town. Elin was no stranger to the digital divide. In her former role at the Office of Consumer Counsel for the State of Connecticut, she battled private telecom companies to bring more access to her state, which she believed was lagging in digital access. For Elin, municipal broadband—which has instigated long, contentious battles with private telecom companies—was central to closing the digital divide for her residents. Alongside this cause was the need to bring more internet access to public schools.

In 2018, Elin testified before Congress's House Energy and Commerce Subcommittee on Communications and Technology, where she shared the findings of a previously commissioned report on Connecticut's digital divide, pointing out in her testimony the lack of access for students in the North End of Hartford, who must walk to a local McDonald's restaurant to complete their homework. The North End is predominantly African American and lower income. While calling out the homework gap among her state's students, she also implied that the city had created broadband deserts that force students to "continually search for safe, reliable broadband service connections outside of their homes."[26]

Even though students used local fast food restaurants to complete homework, she explained on that certain establishments had changed their policies and even limited their hours and space for students. Further, she detailed the unsafe conditions that students traveled to gain access to a free Wi-Fi signal and how certain schools even shut down their connectivity to reduce the use of their networks. And it did not end there; Elin noted long lines at public libraries; broadband service shut-offs for low-income households; and insufficient, feature-based smartphones that heightened the frustrations of low-income users who need to do much more via these devices. In other words: Hartford was in a digital crisis.

When I eventually visited Hartford, Elin arranged for us to meet her friend and community activist Janice Flemming-Butler, a Black woman who grew up in the city and currently lived in its largely black North End. She was also Elin's unusual bedfellow in this quest for equitable digital access. Janice founded Strategic Outreach Services (SOS), a community-based communications company in Hartford, and was the CEO of the Voices of Women of Color, a social justice organization that teaches leadership skills to women of color. A longtime community organizer and political consultant, Janice recently started working with Elin on citywide digital equity issues, including strategies for bringing more access to the Hartford Public Schools.

As I pulled in front of her home, Janice, with her full afro, stood next to Elin, a slender Jewish woman with curly hair, on the top of the stairs. After welcoming me to her home and city, she passionately referred to Elin as her "sister" in this fight, before signaling us to her outdoor table. Bill, who worked with Elin and is an older white male, also joined us at Janice's home.

"Someone has to do this because our students matter," Janice started the conversation. "In our communities, some of the school buildings are so old, they can't even get Wi-Fi. On top of this, some of these schools are partially vacant and are at risk of closure."

Data from Broadband Now, an independent nonprofit that assesses broadband competition and speeds, found that DSL and cable were the primary providers of internet service in Hartford around the time of my visit.[27] Broadband speeds in the city were above average when compared with the state, at around 20 percent higher. But 5 percent of residents had one or fewer providers for the internet as of 2020, compared with two or more offered in other parts of the state. But not all parts of the city were created equal when it came to broadband service and speed. The North End of the city has much slower rates than other zip codes in the area.

The community—which sits just a few miles away from the city's capitol buildings—is also experiencing its own share of problems. Since the 2000s, this area has been losing residents at a rate of negative 19 percent and has an annual residential turnover of 13 percent. The median income in the area is $32,000, with most of the households having children.

Compared with other cities like New York and Chicago, Hartford is relatively safe; but within the state of Connecticut, it has the highest crime rate. One in 93 residents face the chance of becoming victims of violence in the city.

Janice, who has lived here all her life, shared: "We are making progress in the city a little bit at a time. We are just being affected by the loss of homeowners in the community and the fact that times have changed around here for the black community."

When researching the digital crisis in her community, Janice points out the missed opportunities for students of color, especially those from low-income families: "They are losing the game if they do not have equal access to the resources that other children have in other communities." She went on further to suggest that not having an internet connection is like not having books in schools.

After a while, we left her comfortable porch to grab lunch. On the way to the area on the edge of downtown, I could tell that Hartford is an older city with pockets of affluence in the past and perhaps now, especially as some residents have begun to renovate some of the older housing stock. As we got closer to the restaurant, we made a few stops on the way, including to a local barber shop, where the owner—who was busy cutting a client—saw no need for the internet simply because it was not reliable enough for what he needed to do, after I inquired. The owner of the local Caribbean restaurant where we eventually ate shared a similar complaint about his broadband service, which he had upgraded several times without much change. Between these two local businesses, the theme appeared to be along the lines of "we will take what we got, because this is all that we know when it comes to being connected."

Abruptly, Elin and Bill had to leave our gathering just as we received our hearty Jamaican dishes. There was a film screening at the local library that Elin and Bill were leading with the Mayor's Office, which was commissioned by Verizon about the digital divide in schools. They asked if I could stay in town a few more hours to attend, and Janice volunteered to take me back to her place to rest before the screening and ride back to Washington. Of course, Janice and I ate our food, talked, and laughed as if we had known each other for years.

As we wrapped up lunch, Janice leaned in and shared, "Elin doesn't care if she gets in trouble. She just wants to do the right thing for the kids in this district."

This exchange had me rethink the relationship between this unusual friendship: one woman, who shared that she was born into a more privileged society and family; and the other woman, who shared her constant dedication and struggle to advocate on behalf of her people, who are underserved. But together, they were fighting the enormous battle of making the consequences of being online more visible to city, state, and federal leaders.

When I first met Elin for lunch in D.C., she said something that has stayed with me: "We have never said to children whose parents cannot afford textbooks, sorry, you don't get to learn math or history or science." Meaning that more vulnerable populations should not have to choose between having broadband access or food on the table. Being in her environment, and among her people, made me believe that she was firmly committed to closing the digital divide.

Janice seemed to have the same fervor that day, and I could see that by them working together, these two women epitomize what it means to be on one accord—a lesson for policymakers who have played political ping pong with this issue for decades.

We both thanked the owner for the delicious meal, and on our way out of the restaurant, Janice stopped in a hair salon that also had a clothing store on the other side of the parking lot. Knowing my mission, Janice asked the owner, "Hey, my sister, my friend here is wondering what you think internet is like in our city?"

"Oh, I don't trust the internet. I'm not on it and will never be," the clothing store owner slash beautician quickly responded.

"Well, how do your customers pay you, though, when they are done?" was my follow-up question.

"Of course, they pay cash, but when they don't have anything on them, I take Cash App," she replied. The interaction reminded me of the Joseph's mom in Staunton, Virginia, who referred to the internet as "the Facebook." Some people still do not quite understand the intersection between having broadband access and taking advantage of the applications that run over high-speed networks. Nor do they get that without their personal data and use, the modern-day internet would not flourish.

When we got back to Janice's home, she led me to a guest room, where I was able to take a short nap before the evening film screening. We arrived at the downtown, well-resourced library on time. As with any library, it was eerily quiet upon entering. We followed the signs leading to the auditorium after passing the few people on the computer workstations and printers, many of them homeless with overstuffed bags at their feet. To my surprise, the audience in the theater was mostly white, older senior women who looked like they read the announcement about the screening on a library bulletin board. Walking in with Janice in her sleek Afro and cotton sweatshirt was all that I needed, who whispered to me as we wandered around the room, "Meet the other side of my city." People in the room knew her, and when the mayor walked into the auditorium, he flocked to her first for greetings to which she responded with a smile because she knew her importance to the city's mission.

Elin formally introduced me to the mayor as she walked right over, and after hearing about my project, he invited me back to talk more about what their resources could do to finally close the digital divide. Soon after, he went to the podium and he kicked off the event before introducing Elin, who came to the podium and acknowledged her friend Janice.

There were no students at this film screening on the state of the educational digital divide. There were no families of color from the North End. There were just middle-aged, older, white library goers who appeared to be emphatic to the need to accelerate broadband access for students. Leaving the city that night, I rode back through the mostly Black North End community to get a sense of what it was like to grow up digitally invisible here.

In the darkness of the streets, I imagined what it was like for a student to be walking home from McDonald's after the streetlights went out, all for the purpose of finishing homework. That was in 2019, before this became a new normal for thousands of students without internet access during the nation's shutdown.

Compared with Marion and Phoenix, Hartford was no different in the mismatch in opportunities that young students of color who grow up on the wrong side of town, or with an immigrant status that places them in unequal educational systems, face every day. These communities were also quite similar around the premise that schools alone cannot close the digital divide, and that they need local champions to help with the sprint toward greater connectivity. These places also hit me the same way—that being disconnected from the internet was like living during school segregation in the 1960s and how the coordinates of where one lived affected the quality of life.

Addressing the Digital Crises in Schools and Communities

In all these examples, a natural resource metaphor for inequity becomes clear: Schools appear to have gallons of water, but many and certain communities—though rich in motivation and aspirations—are dehydrated and thirsty. In some instances, people do not know that they are dehydrated because they are always constantly thirsty, including the people in Hartford and business owners who did not understand that their broadband access was insufficient.

In all the federal interventions to end the digital divide, we have never adequately acknowledged the local digital infrastructure divides, where the resources within schools are not often exported into the surrounding communities, and vice versa. In Marion and Phoenix, the principals had shared goals when it came to the effective integration and adoption of technology by students, faculty, and some parents. But they required the community, despite not having a mechanism to bring them additional resources to support their connectivity efforts.

Educational models and funding formulas tend to restrict technology use to their facilities, and as a result, they are forced to attend to the measurements expected by their districts and state boards. In places like Hartford, the entrapment is also facilitated by old school buildings that are unable to be retrofitted with new technology because the concrete walls block the transmission of wireless signals. And since we are not building any new school facilities in places like the North End, travel to the local stoops of fast food restaurants becomes normal.

It Starts with Local Digital Infrastructure

Alongside every school must be a complementary local digital infrastructure that includes libraries, community-based organizations, businesses, churches, and local champions like the owner of The Social in Marion, or the barbershop owner in Staunton whose open Wi-Fi could be used while the kid got a haircut. In their research, Rideout and Katz pointed to the benefits in creating such local support, primarily because they advance intergenerational cooperation and adoption of new technologies. Thus, there is a logical need for more engagement by local institutions, including libraries, community centers, and other gathering places, for families without home access to get online.[28] Intergenerational engagement matters, especially in communities of immigrants and other people of color who exercise resilience each and every day.

Francis Marion was an exception when it came to home use of school devices. Not all schools can provide an in-home resource or have technology available at all, leading to increased inequalities that will only widen as the information economy becomes more entrenched. And you have to wonder why, when in higher income school districts, that is never a question. My daughter held her school lap top over the summer until her school requested that she bring it back for upgrades.

Local libraries are not only the most visited when it comes to public computing, but they are also the most utilized asset by individuals without home internet access.[29] In most rural communities, the library is normally the anchor of local activities, such as government services, benefits enrollment, and tax preparation services. Yet some local libraries are still far away from where some local people live, work, or go to school. Librarians and other staff members are also tasked with a variety of functions, from checking out materials to helping individuals apply for jobs and access government services. Challenged by limited funding, staff, professional development opportunities, equipment, and software, local libraries can themselves become barriers to adoption and use. To curb the burnout of librarians, federal and state governments should be resourcing programs, staff, and related resources to make the experiences more seamless for these institutions.

Community-based organizations, including technology centers, and local businesses are also other local resources that permit free Wi-Fi use, including small businesses like The Social. In the end, schools need connections to reliable, convenient, and safe local digital infrastructure—inclusive of libraries, community-based organizations, and even households—to bolster their activities. This can address the growing divides that are quickly widening within low-income and rural communities. But not since Bill Clinton have we seen the type of expansive investments in community-based technology efforts. In the current broadband infrastructure appropriations under Biden, monies have been allocated toward digital equity, but it is a slithering of funds compared to what I call the "hardscaping" of fiber assets to improve the propagation of services. Funds towards the affordability of broadband are also great, but that is a more individualized solution for households without internet access.

Our national goal should be to make community internet access available 24/7 to low-income students and their communities. And I am not referring to stoop-side digital access. Several U.S. cities have deployed lending programs for Wi-Fi hotspots, in addition to providing computer centers. The New York Public Library launched a lending program in 2014 in response to a survey revealing that 55 percent of library patrons did not have internet access at home. For families making under $25,000, the percentage increased to 65 percent. Initially seeded through a $500,000 Knight News Challenge Grant, the pilot focused on public school students who lacked home broadband access and through additional donations targeted 10,000 households with internet access. The Chicago Public Library has also deployed a similar initiative in three libraries that allow residents to check out a Wi-Fi hotspot as they would a book. By mid-2016, the library had 973 wireless internet hotspots for checkout through its Internet to Go program.

Other creative solutions involve the wiring of local school buses. In 2013, the rural Coachella Valley Unified School District (Coachella Unified) in California was the first to provide iPads to every K-12 student as part of their mobile learning initiative. Because 95 percent of students live below the poverty line, they are challenged in their transportation to local institutions or do not have the economic means to subscribe to a monthly broadband service. In 2016, the school district equipped its school buses with solar-powered Wi-Fi routers to provide internet access while in transit. When stationary, the buses were parked within underserved neighborhoods to offer 24/7 Wi-Fi coverage. Coachella Unified's Wi-Fi on Wheels project has enabled broadband internet where students live to minimize the obstacles that disrupt use between the school and community. The program resulted in a jump in district graduation rates from 70 to 80 percent, according to one study.[30] I have mentioned Google's similar initiative, Rolling Study Halls, in the Berkeley County School District that enables broadband on twenty-eight school buses. The program has since been expanded to sixteen additional school districts and provides Wi-Fi routers, data plans, and devices for students to use while in transit. In the fall of 2023, now–chairwoman Rosenworcel of the FCC proposed to put Wi-Fi access on every school bus for students to use for homework.

As early as 2018, policymakers knew the importance of diversifying school access. Before the pandemic, senators Tom Udall (D-NM) and Cory Gardner (R-CO) introduced a bipartisan bill to equip school buses with internet access.

The bill extends the Federal Communications Commission's E-Rate program—which provides schools and libraries with affordable broadband services—to reimburse school districts for the cost of outfitting their buses with internet access. In a press release on the bill, Senator Udall stated, "It's time to end the homework gap. Our legislation will help give all students the ability to get online to study and do homework assignments while they're on the bus—a common sense, 21st-century solution."

One year later, in 2019, Representative Grace Meng (D-NY) introduced a similar bill to reduce the homework gap. Meng's bill, the Closing the Homework Gap through Mobile Hot Spots Act, would develop a $100 million grant program for libraries, schools, U.S. territories, and federally recognized American Indian Tribes for the purchase of mobile hotspots. According to Meng's press release, the mobile hotspots program would be established for students in need of internet access for homework completion. In her statement, she reinforces the need for such action: "Every child deserves their best chance at pursuing an education. But it breaks my heart knowing that millions of kids, every night, are unable to finish their homework simply because they are without internet access. Before the internet became ubiquitous, students completed their homework with pen and paper-today, that is no longer the case."

Taken together, these bills and others could have helped scale up and sustain many of the pilot programs being instituted within local communities, while closing the homework gap and preparing the country for the unforeseen educational consequences of the pandemic. But they are still drafts—nothing more. We could have also had some type of program to bring Wi-Fi to the overwhelming number of students who live in public and/or federally-subsidized housing who were unable to leave their communities during the pandemic. But the truth is that most of these programs created during the pandemic relied on philanthropic and private sector support and continue to do so. The adoption of federal legislation would bring more certainty in terms of appropriations and deployment, making these programs less vulnerable to political changes. With all these activities focused on school connectivity, we need to ask why are we so far behind? When Trump came into office, the ConnectED program was eliminated even though it was really just getting started.

Second, it is critical to the complementary use of digital technologies between schools and communities to foster more intergenerational value, as I reflect on my conversation with Frances. Between 2008 and 2011, the Mooresville Graded School District in North Carolina issued 4,400 Apple MacBooks to students in grades four through twelve. Subsequent gains were seen in graduation rates from 80 percent to 91 percent, and students exhibited greater proficiency in reading, math, and science—73 percent to 88 percent overall. But their story, as some suggested, had less to do with the availability of hardware and more to do with the leadership and their plan for technology deployment. According to its website, the district continues to distribute laptops to its students. But the other keys to success are online content, teacher development, and parent engagement that the school has pushed for.

What is even more comparable to the goals of Mooresville and the two schools that I physically visited is the time spent creating the trust of technology among students, teachers, parents, and other community members. In communities of color, intergenerational connections are fundamental to this process, especially as the parents and caregivers of students experience a host of other social problems. For example, when Dr. Trimble decided to allow her students to bring home their iPads, she was appealing to the intergenerational relationships within her community while enabling additional online activities for other family members too, such as job searching, distance learning, among other functions.

Research has long supported the role of students in influencing parents to engage new technologies.[31] When young people become "brokers" to new technologies for their parents and other caregivers, there is a higher likelihood of broadband adoption within the home and a greater exploration of the functionality of the internet (e.g., for health care, employment, and other critical decisions). Children are often seen as the most trustworthy source for families when it comes to internet use. One researcher, Teresa Corea, found that despite one's demographic status (as defined by socioeconomic status, income, and family structure, among other variables), young people are the key agent for introducing and integrating technology into the home.[32] Thus, the imperative to create more robust local programs that enhance intergenerational engagement could be one of the bridges between schools and local communities. The fifth-grade research project highlighting Latina women around the Pendergast community was also an attempt to pull the community into the school, which is an incremental step in creating a more digitally enabled community.

Other nationally known programs are attempting to build such bridges. For the last six years, Comcast's Internet Essentials and other digital bridge programs have been offering low-cost broadband to low-income families, using young people as digital connectors or local ambassadors for training and service within their respective communities. In some affiliate programs, students receive community service credit or a small stipend for their efforts. The company has also created Lift Zones across the United States to bring free Wi-Fi in safe and familiar spaces, including local community centers, to students. Establishing both trust and purpose for the technology are important for schools, community-based organizations, and other local institutions introducing digital resources. It also returns to my original theory that energizing spaces and places are critical components of digital equity.

Technology must be considered a catalyst for increased student engagement between schools and their communities. But even when resources are available and connections are made, schools like Francis Marion and Pendergast are assessed by stringent metrics, including student grades, test scores, and college enrollment often dictated by historical and present racial expectations. Low-income schools start with a deficit and consequently must catch up with more affluent institutions. While an in-school technology program and available local resources should be ingredients for more effective learning, such goals are often unrealistic given the basis of cognitive retention around test scores and the institutional funding and staffing constraints for certain communities.

The principals of Francis Marion and Pendergast faltered at changing overall student achievement because they are constrained due to the complexion of their students. In the future, more research is needed to understand how technology can be used to improve test scores, or if the reliance on test scores represents student performance writ large. We also need more sociological inquiry into whether racial and economic disparities are still driving said outcomes, and thereby are creating limited room for creative expansion in poorly performing schools.

Technology deployment at those two schools awakened some of the dormant realities of their students, who were simultaneously navigating through distressed economic and social circumstances. On this point, a Francis Marion high school student shared, "I really didn't know what I could do for myself until we received an iPad."

While test scores may not be have changed, student engagement within the schools did. In the 1960s, this type of educational quagmire was understood in the failures of *Brown v. Board of Education* to create parity within public schools. Facilities were still separate and unequal, despite the legal mandate of desegregation. As a result, low-income and rural poor schools faced the academic repercussions of these inequalities, as demonstrated in poor student achievement and growth.

In many ways, schools in Marion, Phoenix, and Hartford are still experiencing the intersectional effects of educational and place-based segregation. Yet technology access has the potential to enliven dissatisfied and disassociated teachers, as well as students whose socioeconomic status often dictates predictable (or discouraging) life outcomes.

Moving toward an ethos that assesses how technology affects student, parent, and teacher engagement should count for something. The increased inquiry and activity happening within America's low-income and remote rural schools can be considered progress, especially if more students are enrolling in college or, at least, enhancing their critical thinking and problem-solving skills. Further, measuring increases in student engagement as a corollary to boredom or disengagement should be added to the conversation on school performance. In both case studies, each principal was excited about the potential of technology to change the course of their students' life trajectories.

Policymakers, state education officials, and educators should explore ways to measure how schools are adapting to the skills necessary for twenty-first-century advancement. Further, educational districts should be calling upon their affiliated schools to explore these opportunities to ensure that parents and other caregivers are provided with the same type of interest and proficiency in new digital skills. As summarized in an old cliché, "it takes a village."

Technology access is critical for students as it slowly enables them to develop the values, norms, and skills needed for future participation in our emerging online economy. Two years after the DeVos press conference, most public school students were still at home, or were experiencing major learning losses due to the disparities in broadband access. What the coronavirus surfaced about the digital divide should be lesson to us all—particularly, that we need broadband to be more of a lifeline for the millions of school-age children on whom we are counting to further the future global competitiveness of our nation. And even as students returned to their respective classrooms, we learned very little during this technological impasse, except that without internet access, we have a lot more catching up to do.

Notes

Part IV epigraph: Jessica Rosenworcel, "Closing the Digital Divide," speech, Aspen Ideas Festival, Aspen, June 30, 2016.

1. Federal Communications Commission, "Fact Sheet: Update of E-Rate for Broadband in Schools and Libraries," July 19, 2013, https://www.fcc.gov/document/fact-sheet-update-e-rate-broadband-schools-and-libraries.

2. Google for Education, "Rolling Study Halls," https://edu.google.com/intl/ALL_us/why-google/our-commitment/rolling-study-halls/.

3. Monica Anderson and Andrew Perrin, "Nearly One-in-Five Teens Can't Always Finish Their Homework Because of the Digital Divide," Pew Research Center FactTank (blog), October 26, 2018, https://www.pewresearch.org/short-reads/2018/10/26/nearly-one-in-five-teens-cant-always-finish-their-homework-because-of-the-digital-divide/.

4. Colby Leigh Rachfal and Angele A. Gilroy, "Broadband Internet Access and the Digital Divide: Federal Assistance Programs," Congressional Research Service, October 25, 2019, https://fas.org/sgp/crs/misc/RL30719.pdf.

5. Kim Hart, "The Homework Divide: 12 Million Schoolchildren Lack Internet." Axios, December 1, 2018, https://www.axios.com/the-homework-gap-kids-without-home-broadband-access-3ad5909f-e2fb-4208-b4d0-574c45ff4fe7.html. This definition differs from the traditional educational reference to an achievement gap. It primarily explores students' access to broadband at home and within the community.

6. Alabama Department of Education, "Alabama State Department of Education," 2019, http://reportcard.alsde.edu/Alsde/OverallScorePage?schoolcode=0000&systemcode=000&year=2019.

7. "State Profiles," Database, The Nation's Report Card, 2019, https://www.nationsreportcard.gov/profiles/stateprofile?chort=1&sub=MAT&sj=AL&sfj=NP&st=MN&year=2019R3.

8. Alabama Department of Education, "Francis Marion School," 2019, http://reportcard.alsde.edu/Alsde/OverallScorePage?schoolcodc=0025&systemcode=053&year=2019.

9. *United States v. Perry County Board of Education, Maury Smith*, U.S. District Court for the Southern District of Alabama 1971.

10. BroadbandNow Team, "Report: U.S. States with the Worst and Best Internet Coverage 2018," August 14, 2018, https://broadbandnow.com/report/us-states-internet-coverage-speed-2018/.

11. Aimee A. Howley, Lawrence Wood, and Brian H. Hough, "Rural Elementary School Teachers' Technology Integration," *Journal of Research in Rural Education* 26, no. 9 (2011), http://jrre.psu.edu/articles/26-9.pdf.

12. Tandra L. Tyler-Wood, Deborah Cockerham, and Karen R. Johnson, "Implementing New Technologies in a Middle School Curriculum: A Rural Perspective," *Smart Learning Environments* 5, no. 1 (October 10, 2018): 22, https://doi.org/10.1186/s40561-018-0073-y.

13. Monica Anderson, "Racial and Ethnic Differences in How People Use Mobile Technology," Pew Research Center FactTank (blog), April 30, 2015, https://pewresearch-org-preprod.go-vip.co/fact-tank/2015/04/30/racial-and-ethnic-differences-in-how-people-use-mobile-technology/.

14. John Horrigan, "Connections, Costs and Choices," Pew Research Center: Internet and Technology (blog), June 17, 2009, https://www.pewresearch.org/internet/2009/06/17/connections-costs-and-choices/.

15. Daniel O. Beltran, Kuntal K. Das, and Robert W. Fairlie, "Home Computers and Educational Outcomes: Evidence from the NLSY97 and CPS," International Finance Discussion Paper 958, November 2018, 47.

16. Tabassum Rashid and Hanan Muhammad Asghar, "Technology Use, Self-Directed Learning, Student Engagement and Academic Performance: Examining the Interrelations," *Computers in Human Behavior* 63 (October 1, 2016): 604–12, https://doi.org/10.1016/j.chb.2016.05.084.

17. Michelle Alexander, *The New Jim Crow: Mass Incarceration in the Age of Colorblindness* (New York: New Press, 2012).

18. Cecillia Wang, "How the People of Maricopa County Brought Down 'America's Toughest Sheriff,'" American Civil Liberties Union (blog), August 3, 2017, https://www.aclu.org/blog/immigrants-rights/state-and-local-immigration-laws/how-people-maricopa-county-brought-down.

19. "Demographics of Mobile Device Ownership and Adoption in the United States," Pew Research Center: Internet, Science & Tech (blog), June 12, 2019, https://www.pewresearch.org/internet/fact-sheet/mobile/.

20. U.S. Census Bureau, "2013–2017 American Community Survey 5-Year Estimates," https://factfinder.census.gov/faces/tableservices/jsf/pages/productview.xhtml?pid=ACS_17_5YR_GCT2801.ST51&prodType=table.

21. Vikki S. Katz, "How Children of Immigrants Use Media to Connect Their Families to the Community," *Journal of Children and Media* 4, no. 3 (August 1, 2010): 298–315, https://doi.org/10.1080/17482798.2010.486136.

22. Katz.

23. Reboot Foundation, "Does Educational Technology Help Students Learn?" June 6, 2019, https://reboot-foundation.org/does-educational-technology-help-students-learn/.

24. Reboot Foundation.

25. Gallup, "Creativity in Learning," 2019), https://www.gallup.com/education/267449/creativity-learning-transformative-technology-gallup-report-2019.aspx.

26. Elin Swanson Katz, "Testimony of Elin Swanson Katz, Connecticut Consumer General," Hearing titled Closing the Digital Divide: Broadband Infrastructure Solutions, U.S. House of Representatives, Committee on Energy and Commerce Subcommittee on Communications and Technology, https://democrats-energycommerce.house.gov/sites/democrats.energycommerce.house.gov/files/documents/Testimony-SwansonKatz-CAT-Hrg-on-Closing-the-Digital-Divide-Broadband-Infrastructure-Solutions-2018-01-30.pdf.

27. BroadbandNow, "Internet Providers in Hartford, Connecticut," https://broadbandnow.com/Connecticut/Hartford.

28. Victoria Rideout and Vikki Katz, "Opportunity for All? Technology and Learning in Lower-Income Families," Joan Ganz Cooney Center at Sesame Workshop, February 3, 2016, https://joanganzcooneycenter.org/wp-content/uploads/2016/01/jgcc_opportunityforall.pdf.
29. Samantha Becker and others, "Opportunity for All: How the American Public Benefits from Internet Access at U.S. Libraries," Institute of Museum and Library Services, January 3, 2010.
30. Cradlepoint, "Cradlepoint Helps California School District Ensure No Child Is Left Offline," 2016, https://www.cosn.org/sites/default/files/Coachella-Customer-Success-Story.pdf.
31. Rideout and Katz, "Opportunity for All?"; Teresa Correa, "Bottom-Up Technology Transmission within Families : How Children Influence Their Parents in the Adoption and Use of Digital Media," December 2012, https://repositories.lib.utexas.edu/handle/2152/22115; Katz, "How Children of Immigrants Use Media."
32. Correa, "Bottom-Up Technology."

V

The Path to a More Just and Equitable Digital Society

I promised to be a president for all Americans, whether or not they voted for me or whether or not they voted for these laws. These investments will help all Americans. We're not going to leave anyone behind.

—President Joe Biden,
Remarks on broadband investments,
June 26, 2023

8

Returning to the Purpose of Universal Service

In 2018, I took my first trip to China with colleagues from the Brookings China Center, led by senior fellow and director Cheng Li. The delegation went to the World Internet Conference, which was hosted in a small, rural water town called Wuzhen that is part of Tongxiang and north of Zhejiang Province. The location was about three hours outside Shanghai, the closet airport destination. It is an understatement to say that the Chinese do it big at the World Internet Conference. Upon arrival at the convention center, a combination of colorful, boastful displays of the government's technological advancements along with a mind-blowing showcase of impressive new products on display in the venue's largest exhibit hall welcomed us. While there, our delegation participated in an all-day gathering with staff members of other international think tanks on the future of technology and the internet. When I first attended the conference, the focus was on 5G; and over the next two years, discussions focused on artificial intelligence.

Each year we went to the conference, I found time to sneak away from the crowds of suited attendees and explore the local area, which looked like a ghost town around the time of the conference—there were virtually no cars or people on the streets. Given the tenor of political control in China, it was probably not the choice of residents to stay off the main streets. The small Chinese town was also quite interesting because there were no Black people here except for some attendees from Africa and me, of course. When I first walked alone down one of the main streets, I felt like I was the storyline behind Director Jordan Peele's 2017 movie *Get Out*. In the movie, the main character, who is Black, arrives at

157

the home of his girlfriend's parents. Everyone is white, and when he gets out of his car to meet them in this very wooded and secluded area (mistake number one), they all stare for what seems like hours as opposed to minutes. Later in the movie, he is preyed upon and tortured by them, and he is even the subject of a botched lobotomy—a plan that is ultimately thwarted when he kills everyone in the house and escapes.

I momentarily worried about this plot line as I walked along the empty streets of this town. The profound stillness and silence of my excursion were enough to elevate my anxiety, especially when an old Chinese man on a bike stopped in the middle of the deserted street and stared at me before quickly cycling away. But soon I realized that I was on display like a mannequin in a grandiose department store. Here, that man had probably never, ever seen Black people before me, except on televisions, if the Chinese government welcomed such programming.

Nevertheless, I kept walking until I discovered a stairway leading to a bottom walkway underneath the bridge on which I was standing. After making it to the bottom of the stairs, I encountered a river and a robust community of people sitting in front of tightly stacked homes. There was also local market of Chinese goods, including textiles like wool and cashmere, cultural trinkets, and various foods and spices. At every step of my short journey through this tiny hamlet, people continued to stare at me and sometimes snapped a photo, probably with intentions of showing it to family and friends who also had never seen a Black person before. Just when it could not have gotten more interesting, as I walked through the bustling area a young man behind me whispered to his friend *"Michelle Obama?"*—despite me being way shorter and less prestigious than the former first lady of the United States.

After a few minutes of walking, I stumbled on a very narrow sidewalk that doubled as a road where motorcycles whizzed past me, sometimes dangerously. It was there that I would meet an eighty-eight-year-old woman, whose shop was adorned with everything from cashmere scarves and hats to all types of Chinese souvenirs. With her wrinkled face and stylish clothes, she welcomed me into her literal hole-in-the-wall store, and I picked out several items to buy with the local currency. But things changed when she pulled out her new Apple iPhone and swiped it up to reveal an electronically generated quick response (QR) code, which looked like a symbol that you would scan at a restaurant. Because we could not understand each other's native language, she pointed to the QR code, which had the emblem for the Chinese social networking tool WeChat at its top corner. WeChat is the Chinese equivalent of Facebook/Meta, PayPal, WhatsApp, and Open Table all in one application, but also with incredible abilities to bank, transact, and validate one's identity in this highly surveilled country.

Of course, I did not have a QR code; nor was I on WeChat. All that was in my possession was paper currency, and she ultimately ended up taking most of it because she did not have change.

In the United States, electronic financial tools like Cash App, ApplePay, and Venmo have more recently integrated QR codes into their platforms. In the United States, these online tools are not banks; rather, they are online social networks built upon the trustworthiness of relationships in financial transactions. Venmo started the craze after college students used the tool to exchange money for cabs, dinners, and other forms of late night entertainment. CashApp capitalized on the potential of peer-to-peer payments in 2013, and it targeted low-income consumers to be more of a market for them, especially in the city of Atlanta, where the product was first launched. While these financial social networks are more widely used than ever, with more than 80 million users across a range of them, they are transactional and do not address concerns of the wealth gap, income divides, or explicit racism when it comes to banking and other financial services products, such as home loans or short-term credit. In the United States, they stand alone from the more protected and federally insured banking systems available today, but they make purchases readily available to many people, including the unbanked.

However, for this local older woman, whom I ended up seeing every subsequent year that I came to the conference, WeChat was her all-encompassing app. It served as her social networking app, as well as providing her with financial services, commerce, and civic engagement needs. The platform was very much part of the industrial goals of the Chinese government, working alongside its developer, Tencent, that has integrated the functionality of payment, commerce, and social networking into one singular system, whereby a Chinese subscriber can do just about everything, although with the caveat of having the government likely keeping track of their various digital activities.[1]

Internet user penetration is on a steady upward trajectory in both urban and rural regions of China. Seventy-nine percent of urban residents have access to the internet, compared with a growing 56 percent of rural ones.[2] That is why my new friend in the market has a QR code in her small community and uses it to run her business. How China is making the transition to the digital economy is worth its own book, but the whole experience sheds some light on the progress China is making on universal service.

During the Obama administration, I joined an advisory board at the U.S. State Department established by my friend Ambassador Daniel Sepulveda, who had previously served in the Senate as senior adviser to the former secretary of state, Senator John Kerry (D-MA). Obama appointed him to this role, and later he transitioned to the Economic Bureau before leaving government. As a member of the advisory board, I heard presentations from members of the private sector on how they were leveraging technology to thwart things like the Ebola epidemic in Africa. At other times, we heard testimony from staff members of global nongovernmental organizations who were working to address the impact of digital disruption in some of less developed countries in Africa, Asia, and parts of Latin America.

The Global Digital Divide

My time on the advisory board was thought-provoking and helped me to gain a better understanding of digital exclusion in developing countries and how that compares with places experiencing underinvestment and disinvestment in the United States. For example, Anacostia—just south of downtown Washington—was one of the poorest neighborhoods in the city. The *Washington Post* reported that Anacostia residents were the least likely in the city to have broadband access and related digital benefits, like access to Uber and other ridesharing services. One part is due to its income disparities and the other is due to the racism that makes ridesharing companies less incentivized to cross the river.

So, to think that I was being exposed on the advisory board to how to address global disparities of the digital divide was both exciting and disheartening at the same time. Take the African Union as an example. Through persistent bilateral trade relationships with China through its Belt and Road Initiative, Africa's wireless industries had experienced tremendous growth over the years. In 2017, there were 250 smartphone connections there, but they are expected to rise to 440 million by 2025.[3] Behind these numbers have been decades of available low-cost equipment, affordable prepaid plans, multiple IM cards, and the tethering of applications with mobile providers, especially in the areas of banking, mobile money, and other forms of commerce, as well as health care.[4] Compared with U.S. investments in fiber to primarily bolster internet service, Africa has been largely focused on phone technologies (USSD/SMS) to reduce the cost of mobile services and to diversify its routes to internet access.[5] Reflecting on the forthcoming investments in fiber without some support for wireless today has me scratching my head.

The United Nations puts the number of people in the world not connected to the internet at about 2.7 billion, which demonstrates that more needs to be done multilaterally to tackle this access problem. But even the U.N. is shifting how it defines and speaks about the digital divide. At an annual U.N. forum in November 2022 in Addis Abba, Secretary Antonio Guterres shared in a press release: "With the right policies in place, digital technology can give an unprecedented boost to sustainable development, particularly for the poorest countries. This calls for more connectivity, and less digital fragmentation. More bridges across digital divides; and fewer barriers. Greater autonomy for ordinary people; less abuse and disinformation."[6]

Currently, 60 percent of the African population does not have internet access, and the United Nations' reframing of the "digital divide" to a conversation about "digital poverty" is a new way of thinking about the remaining people without technology access. Internationally, seeing the digital gap as a condition of poverty as opposed to solely a problem of incumbents generates healthy table stakes for the direct and indirect problems associated with it. Not that the United States is completely failing in its attempt to eliminate digital disparities, but its global counterparts are further ahead in thinking about how broadband internet and related technologies are critical for economic development and human rights, because the U.N. secretary general continued to opine in that same press statement that "a human-centered approach protects free speech and privacy; and the safe and responsible use of data."[7]

Therefore, a candid conversation on universal service is timely and needed in the United States. Without it, we are essentially throwing up the same wish list that we had decades ago, in hopes that we can finally do something different— or, as President Biden declared, that we can, finally, finish the job. Such a conversation is also pertinent as spaces maintain certain racialized and/or vulnerable postures, where commitments can help to alter the trajectory for proposed digital access by making it more available.

It Is Time to Modernize the Universal Service Program in the United States

Throughout the book, I have offered some insights into what should constitute universal service in the United States, but it is probably worth a deeper dive into how we codified it decades ago. It began in 1913, with the "Kingsbury Commitment," which was a deal between the former AT&T (before it was reconstituted) and the U.S. Department of Justice after an investigation into the company's market power over telephone service, especially long distance.[8] That would be around the same time that the CEO, Theodore Vail, started talking about universal service after the settlement opened up AT&T's long distance network for independent telephone companies, set up the company's divestiture of the money exchange service Western Union, and stopped the company's ability to purchase other companies if there were objections from the Interstate Commerce Commission, which was the telephony regulator at the time.[9] In many respects, the deal between AT&T and the Justice Department set the stage for the original provision of universal telephone services for all Americans, which was included as a statute in the Communications Act of 1934, after creating the Federal Communications Commission (FCC) as the known regulator over these services. In addition to the language that I previously shared from the statute, it was also the intent that universal service be made "available . . . to all the people of the United States . . . to a rapid, efficient, Nation-wide, and world-wide wire and radio communication service with adequate facilities at reasonable charges."[10] In the 1970s, AT&T was accused of becoming a legal monopoly, and with antitrust complaints from the U.S. Justice Department under the Sherman Antitrust Act, the company ultimately spun off portions of the business in 1984, making way for seven "Regional Bell Operating Companies" to provide consumers with lower rates, more choices of telephone service, and less reliance on AT&T's control over hardware, whereby it had formerly forced consumers to rent phones rather than purchase them.

In 1985, the Lifeline program, with which you are now extensively familiar based on the number of times I have spoken about it, emerged and offered discounted local phone service to low-income consumers. When the communications act was later amended in 1996, the language on universal service was also changed to enable the FCC to "make available, so far as possible, to all people in the United States, without discrimination on the basis of race, color, religion, national origin, or sex, a rapid, efficient, Nation-wide, and world-wide wire and radio community service."[11] The FCC also convened a joint Federal and State Board to ensure compliance with these program caveats that are outlined in the 1996 legislation:

—Quality service at rates that are just, reasonable, and affordable should be available.

—All regions of the Nation should have access to advanced services available in telecommunications and information.

—Telecommunications and information services should be accessible by consumers (including low-income) in all regions of the Nation, including rural, insular, and high-cost areas at rates reasonably comparable to those in urban areas.

—All providers of telecommunications services should make an equitable and nondiscriminatory contribution to preserve and advance universal service.

—Specific, predictable, and sufficient support mechanisms at the Federal and State levels are necessary to preserve and advance universal service.

—Access to advanced telecommunications services for elementary and secondary schools, health care providers, and libraries should be available.[12]

As noted in earlier chapters, the flexibility of the statute allowed for changes to the program, which happened in 2005 under President George W. Bush, to include wireless carriers as "eligible telecommunications carriers" (known as ETCs) to pay into and offer discounted mobile services to low-income consumers—to say it the third time as a charm, this is the reason why the program should not be called the "Obamaphone." Further, the FCC lifted the facilities requirement, which were a requirement for wireless carriers to be eligible that led to more competition from companies like Tracfone, one of the nation's largest Lifeline service providers for wireless, which brokered deals with Sprint and other major incumbents. In the 1990s, Northwest Tower residents were beneficiaries of universal service, but they also were subjected to the "telecommunications tax" that providers passed onto them as part of their legal obligation to this compulsory universal service tax.

One other change worth noting in the telecommunications sector was its expanded inclusion of companies handling interconnections, which facilitated the use of different networks for domestic and international calls. The process also expanded the ecosystem of telecommunications and led to increased contributions to the Universal Service Fund (USF). Some refer to this proportionate distribution and increasing value of telecommunications as "Metcalfe's law," which was attributed to Robert Metcalfe, who also founded the Ethernet, in 1980. As more devices entered the network—including telephones, fax machines, computers, and later the internet—more value was accrued in their networking; that is, two fax machines communicating with one another to send and receive documents contributed more dynamism to telecommunications.[13] The Ethernet, or the combination of wired networking technologies to facilitate local to wide-area networks, helped to facilitate these types of connections, and was later commercially standardized in 1983 as IEEE 802.3.

After Reagan put in place universal service and entrusted the FCC with its oversight and expansion, President George H. W. Bush opted for light-touch regulation as communications transitioned from analog to more mobile, digital services and devices. He was also the first to introduce email into the White House in 1992, as he dealt with a variety of notable domestic and global events—including bailing out big banks, the Exxon Valdez oil spill, the massacre in China's Tiananmen Square, and the fall of the Berlin Wall—none of which were posted and shared online, since the internet was not fully commercialized. In 1994, President Clinton published the White House's first website, and he was also the first to introduce the concept of the digital divide to the American public. In the background were large tech companies, like IBM and Microsoft, which were dominant players, setting the stage for companies like Apple, whose early Macintosh products brought competition to Microsoft's personal computers and whose later innovations within advanced communications outpaced Motorola's inaugural set of mobile phones.

The early 2000s made way for tech start-ups, like Google and Mozilla, to leverage emerging internet-enabled platforms to engineer more products and services that revolutionized online search. Simultaneously, companies like Cisco, which was focused more on sensors and devices powering internet networks, like routers, activated the broad ecology of the internet of things with new capacities that can found installed within consumer appliances and even automobiles. To keep up with this growth, voluntarily, some internet service providers (ISPs) provided broadband speeds upward of 124 Megabytes per second (Mbps), which has made technologies like digital subscriber lines, at 35 Mbps, dinosaurs during a time when copper telephone lines are near full retirement, and fiber-optics the fastest broadband conduit, at 1,000 Mbps, or gigabit speeds in many places across the United States.

In April 2021, I testified before the U.S. House of Representatives' Committee on Ways and Means' Subcommittee on Trade about inclusive technological growth. In my written remarks and oral presentation, one of my recommendations to the members was the need to modernize and reform the universal service program— something that I said as early as 2013 in a publication with my former colleague at the Multicultural Media, Telecom, and Internet Council, David Honig, called "Refocusing Broadband Policy: The New Opportunity Agenda for People of

Color."[14] We argued in that white paper that the initial enactment of the U.S. Communications Act of 1934 implored Congress to maintain equity and parity in available technologies, and despite not projecting the capacities of broadband, it has managed not to do this well.

The $8 billion USF is still highly dependent on a compulsory "telecommunications tax" from declining numbers of incumbent telephone and interconnection companies. I briefly mentioned this above: that the fees collected manage, fund, and deploy the four programs that are obligatory to the statute: (1) the Connect America Fund (formally known as the High-Cost Program) to support qualifying telephone companies for broadband deployments in rural areas; (2) Lifeline for eligible, low-income consumers to offset the cost of phone service, including for those on Tribal lands; (3) E-Rate for the deployment of the internet and related resources to schools and libraries; and (4) rural health care, particularly the investments in modern-day telehealth to ensure remote and real-time access to good-quality care in rural areas.

But much has happened in the telecommunications and technology marketplaces to affect the usefulness of universal service. The innovation sector, consisting of high-tech companies, has grown exponentially, and there have been growing monopolies among companies that have been obligatory USF contributors, including the range of wireline and wireless telecommunications carriers, and interconnected Voice over Internet Protocol (VoIP) providers like cable companies that provide voice service. Wireline services have also dwindled alongside the elimination of legacy analog services.

Given such shifts, the universal service program as we know it today is dying, much like the death of analog services and systems with rapid digitization, and consequently support to close the digital divide occurs on the edges of the existing program without any major reform. Further, universal service is not solely based on what and how much you give people, but rather it should be focused on how you treat them. In Garrett County, for example, people were elated to be connected to the internet via the alternative technology of TV white spaces because of how Barry helped them to understand their needs and worked with them individually to solve their connectivity challenges.

This Is Not Your Grandma's USF

For decades, policymakers have perceived universal service as a "one-size, four priorities" program, and they have presented it as a wholesale solution to myriad unique community challenges. Because it was and still is rooted in traditional telephony, universal service has pretty much favored rural areas, with large amounts of monies allocated to them via the Connect America Fund and rural health care programs. Rural areas have also gotten a boost from the complementary resources of the U.S. Department of Agriculture, while urban areas are more situated to benefit from the E-Rate expansion and Lifeline programs.

In the summer of 2023, President Biden crafted a new term, "Bidenomics," which argues that investments in the working and middle classes of America will eventually make it to the masses of less fortunate populations. Not surprisingly, this concept is being applied to the trillions of dollars being allocated to high-speed broadband. During his June 26 press event at the White House, he shared stories of rural, working-, and middle-class residents who wanted to pay less for higher-quality broadband service, and immediately after the formal event, it was announced that about two-thirds of the Broadband Equity, Access, and Deployment (BEAD) monies went to majority-Republican states and households.[15] Senator Tommy Tuberville (R-AL) tweeted his excitement about his state of Alabama being in the top five of BEAD funding recipients, despite voting against the Infrastructure Investment and Jobs Act on the congressional floor in 2021.

While this could very well be an indication of the necessary bipartisan support that Biden needs for reelection in the 2024 presidential election, the short-term gains for the Republicans may do very little to impress social and economic changes for individuals in Perry County, the most impoverished part of Representative Tuberville's state, and the program may be diverted and potentially eliminated if a Republican president takes office after the next presidential election in November 2024. With the current state of political affairs, time will tell.

When I think about the elderly woman in the small Chinese market, it was pretty obvious what China had done to ensure her status as a first-class digital resident, which enabled her to be an entrepreneur. Mind you, countries like China have very little competition when it comes to mobile carriers. China Mobile, the largest operator in the country, has 950 million mobile subscribers and 172 million wireless broadband connection customers.[16] Compare this with the consumer base of the three largest U.S. mobile operators in 2022: AT&T is the largest, with 217.3 million wireless subscribers; while Verizon is at 143.3 million and T-Mobile is at 110.2 million wireless subscribers.[17] All three also pay into the USF, somewhat begrudgingly.

USF Contribution Reform

In 2012, when Obama was in office, his first FCC chairman, Julius Genachowski, opened a Notice of Proposed Rulemaking to address existing USF contribution reform. He pointed to the growing availability of wireless and the variation of voice, data, and video services available over internet protocol–based services, which was the preface to broadband and its streaming capabilities. Genachowski saw the shrinking contributions to the USF and heard from providers about the extraordinary burdens placed on the remaining companies that were obliged to satiate the fund.

While no actions were taken after the comments in the Notice of Proposed Rulemaking, the efforts to modernize the USF's contribution levels over a decade ago were significant. But the conversation that is more pertinent today involves both physical infrastructures and the applications and services that are tethered to the networks, and whether there is enough spectrum to support the increasing consumer, enterprise, and government demands. A comparison of the effects of technology on the U.S. Postal Service is worthy of comparison.

U.S. post offices have survived from both the delivery of letters and packages, but more important from the purchase of stamps and other services, including money orders and express delivery. Then came email and accelerated package delivery for a higher price. When you think about it, first, companies like United Parcel Service and Federal Express upended the Postal Service's existing business models on modes of delivery; and soon after these companies were affected by Amazon, which raised the bar through the two-day delivery schedule as part of its Prime service. At the very least, this is what is currently happening to USF.

Reforming the methodology for contributions into the USF entails a much longer conversation, one that should be of interest to Congress, as more broadband assets are deployed using federal dollars. And getting people access to more reliable broadband and internet-enabled devices may be more urgent than originally realized more than six presidential administrations ago. You are a dinosaur, and a very thirsty one, without being part of robust, online ecosystems that further one's quality of life. Given the state of the marketplace and the shrinking capacities of the few companies still contributing to USF, the United States is at an impasse—whether we like it or not—and for this reason, I offer three recommendations to grow and effectively sustain universal access.

It Is Time for Big Tech Companies to Open Their Wallets

First, it is time for Big Tech companies that amass tremendous profit from available and accessible broadband networks to provide their proportionate share of resources to universal service and/or the USF. Changing the current Communications Act to include every company that builds, supports, and benefits from online connectivity—including the Big Tech companies—could be game changing in the race to equitable online access.

In a 2022 an op-ed in the *Hill*, Matthew Weinberg, who is a partner at an early-stage venture capital firm and a former Obama appointee at the U.S. Small Business Administration, argued that revenue from existing carriers that pay into the USF have eroded from "a peak of $80 billion in the early 2000s to less than

Figure 8-1. *Internet-Edge-Providers' 2022 Advertising Revenues* (billion dollars)

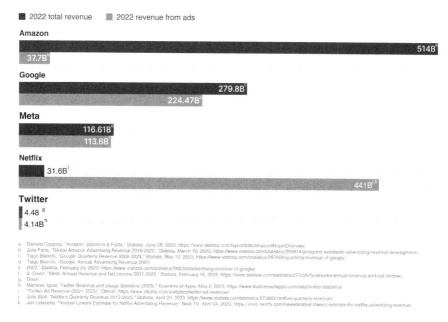

■ 2022 total revenue   ■ 2022 revenue from ads

Amazon
514B[a]
37.7B[b]

Google
279.8B[c]
224.47B[d]

Meta
116.61B[e]
113.6B[f]

Netflix
31.6B[j]
441B[j,k]

Twitter
4.48[g]
4.14B[h]

a. Daniela Coppola, "Amazon: Statistics & Facts," Statista, June 28, 2023, https://www.statista.com/topics/846/amazon/#topicOverview.
b. Julia Faria, "Global Amazon Advertising Revenue 2019-2022," Statista, March 10, 2023, https://www.statista.com/statistics/259814/amazons-worldwide-advertising-revenue-development/.
c. Tiago Bianchi, "Google: Quarterly Revenue 2008-2023," Statista, May 10, 2023, https://www.statista.com/statistics/267606/quarterly-revenue-of-google/.
d. Tiago Bianchi, "Google: Annual Advertising Revenue 2001-
e. 2022," Statista, February 24, 2023, https://www.statista.com/statistics/266249/advertising-revenue-of-google/.
f. S. Dixon, "Meta: Annual Revenue and Net Income 2007-2022," Statista, February 16, 2023, https://www.statista.com/statistics/277229/facebooks-annual-revenue-and-net-income/.
g. Dixon.
h. Mansoor Iqbal, "Twitter Revenue and Usage Statistics (2023)," Business of Apps, May 2, 2023, http://www.businessofapps.com/data/twitter-statistics/.
i. "Twitter Ad Revenue (2021-2023)," Oberlo, https://www.oberlo.com/statistics/twitter-ad-revenue/.
j. Julia Stoll, "Netflix's Quarterly Revenue 2013-2023," Statista, April 20, 2023, https://www.statista.com/statistics/273883/netflixs-quarterly-revenue/.
k. Jon Lafayette, "Analyst Lowers Estimate for Netflix Advertising Revenue," Next TV, April 24, 2023, https://www.nexttv.com/news/analyst-lowers-estimate-for-netflix-advertising-revenue.

$30 billion in [2022]."[18] Additionally, consumers also have increased their portion of what they carry on the tax from "11% in 2007 to 23% in [2022]."[19] Brendan Carr, a Republican appointed an FCC commissioner, touted the suggestion that the regressive tax on the revenue of landline telephone customers be revisited—suggesting in a statement that the current contributions to USF are like "taxing horseshoes to pay for highways" because of the antiquated base.

More recently, in March 2023, a bipartisan slate of legislators—including Roger Wicker (R-MI), Ben Ray Lugan (D-NM), Todd Young (R-IN), and Mark Kelly (D-AZ)—reintroduced a bill that they had put forward a year earlier called the Funding Affordable Internet with Reliable (FAIR) Contributions Act, which would direct the FCC to conduct a study into the feasibility of collecting USF contributions from internet-edge-providers (IEPs).[20]

IEPs include any company that is a website, web service, application, online content hosting, or online content delivery service that customers use to get online—such as Google, Amazon, Netflix, and Meta—that ride on the networks built and managed by ISPs. Under the FAIR Act, a portion of the digital advertising and user fees may be assessed as contributable to the fund in a way that seeks parity of use of these networks. For illustrative purposes, figure 8-1 presents both the total 2022 revenue made by a few of the larger IEPs and the portion of profits that can be traced to their ad revenues. Compare their 2022 total revenues with those of the top three U.S. mobile operators: AT&T, $120.74 billion; Verizon, $136.835 billion; and T-Mobile, $79.57 billion.[21]

I will project the precise percentage of ad revenue that should be taxed and/or contributed to the USF. However, I do believe that most of these companies have the financial resources to buffer the impact of the digital divide and help fund existing and increasing gaps in the USF. These companies are also no strangers to programs focused on digital equity and have invested in more recent technologies to do so.

In 2014, for example, Google announced that it would be investing $1 billion to connect the world to the internet through high-capacity satellites that will orbit the Earth at low-level altitudes.[22] Almost ten years later, Amazon launched Project Kuiper, which, according to its website, will "increase global broadband access through a constellation of 3,236 satellites in low Earth orbit (LEO). Its mission is to bring fast, affordable broadband to unserved and underserved communities around the world."[23] Satellite technology is yet another channel for broadband connectivity that is also not included in Biden's "Internet for All" program joining commercial wireless and cable providers.

It is worth noting that for Big Tech companies have always been asked to do more. My mentor, the Reverend Jesse Louis Jackson Sr.—who not only ran for president twice in his lifetime but also marched alongside the late Reverend Dr. Martin Luther King Jr. was the first to publicly expose the disparate hiring practices of telecommunications and Big Tech companies. Later, under the umbrella organization that Reverend Jackson founded in 1971 in Chicago, the Rainbow PUSH Coalition sent a letter to twenty-five large tech companies—including Google, Facebook, Tesla, and Oracle—to openly share their hiring practices, board diversity, and employee retention statistics to be publicly assessed on their progress.[24] His efforts also paralleled the Department of Labor's 2018 inquiry into the same situation, requesting that these same companies complete EEO-1 forms documenting their demographic data for their workforce.[25] After two years of inquiry, tech companies did respond by making their data available and identifying more diverse candidates for their C-suite positions and boards—at least in small increments, since the inquiry started in 2018.

Yet recent challenges and debates over the importance of affirmative action and increasing attention to diversity, equity, and inclusion practices post–George Floyd have also become political. In the backdrop of a recent U.S. Supreme Court decision banning race-based college admissions, dueling letters from congressional chambers on the importance of diversity, equity, and inclusion in *Fortune* 500 companies, the progress made by Reverend Jackson and others could be reversed, especially when technologies like artificial intelligence can easily encroach upon civil and human rights.[26]

Having Big Tech companies open their wallets to contribute to the USF can also ensure that their products and services, especially those leveraging artificial intelligence, are not out of reach from communities without broadband access. Reforming the USF and expanding the contributions to it are both critical to how the United States administers and maintains internet access for all.

It is meaningful to have the money directed at efforts to close the digital divide, which are nonpartisan and always available—and trust me, after years of having a much smaller wish list like brand new computer monitors in the 1990s, it does help to be well resourced. But the engagement of more innovative partners can amplify and modernize outdated systems and processes, and essentially change the current conversations on connectivity.

Take, for example, the stagnant monthly benefit of the Lifeline program that is still offered under a $10 subsidy for existing landline or wireless services. Much more can be done to amplify the program if online access to, at minimum, government content was offered free to anyone who needs them, diminishing the effects on existing data caps through a practice commonly known as zero-rating, or sponsored, data.

Zero-Rating Government Services

There has not been a rush to widely employ zero-rating government services in the United States, largely because it conflicts with widely debated net neutrality expectations. As recent as 2018, a telehealth app called VA Video Connect was offered by the U.S. Department of Veterans Affairs (VA) to allow veterans and their caregivers to meet with VA health care providers via a computer, tablet, or mobile device. Under a 2019 agreement between the VA and wireless carriers, the app is offered free to veterans using their smartphones without counting toward their data caps.[27] But it did not take very long for concerns to be raised about the arrangement that the VA made with several ISPs—including AT&T, Verizon, and T-Mobile—that violated California's newly enacted net neutrality law. The matter escalated to the state's attorney general office for review, despite it being used in a manner consistent with the public interest.

Around the same time, California had passed its own net neutrality law, SB-822, after the Trump FCC overturned the existing Obama rules. When this law went into effect, concerns were raised about zero rating, the practice by which commercial arrangements and unilateral decisions by network operators are exempted from consumer pricing and data caps.[28] Under California's net neutrality law, zero-rating and sponsored data programs were violations because certain content cannot be excluded from consumer data caps, or usage-based pricing.

Most consumers are familiar with zero-rating and sponsored data programs in the mobile marketplace, as popular streaming services for music and movies are often exempted from user data caps or are bundled into unlimited monthly service packages. For wireless service providers, such offerings allowed them to differentiate themselves from other carriers in a highly competitive market and helped to offset consumers' being double charged by application and internet-edge-providers, like Netflix.

But net neutrality relies on online content and traffic being treated equally to deter broadband service providers from restricting it or blocking applications on their platforms. Among many content creators and IEPs, they abhor the use of zero-rating or sponsored data programs, in theory, because internet gatekeepers can still decide who is worthy to be featured on their devices and platforms.

Without getting too prescriptive, the FCC's "general conduct standard" has been in action for decades to evaluate potential products and services like this on a case-by-case basis, including tiered pricing and data caps versus exempted usage metering like zero-rating.

At face-value, the VA app did not appear to be following the California law. Stanford law professor and net neutrality advocate Barbara van Schewick, argued that the real problem rests on ISPs, which should eliminate data caps entirely for consumers or lower the costs of unlimited service plans, which would be allowable under net neutrality provisions.[29]

Veterans—oddly—find themselves in the middle of the regulatory debate about the internet. But so too are Joseph from Staunton and the other people with whom I spoke who have limited data options.

How This Could Reinvigorate the Lifeline Program

The automatic exemption of dot.gov domains from data caps would entail agreements, like the one the VA had with ISPs, whereby federal agencies could subsidize the free data or establish a financial agreement with the Universal Service Administrative Company. In the process, the arrangement could compel higher rates of participation in the Lifeline or future versions of broadband affordability programs, especially those for participants receiving government benefits. Sponsored data programs between government agencies, ISPs, and other providers could introduce other public-interest-oriented content offerings through partnerships with online job search engines or hospitals offering remote patient monitoring to medically underserved patients, where free data facilitates improved communications or could be paid for by hospitals and clinics that may want their patients to stay more connected. These and other programs could happen now under the current FCC, but would be forbidden in California, and potentially at the national level, if we employ a less flexible net neutrality regime. This makes the case for federal legislation to codify the components of a widely agreed-on open internet law.

Another way to look at zero-rated offerings is to think about the needs of wireless customers in rural and urban areas who with such choice to gain free access to government content do not have to choose between streaming a movie or applying for unemployment. This would have been a tremendous boost to the more than 40 million individuals who were told to go to the internet first to apply for unemployment insurance over the course of the pandemic. Or senior citizens on a fixed income who should not have to choose between using data for remote health care over playing online games to break life's monotony. Though some may doubt the ability of the FCC and Congress to do this now, they can make public interest exceptions, especially the agency, which could err on the side of a case-by-case review of zero-rated and sponsored data programs to minimize broadband affordability concerns and offer untethered access to government and government-supported content offerings. Further, Congress will need to take on USF contribution reform, which may in my lifetime happen if they care about the future global competitiveness of the country.

With some leverage of free data, people who have been marginalized by the digital ecosystem, along with others who are budget conscious in their data use, could

—enroll in and complete required workforce training or credentialing via state and federal workforce sites though U.S. Department of Labor's websites.

—find federally assisted housing through the U.S. Department of Housing and Urban Development's portals.

—apply for public benefits online and monitor their health outcomes post-pandemic via the U.S. Department of Health and Human Services and local health departments.

—access early learning and child development services available by the U.S. Department of Education.

Again, such a proposal for the reform of existing universal service suggests that we meet people where they are, making it easier rather than more difficult to access government websites and other online resources, while amplifying a stagnant and noninflationary subsidy.

The Foundation of Online Consumer Privacy

Critical and innovative reform of the universal service program also involves the right to consumer privacy. In China, it is the lack of privacy—despite a national bill to protect it—that was a trade-off for my elderly friend from the local Chinese market because platforms like WeChat are monitored by the government. But Americans made similar privacy trade-offs during the pandemic when millions of people surrendered their data to the websites of private companies to schedule COVID-19 testing and vaccinations. As of this moment, we do not know where and how that information was stored—and if it has been deleted.

The right to online privacy should be embedded in any reform of universal service because it is not solely about getting and keeping people online. It is also about their trust and security of digital systems that reasonably and protect their personal information. In 2012, I wrote an article when I worked at the

Multicultural Media, Telecom, and Internet Council, years after I closed my technology centers in Chicago and moved to Washington for work, that was focused on the online privacy of communities of color. Back then, I stated:

> Today, our online interactions and transactions are being registered, saved, and tracked by online data brokers that use data to improve targeted advertising to online consumers. These companies have created search engines that literally mine the Internet for information, attach this data to consumers, and make projections on future consumer purchases based on these online behaviors. This type of information tracking is no different than when a customer enrolls in a frequent buying club at a commercial establishment or uses a customer savers card at the local grocery. Consumers' enrollment in these programs gives permission to retailers to track their purchasing history, preferred products and services, and frequency of visits to that establishment. In turn, customers receive discounted coupons, buyer surveys and other forms of marketing collateral that essentially help industry improve their advertising and sales strategies.[30]

Further in the article, I argued that the lack of understanding of their online privacy rights for individuals, who at the time were new internet adopters, made them more vulnerable to predatory targeted advertising and other discriminatory activities.[31] Such concerns are even truer today for vulnerable populations excised from analog systems and practices.

At the time of this writing, members of Congress are still unsettled on what the rule of law for federal privacy legislation should be, which has left several states to enact their own legislation, including California and Washington State. My Brookings colleague Cam Kerry, who was a former Obama appointee at the National Telecommunications and Information Administration (NTIA) working on consumer privacy as far back as 2009 and someone whom I have known since then, and who now works with me now at Brookings, shared in a 2022 interview: "Ten years ago, I was knocking on doors on Capitol Hill trying to get people to partner on privacy legislation, and I couldn't find any takers (this includes people who today have their names on privacy bills). Now, lots of members of Congress are involved with privacy legislation. Recent hearings on the Hill concerning privacy are a lot more sophisticated than they were in the past."[32]

Considering the European Union's passage of the General Data Protection Regulations in 2018 and what China has done through the Personal Information Protection Law in 2021, adopting federal privacy legislation is becoming as drawn out as both closing the digital divide and updating universal service. Reminding legislators in the United States about the importance of preserving and protecting the rights of individuals should be considerably aligned with the expansion of broadband and should closely parallel efforts to support digital equity. As the current period prompts the beginning of the next presidential election, how far the United States will come on privacy will probably be set aside as more pressing concerns that result from the lack of transparency and redlines on the data being collected will emerge, as we have already seen with artificial intelligence.

Online consumer privacy is not necessarily within the authority of the FCC—why would it be, since the agency was established soon after the telegraph. Some parts are governed by the NTIA, which has an interest in how data privacy affects trade and the resilience of the digital economy. Guidance on what companies and third-party data miners can collect, share, repurpose, and retain are fundamental for how the United States approaches universal access and adoption. This speaks to what Cam Kerry said many years ago while at the NTIA: that the country needs "clear rules of the road for businesses and consumers that preserve the innovation and free flow of information that are the hallmarks of the internet economy." Even as I write about the need for a national data privacy standard, new systems are continuing to homogenize and erase the experiences and liberties of individuals and communities, and because of both conscious and unconscious partisanship in technology issues, we are not even a smidgeon ahead in advancing comprehensive legislation.

Where we land on universal service in the United States will help us finally close the digital divide, or really finish the job especially when policymakers—particularly those in Congress—recognize that we are wasting time in our attempts to modernize old and outdated public policies. At the end of July 2023, a bipartisan Senate group was established to evaluate the state of the Universal Service Fund, and provide recommendations—which was still an idea before Congress broke for summer recess.[33] Going into 2024, the focus is still on getting out the Democratic-supported funding for broadband networks, especially to avert any sea change in leadership. Grasping on to an agenda that leads with universal service positions people and their communities will enable us to be digitally competitive in our changing world, and should force us to see the actual trees before the forest.

Notes

Part V epigraph: Joe Biden, "Remarks by President Biden on Broadband Investments," White House, June 26, 2023, https://www.whitehouse.gov/briefing-room/speeches-remarks/2023/06/26/remarks-by-president-biden-on-broadband-investments/.

1. Paul Mozer, "Forget TikTok. China's Powerhouse App Is WeChat, and Its Power Is Sweeping.," *New York Times*, September 4, 2020, https://www.nytimes.com/2020/09/04/technology/wechat-china-united-states.html.

2. Sara Lebow, "For the First Time, More than Half of Those Living in Rural China Have Internet Access," *Insider Intelligence*, March 19, 2021, https://www.insiderintelligence.com/content/first-time-more-than-half-of-those-living-rural-china-have-internet-access.

3. Elo Umeh, "Three Reasons Why African Mobile Connectivity Is Misleading," *Africa Report*, June 27, 2019, https://www.theafricareport.com/14567/three-reasons-why-african-mobile-connectivity-is-misleading/.

4. Nicol Turner Lee, rep., "Navigating the U.S.-China 5G Competition," Brookings, April 2020, https://www.brookings.edu/wp-content/uploads/2020/04/FP_20200427_5g_competition_turner_lee_v2.pdf.

5. Umeh, "Three Reasons."

6. *U.N. News*, "UN Forum Tackles 'Digital Poverty' Facing 2.7 Billion People," November 29, 2022, https://news.un.org/en/story/2022/11/1131142.

7. *U.N. News*.

8. Benton Institute for Broadband and Society, "Lifeline: Where Did It Come From?" May 18, 2015, https://www.benton.org/blog/lifeline-where-did-it-come.

9. Jodie Griffin, "100th Anniversary of the Kingsbury Commitment," Public Knowledge, December 19, 2013, https://publicknowledge.org/100th-anniversary-of-the-kingsbury-commitment/.

10. "The Communications Act of 1934," https://transition.fcc.gov/Reports/1934new.pdf.

11. "The Telecommunications Act of 1996," https://www.congress.gov/104/plaws/publ104/PLAW-104publ104.pdf.

12. "Telecommunications Act of 1996."

13. Techopedia, "Metcalfe's Law," May 28, 2019, https://www.techopedia.com/definition/29066/metcalfes-law.

14. David Honig and Nicol Turner Lee, rep., "Refocusing Broadband Policy: The New Opportunity Agenda for People of Color," Minority Media and Telecommunications Council, November 21, 2013, https://mmtconline.org/wp-content/uploads/2013/11/Refocusing-Broadband-Policy-112113.pdf.

15. Joseph Morton, "John Cornyn Highlights Billions in Broadband Funding for Texas—That He Voted Against," *Dallas Morning News*, June 28, 2023, https://www.dallasnews.com/news/politics/2023/06/28/john-cornyn-highlights-billions-in-broadband-funding-for-texas-that-he-voted-against/.

16. ESGN Asia, "China Mobile Is Bridging the Gap Between Rural and Urban Digital Divide in China," July 5, 2021, https://esgn.asia/china-mobile-is-bridging-the-gap-between-rural-and-urban-digital-divide-in-china/.

17. Petroc Taylor, "AT&T: Statistics & Facts," Statista, May 2, 2023, https://www.statista.com/topics/1252/atundt/#topicOverview; Statista Research Department, "Verizon Communications: Statistics & Facts," Statista, January 19, 2023, https://www.statista.com/topics/2599/verizon-communications/#topicOverview; Petroc Taylor, "T-Mobile U.S.: Statistics & Facts," Statista, June 13, 2023, https://www.statista.com/topics/996/t-mobile-us/#topicOverview.

18. Matthew Weinberg, "Saving the Universal Service Fund: Time for Big Tech to Pay Up," *The Hill*, August 25, 2022, https://thehill.com/opinion/congress-blog/3616131-saving-the-universal-service-fund-time-for-big-tech-to-pay-up/.

19. Weinberg.

20. "Wicker, Luján, Young, Kelly Reintroduce Bill to Explore Collecting USF Contributions from Big Tech," wicker.senate.gov press releases, March 16, 2023, https://www.wicker.senate.gov/2023/3/wicker-luj-n-young-kelly-reintroduce-bill-to-explore-collecting-usf-contributions-from-big-tech.

21. Petroc Taylor, "Revenue of AT&T Worldwide 2006–2022," Statista, June 9, 2023, https://www.statista.com/statistics/272308/atundts-operating-revenue-since-2006/; Petroc Taylor, "Verizon's Revenue by Segment 2012–2022," June 16, 2023, https://www.statista.com/statistics/257309/verizon-communications-revenue-from-wireline-and-wireless-services/; Petroc Taylor, "T-Mobile U.S. Total Revenue 2009–2022," Statista, June 9, 2023, https://www.statista.com/statistics/219458/total-revenue-of-t-mobile-usa-since-2006/.

22. Tyler Falk, "Google Is Investing Over $1 Billion to Connect the World to Internet," ZDnet, June 2, 2014, https://www.zdnet.com/article/google-is-investing-over-1-billion-to-connect-the-world-to-internet/.

23. "Project Kuiper," Amazon: What We Do, https://www.aboutamazon.com/what-we-do/devices-services/project-kuiper.

24. Sinduja Rangarajan, "Jesse Jackson Calls Out Silicon Valley 'Empty Promises' on Diversity," Reveal, April 6, 2018, https://revealnews.org/blog/jesse-jackson-calls-out-silicon-valley-empty-promises-on-diversity.

25. U.S. Equal Employment Opportunity Commission, "Diversity in High Tech," https://www.eeoc.gov/special-report/diversity-high-tech#.

26. Cozen O'Connor, "Republican and Democratic AGs Write Opposing Letters to *Fortune* 100 on DEI Programs," JDSupra, July 21, 2023, https://www.jdsupra.com/legalnews/republican-and-democratic-ags-write-8414662/.

27. John Hendel, "VA Asking California If Net Neutrality Law Will Snag Veterans' Health App," *Politico*, March 24, 2021, https://www.politico.com/states/california/story/2021/03/24/va-asking-california-if-net-neutrality-law-will-snag-veterans-health-app-1369440.

28. Matt Binder, "California's Net Neutrality Law Is a Reality; Here's What It Means," Mashable, February 25, 2021, https://mashable.com/article/california-net-neutrality-can-be-enforced.

29. Barbara van Schewick, "Setting the Record Straight: Carriers Can Help Veterans and Comply with California's Net Neutrality Law," Medium, March 25, 2021, https://schewick.medium.com/setting-the-record-straight-carriers-can-help-veterans-and-comply-with-californias-net-neutrality-b25fdd2fa1ff.

30. Nicol Turner-Lee, "New Internet Users and Online Privacy Perceptions," SSRN, March 31, 2012, https://ssrn.com/abstract=2032823.

31. Turner-Lee.

32. Julia Angwin, "Federal Privacy Law Has Momentum, but There's a Catch," Markup, July 30, 2022, https://themarkup.org/newsletter/hello-world/federal-privacy-law-has-momentum-but-theres-a-catch.

33. "Luján, Thune Announce Bipartisan Working Group on the Universal Service Fund and Broadband Access," lujan.senate.gov, May 11, 2023, https://www.lujan.senate.gov/newsroom/press-releases/lujan-thune-announce-bipartisan-working-group-on-the-universal-service-fund-and-broadband-access/.

9

Centering People and Their Communities

The chatter right now is on hardscaping by building more networks and creating more supply for high-speed broadband. Dr. Cathy Trimble— whom I met in Marion, Alabama, in 2019, and who has become a friend—is still struggling to realize her dream of full access for our students, wherever they are. Toward the latter part of April 2020, I emailed her to see how things were going with her students, teachers, and the iPad program. She immediately wrote me back:

> This digital divide is killing us. Currently, as you may know we are out of school and fortunately we do have the iPads that we gave our students, however, some of them do not have the Internet thus we could not go to all out digital education. Companies are offering [broadband] services to homes with school-aged students to help with this digital problem, but neither one of these carriers reach into our communities. Our library is closed in the town along with social distancing it puts our students at a disadvantage.

But the optimism in her that I saw during my trip to Marion was still there. She continued:

> But I am encouraged and determined to help everyone of them. I am working on a plan of action because although they are rural students they are just as important as anyone else. I actually was trying to be proactive and was working on a plan because I knew when this virus surfaced that we would not make the year out. Our superintendent told me he had a committee

working on it and it was going to be a model plan. I stopped and threw my plan in the garbage and then Monday he called a meeting to work on a plan which is okay as we are going to get it done.

Soon after receiving her email, I had the opportunity to speak with Alabama's school superintendent, who had tried to deploy Wi-Fi-enabled school buses in certain vulnerable areas of the town. But he soon discovered that transportation to the locations where the buses were parked was impossible for many of his isolated students. The state tried other things to support the transition to distance learning, but with the challenges of poverty and geographic isolation persisted throughout the COVID-19 pandemic, and nothing appeared to be working for the low-income Black students in Perry County. They were left invisible once again and put right back into the isolated bunkers that many individuals in the Deep South experience.

When I think about people like Dr. Trimble, I return to the reasons why some communities have uniquely survived ongoing digital depravities. It is people like her—and Janice Fleming, Elin Katz, Principal Woosley, Christopher Wood, Daphne Gooding, and others—who are steadfast within their local institutions and communities when everything else is shuttering around them before and after the pandemic. What you come to learn from listening to their stories are their strategies to accelerate internet access, empower local institutions, and contextualize support for their respective communities. You also come to realize that dogmatic policy debates are important, but they should be balanced relative to the needs of local communities. Chairwoman Rosenworcel reintroduced the prior net neutrality proceeding to, I assume, settle the score with the Trump agency appointee who rolled back the Obama administration's rules. All this was while still confronting the sad reality of millions of people still disconnected and struggling to maintain affordable broadband, as evidenced by the now more than 20 million households subscribed to a program that is entangled in congressional partisanship and could potentially end.

That is why, in addition to a more healthy and sustainable universal service program, it is imperative for the United States to codify into law and practice other activities that will withstand any type of political contentiousness. In areas that include education, and the workforce in particular, such leanings into more proactive and productive programs and measures will ensure more robust technology ecosystems across a wide range of spaces and places that are no longer easily subjected to the whims of historical patterns of racial discrimination and waning political will. In particular, I argue that no children or communities left offline and behind should be mantras for the next phases of work to ensure both universal access and digital equity, and that workers should not be left in limbo during digital progress to make the skills of certain workers more invisible and less useful to the twenty-first-century economy that we are creating.

No Child Left Offline

When President Biden made it to office, his administration and Congress acted swiftly to adopt measures to close the digital divide among schools and libraries as part of the American Rescue Plan.[1] In addition to the Emergency Broadband Benefit that predated the Affordable Connectivity Program (ACP), Congress also passed the Emergency Connectivity Fund, which was funded with $7.17 billion as part of the American Rescue Plan to help schools and libraries acquire Wi-Fi hot spots, modems, routers, and internet-enabled devices for students, staff, and library patrons. During the pandemic, states also worked independently of the federal government to address their respective digital needs ahead of the school year. For example, in Virginia and in the midst of inadequate school support, Governor Ralph Northam proposed $700 million in pandemic stimulus funding to deploy high-speed broadband to some of the poorest counties in the state.[2] Other states did the same thing.

During this period, individual school districts brokered their own deals with private telecom companies and some philanthropic organizations to spur low-cost broadband service options for their neediest students.[3] Miguel Cardona, Biden's secretary at the U.S. Department of Education (DOE), expressed concerns about remote learning, and instead advocating for students' full return to classrooms that eventually happened in the fall of 2022. Before that, however, the damage of unequal education had been done. In the early months of the pandemic, DOE reported on virtual education and found that the majority of fourth-grade students of color were remote-only; 68 percent of Asians, 58 percent of Blacks, and 56 percent of Hispanics chose this option, compared with only 27 percent of whites.[4] Differences in school attendance were partly attributed to their family's lack of trust in the handling of the public health crisis, and the disproportionate impact of the virus on communities of color, where the density of housing conditions and the likelihood of a parent as a frontline worker compounded student's school problems. In the early part of the pandemic, when people of color were hesitant to get vaccinated, DOE had no choice but to embrace remote learning—partly due to the pandemic, and partly since concurrently the world also became more remote and more disaggregated, forcing new educational pedagogies.

As was demonstrated in the cases of Marion and Phoenix, achieving educational parity among public school students has always been a challenge. In 2001 under the Bush administration, Congress passed the No Child Left Behind Act (NCLB) to respond to the failures of the educational system to realize equitable achievement among K-12 students.[5] It was an update to the Elementary and Secondary Education Act and was designed to ensure that all students—especially those from disadvantaged backgrounds—had access to special education services, supportive curricula, and accountable learning environments as measured by test scores, teacher evaluations, and professional development opportunities. In 2015, NCLB was replaced by the Every Student Succeeds Act (ESSA), which is the main law governing education in the United States.[6] Compared with the NCLB, ESSA promotes equal opportunities for students, and it appears to be more progressive than NCLB. But it still masks the long-standing history of discrimination in education since the *Brown v. Board of Education* case of 1954.[7]

The conditions of students without home broadband access or a device mirror the broad systemic inequalities of the United States, which is why Congress must do more than offering sporadic and piecemeal funding to K-12 schools, like ensuring hardware access and affordable monthly services. The current times necessitate the need for a comprehensive policy initiative, or perhaps an addendum to the ESSA, that guarantees institution-wide broadband access for improved educational outcomes and preparedness for the future demands of the twenty-first-century workforce.

When the United States prioritizes people in its effort to close the digital divide, it heavily invests in the nation's schools and students, which constitute our future labor force. A No Child Left Offline initiative could coordinate K-12 federal and state resources within school districts by collecting local and national school data on broadband connectivity and adding that information to national broadband maps for accurately tracking blind spots in connectivity for schools, libraries, and surrounding communities. For example, when I met with school administrators and teachers, many of them did not know which internet service providers were in their local footprint, partly because many teachers are not required to live where they teach. A good number of educators and administrators also did not know if their students had internet service at home.

In addition to school leaders surveying student households about their internet access, internet service providers also report the student enrollment data from their low-cost broadband programs because right now some of the data are redacted and not entirely public. No Child Left Offline could also require schools to gather information about home and community device availability and inquire about the need for extra assistance in paying for monthly. With respect for student privacy and anonymity, such data could be shared in aggregate to city, state, and federal officials to facilitate a more truthful dialogue on the granular accuracy of national broadband maps, especially those highlighting access near and around schools and the provision of more resources—whether through the expansion of the E-Rate program or via partnerships between industry-philanthropy and community institutions. Some school districts have started this process to improve their data collection, but this should become part of national standards and best practices.

No Child Left Offline could also commit to the automatic provision of internet-enabled hardware and software for home broadband service and devices for disadvantaged K-12 public school students. As a national imperative, the program could give eligible, disadvantaged students hardware, instructional software, and services (e.g., digital literacy training) for seamless transitions to remote learning while emboldening students for the new digital economy. These benefits would be available to students throughout the school year, and during the summer months, when students need refreshed learning. Whether through the redirection of E-Rate funds to the homes of eligible students or the consolidation of any remaining pandemic response funding, eligible K-12 students without a home broadband connection should have access to free, low-cost, or subsidized offerings, and devices as part of their school enrollment with the option of 12 months possession while enrolled in elementary to high school.

Despite the painful transition to remote learning for educators, working parents, and students, these new digital skills will foster independent learning, collaboration, and multimedia integration, among other competencies, which will prove invaluable to the economy. Educational institutions must continue to foster—not thwart—these activities as the nature of work changes from analog to hybrid or fully digital environments. Cathy and I appeared on the segment for *PBS News Hour* toward the end of 2020, and her comments during her part of the interview were enlightening: "But when you have students just going home [during the pandemic], and it's almost like they're going out of the light into the darkness, because what it does is, it prohibits them or blocks them off from the rest of the world. Without the internet [having a tablet], it was just like a book with no pages." Books without pages are like the analogy of broadband cemeteries that Leon Wilson shared when I visited Cleveland.

To ensure that we never encounter another pandemic, natural disaster, or school shooting that mandates school closures, districts should establish a dedicated Office of Innovation that is constantly promoting digital inclusion and equity at the local level. This is different from the technology departments at schools whose main duties are to fix laptops and desktops. Having leaders that understand technology's value in education and for long-term career development will help schools avoid failure at times when pedagogic traditions are shifting. In fact, school districts should establish an official, which Office of Innovation can facilitate more seamless technology transitions, and build partnerships. As a potential federal program, No Child Left Offline could also facilitate the effective marshaling of resources and programs for schools, students, and families, as well as hope for both communities and industries that we will, as a nation, be able to fulfill vacant roles and positions left empty due to the lack of well-educated and trained students on technology's advances.

In 2022, schools reopened, and pretty much every district made it to the end of the academic year. Yes, other issues awaited them, however—especially the mental exhaustion of teachers who had persevered through the remote learning period, and students whose mental acuities were fractured as they stayed locked in their rooms and glued to social media and other online platforms. My daughter recently shared her experience of succumbing to online pressures to fit the mold of girls she sees on social media. With high rates of teacher attrition, and some children in homes where both the mother, father, and/or another loved one was the casualty of a public health war, the processes associated with traditional learning and support for school-age children will need to be recalibrated. Further, the learning losses that primarily affected students of color, who, in some instances, were already behind in math, science, and reading.

I am personally learning that learning recovery is not easy, especially in math—somehow my daughter, who only physically attended her middle school for two months, must get back on track in high school due to missing Algebra I during the pandemic.

While many of us can pout about the inconvenience of having our children with us nonstop for almost two years, including summers, it was probably the first time for many of us to see and understand our own children—who, too, are invisible when adults decide their futures.

During the pandemic, we learned so much about our communities and our families while understanding the consequences of having a lingering digital divide. More important, we realized that having a laptop or tablet, along with seamlessly available and affordable internet access, is a necessity for our students to learn and do almost anything else but with some type of reasonable explanation. But if the states receiving the huge infusion of cash under the National Telecommunications and Information Administration (NTIA) do not prioritize support for our nation's schools and libraries, what have we really done about the digital divide to secure internet access and a laptop for, at most, the entire nine months of an academic year, along with zero-rated access to educational resources and the tutoring that they can access from their mobile phones. Right now, it is still too soon to see the results.

There is also some time at the time of this book's writing to assess the progress of the industry-led, low-cost broadband programs, and their public commitment to closing the digital divide—many of which are directed toward education. By 2023, many telecommunications had announced their programs:

—AT&T's $2 billion as part of their Bridge to Possibility program, which is focused on digital literacy training via free platforms and free equipment to partner organizations, above and beyond their role in the ACP's low-cost broadband offerings.[8]

—Verizon has committed $3 billion between 2020 and 2025 to digital inclusion programs for education, small businesses, and health care.[9]

—T-Mobile's Project $10 Million is directed at eradicating the homework gap through free service, hotspots, and reduced-cost devices to 10 million households over five years.[10]

—Charter Communications announced on May 16, 2023, that it would be adding $1 million to an existing $8 million to address digital divide issues, especially in the areas of broadband education, training, and technology devices.[11]

—Comcast Corporation pledged $1 billion over 10 years before the pandemic hit to create digital access for students in digital literacy training and equipment, and to additionally resource its existing Lift Zones, which aim to establish Wi-Fi-connected spaces in more than 1,000 community centers.[12]

The hope is that these programs, led by companies that are still paying the "telecommunications tax," will greatly benefit consumers from all economic strata, and will not be swayed by transitions of leadership or waning political interest—especially as the nation is on the heels of another major presidential election in 2024.

No Community Left Behind

I was deeply saddened when I heard that The Social, the ice cream shop in Marion, Alabama, with free Wi-Fi closed. The owner's enthusiasm was no match against the effects of a global pandemic that upended most small businesses, particularly those owned by women. But what if the country prioritized access among local gathering spots, and where people lived?

The lessons that I learned during my travels express why digital access must be easily available in our nation's housing developments. Students who reside in affordable housing require the same resources and capabilities as those from affluent backgrounds. The United States needs to ensure that every child who lives in federally assisted housing can engage new and existing technologies from where they live, at least in the moments when they are not deathly worried about being displaced by city mandates or rapid gentrification.

The country's schools, libraries, churches, community-based organizations, and small businesses filled the gaps when school and commercial buildings were closed across the United States. Organizations shared their Wi-Fi signals from parking stoops, building stairs, or tall stools—all while they struggled themselves to stay connected.

If the United States is going to make the digital divide about universal service and transcend the use of technology to address deeply entrenched social concerns, like meeting people in the places that have been redlined out of economic prosperity, then we will finally be correctly and appropriately addressing the problem. Supporting local institutions should be a no-brainer to a community's internet access. This is even more important for populations like seniors, who have been outsmarted by technologies that they do not know.

This is what should motivate policymakers and other investors in community assets to transform those physical parking lots of local libraries, fast food restaurants, churches, other community-based organizations where students attempted to get online for homework into dignified "digital or open access parks," with benches and tables for communal exchanges online and in person.[13]

It was unfortunate that many of the nontraditional anchor institutions, not supported by the E-Rate program, paid out of their own pockets and slim budgets to bolster their Wi-Fi signals without government funding.[14] They also managed to open their facilities and power on one or two accessible computers with the internet to help an individual schedule an appointment for a vaccination and map out the route on public transportation to the closest facility. Among housing authorities and their partners, they are still getting up to speed. I participated in a panel that right before us featured the deputy secretary at the U.S. Department of Housing and Urban Development (HUD), who shared that they had just started to work with the Federal Communications Commission on the ACP, and this was in the spring of 2023, before it became vulnerable.

In tandem with ensuring that No Child Is Left Offline, we should have a similar interest in promoting community connectivity with recommendations that encourage HUD and other federal agencies to make broadband access available, because public housing is where the nation's most vulnerable students and adults live. HUD can equip new and existing construction with broadband infrastructure and make free Wi-Fi openly available throughout its properties. In my opinion, the widespread availability of the internet in low-income housing may have facilitated universal access for millions of students during the pandemic. In this current age, we are requiring federal agencies to construct plans for cybersecurity, artificial intelligence, and other new innovations—what about having them establish plans on universal access to government services to ensure that no child or community is left offline in provisioning them.

As the recent infrastructure proposal under the Biden-Harris administration only contains references and no funding for "anchor institutions," those entities that directly supported schools and just about everybody within their reach should also be funded for their efforts to keep No Community Left Behind— a powerful and insightful framework for giving local institutions some agency over their role to support ubiquitous access. An initiative focused on more inclusive communities will result in more ready workforces, another suggestion to recalibrate our policy positions toward people. What a powerful statement from the current and future administrations to make this point a necessary caveat in how we administer government here.

No Worker Left Invisible

Well-connected students ultimately result in better trained labor to engineer and maintain the burgeoning digital economy. In 2024, and going into 2025, all fifty states, the District Columbia, Puerto Rico, and sovereign Tribal lands will have received some portion of their average $100 million allotment toward high-speed broadband service. Alongside the infrastructure investments, the Biden-Harris administration also promised to create hundreds of thousands of high-quality jobs—particularly those that were blue-collar, in technology development, semi-conductor production, and advanced manufacturing. Before this announcement, industry associations had already anticipated the creation of 850,000 new jobs in broadband sectors through 2024.[15]

In 2022, Commerce Secretary Gina Raimondo predicted that the Infrastructure Investment and Jobs Act's $65 billion in funding for broadband alone would create between 100,000 and 200,000 new jobs.[16] During the early part of 2023, I hosted an event on what these new jobs for vulnerable workers in the broadband sector looked like, and one of the panelists predicted an increase in about 70,000 construction jobs alone—50 percent at job sites, 40 percent in manufacturing, and 10 percent in design. Added to the projections was a recent report from the Government Accountability Office that believes the Broadband Equity, Access, and Deployment (BEAD) program alone could create 23,000 new jobs just for skilled telecom workers.[17]

But with such a serious digital divide and these many jobs being created that outpace the existing available workforce, the United States must establish digital equity goals that fill worker shortages. Expanding broadband deployment will clearly require more workers in a wide variety of professions at every level of broadband deployment and maintenance: telecom workers, iron workers, skilled manufacturers, customer service agents, and even arborists.[18] Removing obstacles to these jobs and guaranteeing robust employee protections will be crucial not only for increasing equity in the labor market but also for meeting the surge in demand in the first place. Further, avoiding a labor shortage will be essential to deliver the promises of the NTIA's BEAD program, and the Infrastructure Investment and Jobs Act more broadly. On top of this planning, migrating displaced workers from other related industries, like general construction, may help, provided they are nearing the age of retirement, much as in the manufacturing sector.

The absence of standardized broadband job descriptions, workplace and wage protections, and representation of marginalized groups in the workforce are also open items that we need to tick off the list of labor force preparation and replenishment. For two years leading up to the first allocation of federal monies, I wrote with my colleagues about the deficiency of data regarding broadband jobs and the need for better taxonomies of skills and opportunities in broadband occupations. While there is a likelihood, given the urgency of expending funds in a short period of time for the Biden-Harris administration, that more of these jobs will be outsourced to temporary contractors, wage theft and protection will be difficult to manage under known practices of "layering"—where subcontractors hire subcontractors of their own.

The bottom line is that workforce development in the broadband sector and related industries is a fundamental component of digital equity. Referring to Biden's infrastructure plans, Lucy Moore, special policy adviser at the NTIA, stated: "Workforce development and job training in support of the infrastructure workforce is an eligible use of [BEAD] program funding," and the BEAD Notice of Funding Opportunity directs states to prioritize applications from operators who "commit to advancing equitable workforce development and job quality objectives."[19] Again, it is too early to tell if states, particularly the red ones that were opposed to the government's grand spending, will comply with these priorities and work in close partnership with employers to ensure that they are met.

But any federal investment in broadband, and technology more generally, must create unprecedented opportunities for full-time, high-quality jobs—including for workers without advanced degrees—while improving diversity in the broadband workforce. Thus, prioritizing people means taking whole-sector approaches, with state governments, employers, and unions working in concert to engage sidelined workers, develop better taxonomies for existing and emerging jobs, and strengthen social infrastructure to reduce barriers to entry for excluded groups. There also needs to be an aggregation of resources from federal, state, and local governments, philanthropy, and community-directed resources, including those apportioned from banks for the Community Reinvestment Act (CRA), which as a federal law requires commercial banks and savings associations to direct funds to low- and moderate-income communities. On the CRA, Jordana Barton, a community development banker and now senior adviser to the Federal Reserve Bank of Dallas, called for a proposed rule change to allow funds to be directed to digital inclusion activities, including training, workforce, and specific programs like health equity.[20] In 2016, she was perhaps the first person to get high-speed broadband recognized as an infrastructure asset, comparable to water, electricity, and transit systems—years before it became a federal concern.

Getting people immediately into the workforce without any type of social support or social infrastructure is a definite anomaly for low-skilled workers. It is a promise that could never be met because among displaced, dislocated, and de-skilled prospective employees is the need for more help. Right now, there is a short list of ways to enter the broadband sector, including through the National Registered Apprenticeship Program of the Department of Labor, or industry certification in computer refurbishing or network security. There are also levels of opportunities that can support the transformational build out of high-speed broadband networks, and one of these is related to the establishment of trusted digital ambassadors.

In the mid-2000s, when I worked at One Economy, the Digital Connectors program was our opportunity to manage future workforce expectations. High school students who were part of the program helped their neighbors with digital literacy training and were involved in community-wide programs to distribute hardware and other related resources. In the early days, we primarily deployed the program within public and affordable housing and rewarded the students at the end of the year with a personal laptop. Later, some of the Digital Connectors went to work in their local communities.

The idea of having digital navigators has recently resurfaced as part of the lofty broadband goals of the Biden administration. But it is not funded or supported by federal dollars. Instead, the National Digital Inclusion Alliance (NDIA), the nongovernmental entity where Bill Callahan still works, received a $10 million grant from Google.org to establish the National Digital Navigators Corps. This was the largest grant that the nonprofit organization ever received, and in fiscal year 2022, eighteen grant recipient organizations received program funding:[21] the Alaska Federation of Natives; Cayuse Native Solutions, Inc.; Cherokee Nation; Community Broadband Action Network Corporation (Iowa); Community Service Programs of West Alabama, Inc.; Computer Reach (Pennsylvania); Easter Seals of Greater Houston; Forest County Broadband Committee (serving Tribal communities); Gila River Broadcasting Corporation: Digital Connect Initiative (Arizona, serving Tribal); Hocking Athens Perry Community Action (Ohio); Hoopa Valley Public Utilities District (Tribal-led); Lummi Indian Business Council; National Digital Equity Center (Maine, serving Tribal); Northwestern Ohio Community Action Commission; Pottsboro Area Public Library (Texas); Pueblo of Jemez (New Mexico, serving tribal); Shaping our Appalachian Region, Inc. (Kentucky); and Washington State University Extension Grays, Harbor County (Washington State, serving Tribal). With the majority of regrants going to Tribal-led, or Tribal-serving, organizations, the goal of the Digital Navigators program is to create a replicable framework for entities already providing digital inclusion services, or for those entering the digital inclusion space to ensure that their constituents can connect with them online.[22] Grants to these organizations will total $6.6 million and be available for over two-and-one-half year periods, and will provide between $320,000 and $400,000 per organization.

The NDIA was founded by Angela Siefer, who was a former employee at the NTIA when I first met her in the mid-2000s. Under her leadership, the organization has coordinated more than 850 digital inclusion practitioners, and it advocates for broadband access, tech devices, digital skills training, and tech support. While the Digital Navigators program has acquired overwhelming support as well as resources, and managed to make digital equity about public service, the longer-term sustainability of such efforts will be determined by a political willingness to codify, again, how we support the universal service and care of certain communities. If I had a crystal ball—which I probably do have somewhere in my attic—I would transition the Digital Navigators to an official Digital Service Corps to ensure greater sustainability and funding.

A New Digital Service Corps

For the last two years, I have proposed a new Digital Service Corps, one that would be under the purview of the U.S. Corporation for National Service, which is the federal agency that leads service, volunteering, and grant-making efforts in the country. The last major update of the program was in September 1993, when President Clinton signed the National and Community Service Trust Act, which brought the Northwest Tower computer lab, Simeon, our Americorps VISTA. Between 1997 and 1998, more than 40,000 individuals were part of the Americorps program, with approximately 15,000 of them enrolled in the Education Awards program to get help with expenses. These formally placed volunteers serve in thousands of settings, including nonprofits, the public sector, local government, colleges and universities, Tribal communities, and faith-based organizations conducting various useful tasks, from teaching, building, and supporting existing and forthcoming programmatic activities.

As part of the existing Biden-Harris broadband investment, $2.75 billion has been allocated as part of the Digital Equity Act, which established three grant programs to promote digital equity and inclusion, like skills training for all ages and communities, and other activities that support technology adoption. In March 2023, the NTIA issued a request for comment on what types of projects should be funded to ensure that "everyone in America has the digital skills and devices they need to realize the full potential of high-speed internet access."[23] Clearly, the resources from the federal government are no match to the $10 million that Google provided to NDIA, but it is worth making digital public service in local communities a mandate that is part of the country's quest for widespread technology adoption and use. CRA funds could be leveraged to support community-building efforts, provided that the Federal Reserve permits such activities uniformly across its entities.

For years, the United States has had various public service initiatives to better integrate technology expertise into federal agencies. A recent example of this is the U.S. Digital Corps, which is a two-year fellowship program for early-career technologists who can work within any participating agency to leverage their skills in software engineering, data science, product management, design, and cybersecurity. The goal of the program is focused on skills transfer, with some hope of recruitment and retention in the federal government. The program is managed by the General Services Administration, which is a likely bedfellow because it supports the integration of technology into the government's daily performance and operation. Other programs, including the Presidential Innovation Fellows and, external to government, Code for America, work to bridge the gaps in skills and employment related to technology implementation and use.

Within the U.S. Corporation for National Service, there ought to be a national Digital Service Corps, perhaps an expanded component of the Americorps VISTA program, where the focus is building local capacities to help residents not only gain basic literacy training but, more important, the navigational skills required to counter economic and social barriers to entering our increasingly digital society. During the pandemic, a bipartisan group of legislators—including sponsoring senators Chris Coons (D-DE) and Roger Wicker (R-MS) and twelve other legislators—signed the CORPS Act (Cultivating Opportunity and Response to the Pandemic through Service Act), which was designed to support an expanded Ameri-Corps–AmeriCorps Seniors for all types of pandemic-related community supports by working in nonprofit organizations.

In 2021, Biden also increased the national service budget by $1 billion to drive transformational change in this area, a move lauded by the nonprofit group Voices for National Service after the bill's adoption.[24] It was also the first time that the volunteer program received a raise since 1994. If the United States is really focused on closing the digital divide, funding a more permanent Digital Service Corps would be a way to support many of the people and communities highlighted in this book, from walking them through sophisticated government websites to helping them transition their largely analog businesses to digital.

When I was in Cleveland, I met a barbershop owner, with whom I spoke to for many hours. He was interesting because at every juncture where I asked about his online use, he pushed back by suggesting the deterioration of communities with the explosion of new technologies. As I mentioned, this conversation lasted for hours, until I inquired about how his clients pay for his services, and he quickly mentioned CashApp, which he swore was not part of the internet as we know it. But over the course of the pandemic, he must have struggled to keep his physical doors open. If we had a Digital Service Corps, we could have helped him to understand what was needed to thrive in a digital economy as an entrepreneur, and within his particular ecosystem.

A Digital Service Corps could include members of the community, who can help answer questions, and figure out what solutions work best for the communities where they live and work. These same service corps members can also learn skills in the meantime that make them more competitively aligned with the goals of a growing digital economy, including new forms of artificial intelligence that can have detrimental effects on communities of color through widespread disinformation. Some members of the Digital Service Corps may find themselves interested in the more blue-collar jobs in the sector and could transition into National Registered Apprenticeships that bring both good jobs and competitive wages to workers, others who have been able to experience why connecting their communities to broadband matters may be enticed to pursue higher education, especially given the educational rewards offered at the end of the annual year of service. They could opt to become a sociologist like me, who through on-the-ground experiences fell in love with community technology.

Biden closely suggests something similar in his work when he compares his goals for a reinvigorated America with those of President Franklin Delano Roosevelt after the Great Depression. But Roosevelt's New Deal was not designed to be inclusive and resulted in deepening racial inequality, whose remnants are still experienced by Black people and their communities.

Not Another New Deal

We do not really need another New Deal. For example, President Roosevelt's establishment of the Civilian Conservation Corps (CCC) was the part of his New Deal federal programs that encouraged paid service for the good of the United States after a devastating economic depression. But the CCC, despite providing jobs to hundreds of thousands of unemployed men, barely enrolled any Black men in its first year, 1933. Responsibility for recruitment was delegated to state and local government officials, who often systematically excluded Black men, especially in the South. After lobbying by what was called the Black Cabinet—the popular name for the Federal Council of Negro Affairs, founded by Mary McLeod Bethune—and civil rights organizations,[25] the CCC expanded its recruitment of Black men, and 200,000 black men participated by 1940. However, the CCC also instituted a policy of official segregation, housing Black men in segregated dormitories and barred them from most administrative positions.[26] This example is illustrative of the experience of the Black Cabinet, which pressured New Deal programs to address racial bias and won meaningful victories without addressing the nation's systemic racial inequalities.

More explicit racial discrimination during the execution of the New Deal was evident when Black workers were denied participation in social security. When enacted, the Social Security Act excluded farmers and domestic workers—87 percent of all black women and 55 percent of all black workers—and was not broadened until the 1950s.[27] The Tennessee Valley Authority (TVA), which focused on the economic uplift of the Tennessee Valley region, provided cash settlements to farm owners whose land was submerged when the TVA flooded 730,000 acres, but the TVA provided no reparations to tenant farmers, many of whom were Black.[28]

Some scholars, like Adolph Reed Jr., a professor emeritus of political science at the University of Pennsylvania who is Black, have defended the legacy of the New Deal in their research, pointing to the ways in which many Black Americans were able to benefit from New Deal programs. He notes that the percentage of Black workers in the Works Progress Administration (WPA) and the CCC were higher than the Black percentage of the population. He also points out that the Public Works Administration (PWA) established quotas to ensure Black workers were hired, and that by 1936 Black workers were more than 30 percent of the PWA's payroll and more than 15 percent of skilled workers in the program.

But there is a lot to unpack in the New Deal, which is why it is not a good comparison to what we are trying to do now with national infrastructure. Inherent in the Roosevelt administration's federal programs and practices was a dismissal of the importance of equity, which would be entrenched in systems of inequality in the following decades. For example, the Black percentage of the WPA and CCC workforces, though greater than the Black percentage of the total population, was smaller than the Black percentage of those in greatest need of work. While many New Deal programs simply failed to address systemic racial inequality, it was the effects of resulting and remaining policies, including the Home Owners' Loan Corporation and the Federal Housing Authority programs that have led to deliberate redlining and devastating effects on Black families' ability to accrue wealth and economic stability. As was noted in previous chapters, these agencies expanded home buying opportunities for white Americans but, as a deliberate matter of policy, refused to underwrite loans for homes in Black neighborhoods through the practices of redlining.[29] The combined effects of these New Deal policies have exacerbated the African American wealth gap, which is just 5 percent of white wealth.[30]

In a 2021 op-ed in Bloomberg, right before the full passage of the Bipartisan Infrastructure Law, Willow Lung-Amam wrote: "For Black Americans, the New Deal left an ambivalent legacy that does not offer an easy template for change."[31] President Biden's gestures to the New Deal as inspiration for his own agenda is both encouraging and troubling. While he aims to be transformational in his economic policies, he cannot make the mistakes of Roosevelt's New Deal and steer clear of its reference because it reeks of inequality.

At the onset of the pandemic, I, too, was excited about this idea of New Deal paradigms and nostalgia until Representative James Clyburn, who has long represented South Carolina, where most of the slaves were transported from West Africa, shared on a podcast that I host, "Roosevelt wasn't concerned about racial equity. It took Lyndon B. Johnson to correct his wrongs."

While Biden, who is a close friend of Clyburn, is not seen in the same vein as one of the good old boys in the Confederate network, it is best that, working alongside the first Black woman vice president, he engineers new frameworks and priorities when it comes to making racial equity a huge part of his massive broadband spending. Moreover, closing the digital divide is not a New Deal, as Biden and others have suggested. It is a transformative and crucial deal because people have been erased and made to be increasingly invisible as analog systems have dissolved.

There is also this perverse reference to broadband as the new rural electrification moment, returning to Roosevelt's New Deal again as he responded to the disadvantages experienced by rural residents without practical and more innovative electrical systems. Coined as the electrical divide, the differences between rural and urban areas when it came to power was significant, and in the 1930s, promoting this modernization became part of Roosevelt's presidential campaign. What was becoming known was that electricity fueled efficiencies, and it allowed farmers to stay on family farms, much like what Jon Yoder wanted to do in Garrett County. But when it came down to building and expanding rural electricity, Black populations were cut out from those jobs—largely because they lived in urban areas. Some other interesting activities emerged as rural America became electrified; for example, the Rural Electrification Administration, established by Roosevelt as the primary agency responsible for the initiative, hired a bunch of advisers to go around the country staging "electric circus" tours, where they touted the importance of the improvements.

I now see why the Biden administration has taken on this history to drive its own goals for broadband. Sparsely populated rural areas were largely abandoned by existing utility companies in the 1930s, and consequently, farmers were being left behind to acquire the basic qualities of life, including efficiencies with everything from production to household chores.

And with the Rural Electrification Administration repurposed into the Rural Utilities Services, we see large sums allocated to rural areas. These investments will continue for the duration of existing Universal Service Fund programs, except for Lifeline and E-Rate, which can be provisioned just about anywhere.

This is not about a New Deal for broadband and other infrastructure, but rather a path toward a more just and equitable digital society that will benefit everyone and every community—not just rural but also urban and suburban, as well as tribal lands. To elevate those who have been traditionally exploited and passed over by government, industry, and some civil society organizations, there is no other way but to see the problem of twenty-first-century broadband as everybody's issue, including the Big Tech companies that are fairly recent to the problem but are equally responsible for its existence.

But this will not happen until conversations about the digital divide shift from focusing on networks to focusing on the people and their communities that are being made invisible by existing and emerging technologies—making it a conversation about race, place, and space, especially those that are the remnants of racialization and discrimination. That is, until those working to redress the lack of internet access among people of color and other vulnerable groups acknowledge such realities, the outcomes will continue to devalue the worth and residence of millions of Americans, while piercing their capacities to thrive in our global economy. Closing the digital divide is about unleashing our full potential as a nation to democratize technology in ways that embolden participation among individuals and their communities.

Notes

1. White House, "President Biden Announces American Rescue Plan," January 20, 2021, https://www.whitehouse.gov/briefing-room/legislation/2021/01/20/president-biden-announces-american-rescue-plan/.
2. Tyler Arnold, "Northam Proposes $700 Million in Federal Money for Virginia Broadband 'The Center Square,'" July 19, 2021, https://www.thecentersquare.com/virginia/northam-proposes-700-million-in-federal-money-for-virginia-broadband/article_00de7cec-e8c8-11eb-8449-5fa1d1d41a7d.html.

3. Benjamin Herold, "Millions of Students Got Free Home Internet for Remote Learning; How Long Will It Last?" *EducationWeek*, March 10, 2021, https://www.edweek.org/technology/millions-of-students-got-free-home-internet-for-remote-learning-how-long-will-it-last/2021/03.

4. U.S. Department of Education, Office for Civil Rights, *Education in a Pandemic: The Disparate Impacts of COVID-19 on America's Students*, June 9, 2021, https://www2.ed.gov/about/offices/list/ocr/docs/20210608-impacts-of-covid19.pdf.

5. U.S. Department of Education, "No Child Left Behind," https://www2.ed.gov/nclb/landing.jhtml.

6. U.S. Department of Education.

7. *Brown v. Board of Education*, National Archives, https://www.archives.gov/education/lessons/brown-v-board.

8. AT&T, "Digital Divide," https://about.att.com/pages/digital-divide.

9. Rich Young, "The Facts on Verizon's Broadband Deployment," Verizon, January 20, 2023, https://www.verizon.com/about/news/facts-verizons-broadband-deployment.

10. Kiesha Taylor, "It's Time to Close the Digital Divide," T-Mobile, May 22, 2020, https://www.t-mobile.com/business/resources/articles/bridge-the-digital-divide.

11. Charter Communications, "Charter Commits $1 Million to 2023 Spectrum Digital Education Program, Raising Total Investment to $9 Million," press release, May 16, 2023, https://corporate.charter.com/newsroom/charter-commits-1-million-to-digital-education-program-in-2023.

12. Linda Hardesty, "Comcast Pledges $1B Over 10 Years to Close Digital Divide," Fierce Telecom, March 24, 2021, https://www.fiercetelecom.com/operators/comcast-pledges-1b-over-10-years-to-close-digital-divide.

13. Cecilia Kang, "Parking Lots Have Become a Digital Lifeline," *New York Times*, May 5, 2020, https://www.nytimes.com/2020/05/05/technology/parking-lots-wifi-coronavirus.html.

14. Ali Tadayon and Sydney Johnson, "California Schools Build Local Wireless Networks to Bridge Digital Divide," *EdSource*, January 4, 2021, https://edsource.org/2021/california-schools-build-community-wireless-networks-to-bridge-digital-divide/645919.

15. Scott Jensen, Kelly Rogers, and Kate Finnerty, "Key Steps in Creating a Diverse Broadband Workforce," *Route Fifty*, March 28, 2023, https://www.route-fifty.com/management/2023/03/key-steps-creating-diverse-broadband-workforce/384537/.

16. Diana Goovaerts, "Commerce Chief: $65B in Broadband Funding Will Create 200,000 Jobs," Fierce Telecom, February 1, 2023, https://www.fiercetelecom.com/broadband/commerce-chief-65b-broadband-funding-will-create-200000-jobs.

17. U.S. Government Accountability Office, "Telecommunications Workforce: Additional Workers Will Be Needed to Deploy Broadband, but Concerns Exist About Availability," December 15, 2022, https://www.gao.gov/products/gao-23-105626.

18. Chris Teale, "'Whole Nation' Effort Needed to Build Broadband Workforce," *GCN*, February 13, 2023, https://gcn.com/cloud-infrastructure/2023/02/whole-nation-effort-needed-build-broadband-workforce/382886/.

19. Applying BEAD Monies to Workforce Development," *Optics*, December 8, 2022, https://optics.fiberbroadband.org/Full-Article/applying-bead-monies-to-workforce-development-1.

20. Federal Reserve Bank of Dallas, "Closing the Digital Divide: A Framework for Meeting CRA Obligations," July 2016 (revised December 2016), https://www.dallasfed.org/-/media/Documents/cd/pubs/digitaldivide.pdf.

21. Yvette Scorse, "NDIA Awards 18 National Digital Navigator Corps Grants in Rural & Tribal Areas," *NDIA*, September 7, 2022, https://www.digitalinclusion.org/blog/2022/09/07/ndia-awards-18-national-digital-navigator-corps-grants-in-rural-tribal-areas/.

22. Scorse.
23. "Biden-Harris Administration Requests Input on Upcoming Digital Equity Programs," NTIA BroadbandUSA, March 1, 2023, https://broadbandusa.ntia.doc.gov/news/latest-news/biden-harris-administration-requests-input-upcoming-digital-equity-programs.
24. Annmaura Connolly and Rye Barcott, "National Service Is a Bipartisan Priority," *The Hill*, June 23, 2021, https://voicesforservice.org/news/voices-blog/national-service-is-a-bipartisan-priority/.
25. Mary-Elizabeth B. Murphy, "African Americans in the Great Depression and New Deal," *Oxford Research Encyclopedias: American History*, November 19, 2020, https://oxfordre.com/americanhistory/display/10.1093/acrefore/9780199329175.001.0001/acrefore-9780199329175-e-632;jsessionid=897C7418627363E4555932A11FE10193.
26. Sam Wotipka, "How Racism Reshaped the Civilian Conservation Corps," *Crosscut*, March 29, 2023, https://crosscut.com/equity/2023/03/how-racism-reshaped-civilian-conservation-corps.
27. Murphy, "African Americans."
28. Jim Powell, "Why Did FDR's New Deal Harm Blacks?" Cato Institute, December 3, 2003, https://www.cato.org/commentary/why-did-fdrs-new-deal-harm-blacks.
29. Terry Gross, "A 'Forgotten History' of How the U.S. Government Segregated America," NPR, May 3, 2017, https://www.npr.org/2017/05/03/526655831/a-forgotten-history-of-how-the-u-s-government-segregated-america.
30. Gross.
31. Willow Lung-Aman, "The Next New Deal Must Be for Black Americans, Too," Bloomberg, January 18, 2021, https://www.bloomberg.com/news/articles/2021-01-18/the-next-new-deal-must-be-for-black-americans-too.

Postscript

When I started in community technology, both of my children were not even conceived even in my thoughts because I was a young graduate student fresh out of college. Today, my oldest is almost twenty-two years old, and my youngest is nearing eighteen. During their lifetimes, they have watched me evolve from "computer lady" to a scholar and activist focused on addressing the digital divide and promoting more equity in a space that has been recently filled by newly minted state broadband leaders and other appointed officials. Throughout my lifetime, I have witnessed firsthand how important it is to be connected—from the early interactions at Northwest Tower to watching my own two children confined to computer screens for over two years after the onset of the COVID-19 pandemic.

Writing this book was not easy. Before the tour, I had to figure out how to finance the trips to various cities, and my curiosities were overwhelming because I spoke to just about everybody I met—even when I was not actively working on the book. I also realized, as part of the research, that there is still much more to be discovered in this space. For example, I tried to visit a couple of Indigenous, Tribal communities, but the timing was not right before the pandemic, and as the country resettled, I was deep into the writing process. I also hoped to explore further the experiences of Asian American Pacific Islander populations where class, generational order, and country of origin are significantly linked to socioeconomic outcomes. In fact, my friend and civil rights compadre, John Yang, who leads Asian Americans Advancing Justice, helped me to shape the concept of a first-class, digital resident to avoid the explosive rhetoric of citizenship in the United States. In the future, I owe it to him and the Asian American Pacific Islander community to dive deeper and make more visible their experiences, and those of Indigenous communities, as a researcher.

Clearly, a book of this scope has no ending, which encourages me to continue my field studies.

In the three decades of working, living, and loving so many people in this space, progress has, indeed, been made. The tremendous federal investments in high-speed broadband by the Biden-Harris administration do give me hope that something good will come out of that—especially the heightened attention to a topic that has been festering for decades. I sometimes share with people that before the pandemic, studying the digital divide was like being at a high school prom where no one asked you to dance. Because of the global pandemic, I have suddenly become the life of the party, which does have repercussions, including very long nights and changed arguments with the moving parts from government, industry, the academy, and civil society groups. On top of these commitments are my continued workload as a policy influencer, and dedication to my family, who are the utmost reason why I do this work.

I am realistic that, in the months leading up to the next presidential election, the pendulum can switch and the quietude that once overshadowed the dire urgency to bring parity and equity to our nation's communications ecosystem is always possible.

We ought to proceed in this modern-day digital race by turning the page to a new history that pulls away from nostalgic references to acting upon ubiquitous access to the internet but with some variation in the narrative. The new demons to be faced are completely permissionless and unbounded technologies without regulatory restrictions. Artificial intelligence will constitute our next digital divide, which is frankly why the United States must get this one right at some point— even if that means starting with some hard and truthful conversations on why it has taken so long to make such efforts domestic and international priorities. Just like Ralph Ellison's protagonist, the invisible man, who fell into the bunker and used the time to build up his courage, there are many people like him who are ready to exercise their agency over digital disparities in the places where they live, and the spaces where they find safety and comfort. It is time that we make them part of the broader conversations about their futures both online and in before we are back at the same starting point once again.

Bibliography

Abdullah, Khalil. "Google's Broadband War Redlining Black Communities." *Philadelphia Tribune*, January 6, 2017. https://www.phillytrib.com/commentary/googles-broadband-war-redlining-black-communities/article_78510d50-d377-59ef-8032-2db568d647c4.html.

"Alabama State Department of Education." Alabama Department of Education, 2019. http://reportcard.alsde.edu/Alsde/OverallScorePage?schoolcode=0000&systemcode=000&year=2019.

Alexander, Michelle. *The New Jim Crow: Mass Incarceration in the Age of Colorblindness.* New York: New Press, 2012.

Ali, Christopher. "Opinion: We Need a National Rural Broadband Plan." *New York Times*, February 7, 2019. https://www.nytimes.com/2019/02/06/opinion/rural-broadband-fcc.html.

"Amendment of Part 15 Rules for Unlicensed White Spaces Devices." Federal Communications Commission, March 20, 2019. https://www.fcc.gov/document/amendment-part-15-rules-unlicensed-white-spaces-devices.

Anderson, Monica. "Racial and Ethnic Differences in How People Use Mobile Technology." Pew Research Center FactTank (blog), April 30, 2015. https://pewresearch-org-preprod.go-vip.co/fact-tank/2015/04/30/racial-and-ethnic-differences-in-how-people-use-mobile-technology/.

Anderson, Monica, and Andrew Perrin. "Nearly One-In-Five Teens Can't Always Finish Their Homework Because of the Digital Divide." Pew Research Center FactTank (blog), October 26, 2018. www.pewresearch.org/short-reads/2018/10/26/nearly-one-in-five-teens-cant-always-finish-their-homework-because-of-the-digital-divide/.

Angwin, Julia. "Federal Privacy Law Has Momentum, But There's a Catch." *The Markup*, July 30, 2022. https://themarkup.org/newsletter/hello-world/federal-privacy-law-has-momentum-but-theres-a-catch.

"Applying BEAD Monies to Workforce Development." *Optics*, December 8, 2022. https://optics.fiberbroadband.org/Full-Article/applying-bead-monies-to-workforce-development-1.

Arnold, Tyler. "Northam Proposes $700 Million in Federal Money for Virginia Broadband 'The Center Square,'" July 19, 2021. https://www.thecentersquare.com/virginia/northam-proposes-700-million-in-federal-money-for-virginia-broadband/article_00de7cec-e8c8-11eb-8449-5fa1d1d41a7d.html.

Baldwin, James. *The Fire Next Time.* New York: Dial Press, 1962.

Barton, Jill. "Suit Against AT&T Alleges Broadband Discrimination." *Government Technology*, July 27, 2010. https://www.govtech.com/archive/suit-against-att-alleges-broadband-discrimination.html.

Barwick, Ryan. "Millions Could Lose Low-Cost Phone Service under FCC Reforms." Center for Public Integrity, September 4, 2018. https://publicintegrity.org/inequality-poverty-opportunity/millions-could-lose-low-cost-phone-service-under-fcc-reforms/.

Becker, Samantha, Michael D. Crandall, Karen E. Fisher, Bo Kinney, Carol Landry, and Anita Rocha. "Opportunity for All: How the American Public Benefits from Internet Access at U.S. Libraries." Institute of Museum and Library Services, January 3, 2010. https://www.imls.gov/sites/default/files/publications/documents/opportunityforall_0.pdf.

Beltran, Daniel O., Kuntal K. Das, and Robert W. Fairlie. "Home Computers and Educational Outcomes: Evidence from the NLSY97 and CPS." International Finance Discussion Paper 958, November 2018.

Benjamin, Ruha. *Race After Technology* (Cambridge: Polity, 2019).

Bennett, Jared, and Ashley Wong. "Under Trump, Millions of Poor Lose Access to Cellphone Service." *USA Today*, November 5, 2019. https://www.usatoday.com/story/news/investigations/2019/11/05/under-trump-millions-poor-lose-cellphone-service/2482112001/.

Bianchi, Tiago. "Google: Annual Advertising Revenue 2001–2022." Statista, February 24, 2023. https://www.statista.com/statistics/266249/advertising-revenue-of-google/.

———. "Google: Quarterly Revenue 2008–2023." Statista, May 10, 2023. https://www.statista.com/statistics/267606/quarterly-revenue-of-google/.

Biden, Joe. "Remarks by President Biden on Broadband Investments." White House, June 26, 2023. https://www.whitehouse.gov/briefing-room/speeches-remarks/2023/06/26/remarks-by-president-biden-on-broadband-investments/.

"Biden-Harris Administration Requests Input on Upcoming Digital Equity Programs." NTIA BroadbandUSA, March 1, 2023. https://broadbandusa.ntia.doc.gov/news/latest-news/biden-harris-administration-requests-input-upcoming-digital-equity-programs.

Binder, Matt. "California's Net Neutrality Law Is a Reality; Here's What It Means." *Mashable*, February 25, 2021. https://mashable.com/article/california-net-neutrality-can-be-enforced.

Breidenbach, Michelle. "Syracuse Embarks on $800 Million Plan to End Public Housing as We Know It." Syracuse.com, January 18, 2022. https://www.syracuse.com/news/2022/01/syracuse-embarks-on-800-million-plan-to-end-public-housing-as-we-know-it.html.

Broadband Breakfast. "Broadband Roundup: FCC Announces More Rural Funding, Everyone On Expands Footprint, U.S. Telecom Gets Political." September 12, 2019. https://broadbandbreakfast.com/2019/09/broadband-roundup-fcc-announces-more-rural-funding-everyone-on-expands-footprint-us-telecom-gets-political/.

"Broadband in Garrett County: A Strategy for Expansion and Adoption." Columbia Telecommunications Corporation, May 1, 2012. https://www.garrettcounty.org/resources/broadband/pdf/Broadband-Feasibility-Study.pdf.

Brodkin, Jon. "Verizon Wiring Up 500k Homes with FiOS to Settle Years-Long Fight with NYC." *ArsTechnica*, November 30, 2020. https://arstechnica.com/tech-policy/2020/11/verizon-wiring-up-500k-homes-with-fios-to-settle-years-long-fight-with-nyc/.

Brooks, Khristopher J. "40% of Black-Owned Businesses Not Expected to Survive Coronavirus." CBS News, June 22, 2020. https://www.cbsnews.com/news/black-owned-busines-close-thousands-coronavirus-pandemic/.

"*Brown v. Board of Education*." National Archives. https://www.archives.gov/education/lessons/brown-v-board.

Busby, John, Julia Tanberk, and Tyler Cooper. "BroadbandNow Estimates Availability for All 50 States; Confirms That More Than 42 Million Americans Do Not Have Access to

Broadband." *Broadband Now*, May 5, 2021. https://broadbandnow.com/research/fcc-broadband-overreporting-by-state.

CBR staff writer. "U.S. Senators and One Economy Launch Public Internet Channel." *Tech Monitor*, June 11, 2006. https://techmonitor.ai/technology/us_senators_and_one_economy_launch_public_internet_channel.

CEDC Working Groups. "Recommendations and Best Practices to Prevent Digital Discrimination and Promote Digital Equity." November 7, 2022. https://www.fcc.gov/sites/default/files/cedc-digital-discrimination-report-110722.pdf.

"Census Profile: Syracuse, NY." *Census Reporter*. http://censusreporter.org/profiles/16000US3673000-syracuse-ny/.

Central New York Community Foundation. "How the History of Redlining and I-81 Contributed to Syracuse Poverty: CNY Vitals." May 18, 2018. https://cnyvitals.org/how-the-history-of-redlining-and-i-81-contributed-to-syracuse-poverty/.

Chakravoti, Bhaskar. "How to Close the Digital Divide in the U.S." *Harvard Business Review*, July 20, 2021. https://hbr.org/2021/07/how-to-close-the-digital-divide-in-the-u-s.

Chandra, S., A. Chang, L. Day, A. Fazlullah, J. Liu, L. McBride, T. Mudalige, and D. Weiss. *Closing the K-12 Digital Diver in the Age of Distance Learning*. San Francisco: Common Sense Media; and Boston: Boston Consulting Group, 2020.

"Charter Commits $1 Million to 2023 Spectrum Digital Education Program, Raising Total Investment to $9 Million." Charter Communications, press release, May 16, 2023.

City of Staunton, Virginia. "All About Stan-Ton." https://visitstaunton.com/feature/all-about-stan-ton/.

Clinton, Bill. "The 2000 State of the Union." Speech, Washington, 2000. https://clinton.presidentiallibraries.us/exhibits/show/sotu/2000-sotu.

"The Clinton-Gore Administration: From Digital Divide to Digital Opportunity," White House, February 2, 2000. https://clintonwhitehouse4.archives.gov/WH/New/digitaldivide/digital1.html.

Comen, Evan, and Michael B. Sauter. "The Worst Cities for Black Americans." *24/7 Wall St.* (blog), November 3, 2017. https://247wallst.com/special-report/2019/11/05/the-worst-cities-for-black-americans-5/.

Connolly, Annmaura, and Rye Barcott. "National Service Is a Bipartisan Priority." *The Hill*, June 23, 2021. https://voicesforservice.org/news/voices-blog/national-service-is-a-bipartisan-priority/.

Cooper, Tyler. "U.S. States with the Worst and Best Internet Coverage 2018." *BroadbandNow*, May 9, 2023. https://broadbandnow.com/report/us-states-internet-coverage-speed-2018.

Coppola, Daniela. "Amazon: Statistics & Facts." Statista, June 28, 2023. https://www.statista.com/topics/846/amazon/#topicOverview.

Correa, Teresa. "Bottom-Up Technology Transmission Within Families: Exploring How Youths Influence Their Parents' Digital Media Use with Dyadic Data." *Journal of Communication* 64, no. 1 (December 2, 2013): 103–24. https://onlinelibrary.wiley.com/doi/abs/10.1111/jcom.12067.

Coukell, Allan. "President Trump Signs Bipartisan Bill to Fight Opioid Crisis." Pew Charitable Trust, October 24, 2018. https://pew.org/2CvSCaG.

Cradlepoint, "Cradlepoint Helps California School District Ensure No Child Is Left Offline." 2016. https://www.cosn.org/sites/default/files/Coachella-Customer-Success-Story.pdf.

"Creativity in Learning." Gallup, 2019. https://www.gallup.com/education/267449/creativity-learning-transformative-technology-gallup-report-2019.aspx.

C-Span. "Larry Irving on the Digital Divide." Clip of "E-Mail Accessibility," November 21, 1995; November 22, 1995. https://www.cspan.org/video/?c5073707/user-clip-larry-irving-digital-divide.

"CWA Exposes AT&T's Failures on Broadband and Good Jobs." Communications Workers of America, October 8, 2020. https://cwa-union.org/news/cwa-exposes-atts-failures-on-broadband-and-good-jobs.

de Sa, Paul. "Improving the Nation's Digital Infrastructure." FCC Office of Strategic Planning and Policy Analysis, January 17, 2017. https://docs.fcc.gov/public/attachments/DOC-343135A1.pdf.

Desmond, Matthew. *Evicted: Poverty and Profit in the American City*. New York: Crown, 2016.

Demby, Gene. "50 Years Ago: President Johnson Signed the Fair Housing Act." NPR, April 11, 2018. https://www.npr.org/2018/04/11/601419987/50-years-ago-president-johnson-signed-the-fair-housing-act.

"Demographics of Mobile Device Ownership and Adoption in the United States." Pew Research Center: Internet, Science & Tech (blog), June 12, 2019. https://www.pewresearch.org/internet/fact-sheet/mobile/.

"Digital Divide." AT&T. https://about.att.com/pages/digital-divide.

Dixon, S. "Meta: Annual Revenue and Net Income 2007–2022." Statista, February 16, 2023. https://www.statista.com/statistics/277229/facebooks-annual-revenue-and-net-income/.

Domestic Volunteer Service Act Amendments of 1993. Public Law 103-82, 107 Stat. 785 785 (1993). https://www.govinfo.gov/app/details/STATUTE-107/STATUTE-107-Pg785.

Donovan, Andrew. "Hearing from People Bombarded by Robocalls, Sen. Schumer Co-Sponsors Bill That 'Will Stop It.'" WSYR-TV, May 6, 2019. https://www.localsyr.com/news/local-news/hearing-from-people-bombarded-by-robocalls-sen-schumer-co-sponsors-bill-that-will-stop-it/.

Drake, St. Clair, and Horace R. Cayton. *Black Metropolis: A Study of Negro Life in a Northern City*. New York: Harcourt, Brace, 1945.

Eggerton, John. "AT&T Accused of Digital Redlining in Cleveland." *NextTV*, March 10, 2017. https://www.nexttv.com/news/att-accused-digital-redlining-cleveland-163973.

Editorial Board. "50 Million Kids Can't Attend School; What Happens to Them?" *New York Times*, April 20, 2020. https://www.nytimes.com/2020/04/16/opinion/coronavirus-schools-closed.html.

Ellison, Ralph. *Invisible Man*. New York: Random House, 1952.

Enos, Ryan D. *The Space Between Us: Social Geography and Politics*. Cambridge University Press, 2017.

ESGN Asia. "China Mobile Is Bridging the Gap Between Rural and Urban Digital Divide in China." July 5, 2021. https://esgn.asia/china-mobile-is-bridging-the-gap-between-rural-and-urban-digital-divide-in-china/.

Faberman, Jason, and Marianna Kudlyak. "What Does Online Job Search Tell Us about the Labor Market?" *Economic Perspectives* 40, no. 1 (2016). https://www.chicagofed.org/publications/economic-perspectives/2016/1-faberman-kudlyak.

"The Facebook Files." *Wall Street Journal*, October 1, 2021. https://www.wsj.com/articles/the-facebook-files-11631713039.

Falk, Tyler. "Google Is Investing Over $1 Billion to Connect the World to Internet." *ZDnet*, June 2, 2014. https://www.zdnet.com/article/google-is-investing-over-1-billion-to-connect-the-world-to-internet/.

"Family Claims Klan Encounter in Garrett County." *Garrett County Republican*, December 17, 2020. https://www.wvnews.com/garrettrepublican/news/family-claims-klan-encounter-in-garrett-county/article_10c6fd3b-c09b-5bb5-987f-7bd606712c42.html.

Farhi, Paul. "Bush Vetoes Cable TV Legislation." *Washington Post*, October 4, 1992. https://www.washingtonpost.com/archive/politics/1992/10/04/bush-vetoes-cable-tv-legislation/8697e4ca-5cdb-475c-8cf5-3061d7548425/.

Faria, Julia. "Global Amazon Advertising Revenue 2019–2022." Statista, March 10, 2023. https://www.statista.com/statistics/259814/amazons-worldwide-advertising-revenue-development/.

Faverio, Michelle. "Share of Those 65 and Older Who Are Tech Users Has Grown in the Past Decade." Pew Research Center, January 13, 2022. https://www.pewresearch.org/short-reads/2022/01/13/share-of-those-65-and-older-who-are-tech-users-has-grown-in-the-past-decade/.

FCC: Consumer. "Digital Television." August 9, 2016. https://www.fcc.gov/general/digital-television.

"FCC Authorizes Nearly $2.9 Million for Broadband in Garrett County." *Cumberland Times-News*, August 13, 2019. https://www.times-news.com/news/local_news/fcc-authorizes-nearly-2-9-million-for-broadband-in-garrett-county/article_1389c72d-ecdc-577f-bc2a-20095c57e517.html.

FCC Press Release, September 22, 2015. "Commissioner Rosenworcel's Statement on Digital Learning Equity Act." https://www.fcc.gov/document/commissioner-rosenworcels-statement-digital-learning-equity-act.

FDR Library & Museum. "FDR and Housing Legislation: FDR Presidential Library & Museum." https://www.fdrlibrary.org/housing.

Federal Communications Commission. "Connect America Fund Phase II FAQs." June 14, 2016. https://www.fcc.gov/consumers/guides/connect-america-fund-phase-ii-faqs.

———. "Connecting Americans to Health Care." October 19, 2018. https://www.fcc.gov/connecting-americans-health-care.

———. "Fact Sheet: Update of E-Rate For Broadband In Schools and Libraries." July 19, 2013. https://www.fcc.gov/document/fact-sheet-update-e-rate-broadband-schools-and-libraries.

———. "FCC Announces Increase in Rural Health Care Program Funds for FY 2020." June 30, 2020. https://www.fcc.gov/document/fcc-announces-increase-rural-health-care-program-funds-fy-2020.

———. "FCC Announces Over $700 Million for Broadband in 26 States." November 10, 2021. https://www.fcc.gov/document/fcc-announces-over-700-million broadband-26states.

———. "FCC Fixed Broadband Deployment." https://broadbandmap.fcc.gov/.

———. "FCC OKs $4.9 Billion to Maintain, Improve, and Expand Rural Broadband." August 22, 2019. https://www.fcc.gov/document/fcc-oks-49-billion-maintain-improve-and-expand-rural-broadband.

———. "Implementing the Infrastructure Investment and Jobs Act: Prevention and Elimination of Digital Discrimination." *Federal Register*, January 20, 2023. https://www.federalregister.gov/documents/2023/01/20/2023-00551/implementing-the-infrastructure-investment-and-jobs-act-prevention-and-elimination-of-digital.

———. "Keep Americans Connected." March 17, 2020. https://www.fcc.gov/keep-americans-connected.

———. "Lifeline Program for Low-Income Consumers." January 27, 2012. https://www.fcc.gov/general/lifeline-program-low-income-consumers.

———. "Notice of Proposed Rulemaking in the Matter of Implementing the Infrastructure Investment and Jobs Act: Prevention and Elimination of Digital Discrimination." GN Docket 22-69, December 22, 2022. https://docs.fcc.gov/public/attachments/FCC-22-98A1.pdf.

———. Press release. "FCC Chairman Michael Powell Announces Creation of FCC Digital Task Force." October 11, 2001. https://www.fcc.gov/document/fcc-chairman-michael-powell-announces-creation-fcc-digital-tv-task-force.

Federal Reserve Bank of Dallas. "Closing the Digital Divide, A Framework for Meeting CRA Obligations." July 2016 (revised December 2016). https://www.dallasfed.org/-/media/Documents/cd/pubs/digitaldivide.pdf.

Finnegan, Michael. "City National Bank Accused of Racial Bias in L.A. Home Loans." *Los Angeles Times*, January 12, 2023. https://www.latimes.com/california/story/2023-01-12/city-national-bank-redlining-settlement.

Fishbane, Lara, and Adie Tomer. "How Cleveland Is Bridging Both Digital and Racial Divides." Brookings, March 9, 2020. https://www.brookings.edu/articles/how-cleveland-is-bridging-both-digital-and-racial-divides/.

Fontanella, Cynthia A., Danielle L. Hiance-Steelesmith, Gary S. Phillips, Jeffrey A. Bridge, Natalie Lester, Helen Anne Sweeney, and John V. Camp. "Widening Rural-Urban Disparities in Youth Suicides, United States, 1996–2010." *JAMA Pediatrics*, May 2016, 466–73. https://pubmed.ncbi.nlm.nih.gov/25751611/.

"47 U.S.C. § 151: "Purposes of Chapter; Federal Communications Commission Created." https://www.law.cornell.edu/uscode/text/47/151.

"Francis Marion School." Alabama Department of Education, 2019. http://reportcard.alsde.edu/Alsde/OverallScorePage?schoolcode=0025&systemcode=053&year=2019.

Gant, Jon, and Nicol Turner-Lee. 2011. "Government Transparency: Six Strategies for More Open and Participatory Government." Aspen Institute, February 28. https://www.aspeninstitute.org/wp-content/uploads/files/content/docs/pubs/Government_Transparency_Six_Strategies.pdf.

Gant, Jon P., Nicol E. Turner-Lee, Ying Li, and Joseph S. Miller. "National Minority Broadband Adoption: Comparative Trends in Adoption, Acceptance and Use." Joint Center for Political and Economic Studies, February 2010. https://www.broadbandillinois.org/uploads/cms/documents/mti_broadband_report_web.pdf.

Garrett County Government, Maryland. "DNG Announces Launch of NeuBeam High Speed Internet: Technology." October 20, 2016. https://business.garrettcounty.org/2016/news/10.

———. "Swan Meadow School Receives 2018 Sustainable Maryland Green School Award: Education." April 30, 2018. https://business.garrettcounty.org/education/news/swan-meadow-school-receives-2018-sustainable-maryland-green-school-award.

Garrett County Public Schools. "FIRST Robotics Team 1629 Qualifies for World Championship - Public Information." April 6, 2018. https://www.garrettcountyschools.org/2018/news/04.

———. "Garrett County Public Schools Annual Report and Education Superlatives: 2018–2019." https://go.boarddocs.com/mabe/garrett/Board.nsf/files/BMEL4M54C036/$file/GCPS%20Annual%20Report%20and%20Education%20Superlatives%202018-19.pdf.

———. "School Improvement Plan 2021–2022 Swan Meadow." https://docs.google.com/document/d/1lXDVHACr3IAxGlMvoCxrOf2JgW5AjVtjN5SSF_diyJg/edit.

"GCCAC and Rural Maryland Council Provide Declaration Networks Group with Grant for Internet Adoption: Declaration Networks, Inc." March 15, 2018. https://declarationnetworks.com/press/gccac-and-rural-maryland-council-provide-declaration-networks-group-with-grant-for-internet-adoption/.

Geary, Daniel. "The Moynihan Report." *Atlantic*, September 15, 2015. https://www.theatlantic.com/politics/archive/2015/09/the-moynihan-report-an-annotated-edition/404632/.

Giffin, William Wayne. *African Americans and the Color Line in Ohio, 1915–1930*. Ohio State University Press, 2006.

Goovaerts, Diana. "Commerce Chief: $65B in Broadband Funding Will Create 200,000 Jobs." *Fierce Telecom*, February 1, 2023. https://www.fiercetelecom.com/broadband/commerce-chief-65b-broadband-funding-will-create-200000-jobs.

Gross, Terry. "A 'Forgotten History' of How the U.S. Government Segregated America." NPR, May 3, 2017. https://www.npr.org/2017/05/03/526655831/a-forgotten-history-of-how-the-u-s-government-segregated-america.

Hannah-Jones, Nikole. "Living Apart: How the Government Betrayed a Landmark Civil Rights Law." *ProPublica*, June 25, 2015. https://www.propublica.org/article/living-apart-how-the-government-betrayed-a-landmark-civil-rights-law?token=gTxcPWjXmZYvtz VTlrsurtrCPbPuyFPR.

Hardesty, Linda. "Comcast Pledges $1B Over 10 Years to Close Digital Divide." *Fierce Telecom*, March 24, 2021. https://www.fiercetelecom.com/operators/comcast-pledges-1b-over-10-years-to-close-digital-divide.

Harrington, Michael. *The Other America*. New York: Scribner, 1997.

Hart, Jeffrey A. *Technology, Television and Competition: The Politics of Digital TV*. Cambridge University Press, 2004. http://ndl.ethernet.edu.et/bitstream/123456789/11845/1/69pdf.pdf.

Hart, Kim. "The Homework Divide: 12 Million Schoolchildren Lack Internet." *Axios*, December 1, 2018. https://www.axios.com/the-homework-gap-kids-without-home-broadband-access-3ad5909f-e2fb-4208-b4d0-574c45ff4fe7.html.

Haselton, Todd. "President Trump Announces New 5G Initiatives: It's a Race 'America Must Win.'" CNBC, April 12, 2019. https://www.cnbc.com/2019/04/12/trump-on-5g-initiatives-a-race-america-must-win.html.

Hendel, John. "Democrats Torch Trump Failures on Rural Digital Divide." *Politico*, August 17, 2019. https://politico.pro/2z6zLjA.

———. "VA Asking California If Net Neutrality Law Will Snag Veterans' Health App." *Politico*, March 24, 2021. https://www.politico.com/states/california/story/2021/03/24/va-asking-california-if-net-neutrality-law-will-snag-veterans-health-app-1369440.

Herbert, Geoff. "Syracuse Named One of the 'Worst Cities for Black Americans.'" Syracuse.com, November 28, 2017. https://www.syracuse.com/news/2017/11/syracuse_worst_cities_black_americans.html.

Herold, Benjamin. "Millions of Students Got Free Home Internet for Remote Learning. How Long Will It Last?" *EducationWeek*, March 10, 2021. https://www.edweek.org/technology/millions-of-students-got-free-home-internet-for-remote-learning-how-long-will-it-last/2021/03.

Hess, Stephen. *The Professor and the President: Daniel Patrick Moynihan in the Nixon White House*. Brookings, 2014.

Holliman, Irene V. "Techwood Homes." New Georgia Encyclopedia (blog), June 20, 2008. https://www.georgiaencyclopedia.org/articles/arts-culture/techwood-homes/.

Honig, David, and Nicol Turner Lee, Rep. "Refocusing Broadband Policy: The New Opportunity Agenda for People of Color." Minority Media and Telecommunications Council, November 21, 2013. https://mmtconline.org/wp-content/uploads/2013/11/Refocusing-Broadband-Policy-112113.pdf.

Horrigan, John. "Connections, Costs and Choices." Pew Research Center: Internet and Technology (blog). June 17, 2009. https://www.pewresearch.org/internet/2009/06/17/connections-costs-and-choices/.

———. "Disconnected in Maryland." Abell Foundation, January 2021. https://abell.org/publication/disconnected-in-maryland/.

Howley, Aimee A., Lawrence Wood, and Brian H. Hough. "Rural Elementary School Teachers' Technology Integration." *Journal of Research in Rural Education* 26, no. 9 (2011). http://jrre.psu.edu/articles/26-9.pdf.

Hughes, Langston. "Mother to Son." Poetry Foundation, November 22, 2021. https://www.poetryfoundation.org/poems/47559/mother-to-son.

Husock, Howard. "How Brooke Helped Destroy Public Housing." *Forbes*, January 8, 2015. https://www.forbes.com/sites/howardhusock/2015/01/08/how-senator-brooke-helped-destroy-public-housing/.

———. "Public Housing Becomes the Latest Progressive Fantasy." *Atlantic*, November 25, 2019. https://www.theatlantic.com/ideas/archive/2019/11/public-housing-fundamentally-flawed/602515/.

"Implementing the Infrastructure Investment and Jobs Act, Transportation and Infrastructure Committee." July 19, 2022. https://transportation.house.gov/calendar/eventsingle.aspx?EventID=405951.

"Internet Providers in Hartford, Connecticut." *BroadbandNow*. https://broadbandnow.com/Connecticut/Hartford.

Iqbal, Mansoor. "Twitter Revenue and Usage Statistics (2023)." *Business of Apps*, May 2, 2023. https://www.businessofapps.com/data/twitter-statistics/.

Irving, Larry. "The Digital Divide May Be News, but It's Not New." *Morning Consult*, August 31, 2020. https://morningconsult.com/opinions/the-digital-divide-may-be-news-but-its-not-new/.

Jan, Tracy. "Redlining Was Banned 50 Years Ago; It's Still Hurting Minorities Today." *Washington Post*, March 28, 2018. https://www.washingtonpost.com/news/wonk/wp/2018/03/28/redlining-was-banned-50-years-ago-its-still-hurting-minorities-today/.

Jensen, Scott, Kelly Rogers, and Kate Finnerty. "Key Steps in Creating a Diverse Broadband Workforce." *Route Fifty*, March 28, 2023. https://www.route-fifty.com/management/2023/03/key-steps-creating-diverse-broadband-workforce/384537/.

Joe Biden for President: Official Campaign Website. "Joe Biden's Plan for Rural America: Joe Biden for President." https://joebiden.com/rural-plan/.

Justia Law. "*Bell v. School Board of City of Staunton, Virginia*, 249 F. Supp. 249 (W.D. Va. 1966)." https://law.justia.com/cases/federal/district-courts/FSupp/249/249/1457633/.

Kang, Cecilia. "Parking Lots Have Become a Digital Lifeline." *New York Times*, May 5, 2020. https://www.nytimes.com/2020/05/05/technology/parking-lots-wifi-coronavirus.html.

Kanu, Hassan. "Landmark Housing Discrimination Settlement with Fannie Mae Sets Key Precedent." Reuters, February 11, 2022. https://www.reuters.com/legal/government/landmark-housing-discrimination-settlement-with-fannie-mae-sets-key-precedent-2022-02-11/.

Katz, Elin Swanson. "Testimony of Elin Swanson Katz, Connecticut Consumer General." Hearing titled Closing the Digital Divide: Broadband Infrastructure Solutions. U.S. House of Representatives, Committee on Energy and Commerce Subcommittee on Communications and Technology. https://democrats-energycommerce.house.gov/sites/democrats.energycommerce.house.gov/files/documents/Testimony-SwansonKatz-CAT-Hrg-on-Closing-the-Digital-Divide-Broadband-Infrastructure-Solutions-2018-01-30.pdf.

Katz, Vikki S. "How Children of Immigrants Use Media to Connect Their Families to the Community." *Journal of Children and Media* 4, no. 3 (August 1, 2010): 298–315. https://doi.org/10.1080/17482798.2010.486136.

Kerubo, Jacquelynn. "What Gentrification Means for Black Homeowners." *New York Times*, August 17, 2021. https://www.nytimes.com/2021/08/17/realestate/black-homeowners-gentrification.html.

Kessler, Carson. "Thousands of New York Children Lost a Parent or Guardian to COVID-19, Study Finds." The City, September 30, 2020. https://www.thecity.nyc/health/2020/9/30/21494764/thousands-of-new-york-children-lost-a-parent-to-covid-19-study-finds.

Kiers, Susan. "Mike Lund FOOD." Ox-Eye Vineyards, October 2, 2012. https://www.oxeyevineyards.com/post/mike-lund-food.

Kilgore, Steven. "Los Angeles Land Covenants, Redlining; Creation and Effects." Los Angeles Public Library Blog, June 22, 2020. https://lapl.org/collections-resources/blogs/lapl/los-angeles-land-covenants-redlining-creation-and-effects.

Knauss, Tim. "How a Pandemic Laid Bare CNY's Health Crisis." Syracuse.com, August 13, 2020. https://www.syracuse.com/coronavirus/2020/08/how-a-pandemic-laid-bare-cnys-health-crisis.html.

Kotlowitz, Alex. "Revisiting the Hornets." *Chicago Reporter*, March 13, 2015. https://www.chicagoreporter.com/revisiting-the-hornets/.

———. *There Are No Children Here*. New York: Liveright Press, 1991.

Lafayette, Jon. "Analyst Lowers Estimate for Netflix Advertising Revenue." Next TV, April 24, 2023. https://www.nexttv.com/news/analyst-lowers-estimate-for-netflix-advertising-revenue.

Lazorchak, Madelyn. "Digital Divide Creates a New Underclass." *NeighborWorks America*, August 18, 2021. https://www.neighborworks.org/blog/digital-divide-creates-a-new-underclass.

Lebow, Sara. "For the First Time, More Than Half of Those Living in Rural China Have Internet Access." *Insider Intelligence*, March 19, 2021. https://www.insiderintelligence.com/content/first-time-more-than-half-of-those-living-rural-china-have-internet-access.

Library of Congress. "Reconstruction and Its Aftermath: The African American Odyssey—A Quest for Full Citizenship." February 9, 1998. https://www.loc.gov/exhibits/african-american-odyssey/reconstruction.html.

———. "Valley Railroad, Folly Mills Creek Viaduct, Interstate 81, Staunton, Staunton, VA." Image. https://www.loc.gov/item/va0260/.

"The Lifeline Program Through the Years: From Origins to the Present." CBS Miami, January 19, 2015. https://miami.cbslocal.com/2015/01/19/the-lifeline-program-through-the-years-from-origins-to-the-present/.

Lima, Cristiano. "George H. W. Bush's Legacy on Tech & Telecom." *Politico*, December 5, 2018. https://www.politico.com/newsletters/morning-tech/2018/12/05/george-hw-bushs-legacy-on-tech-telecom-442744.

Lohmann, Patrick. "Syracuse Housing Authority Plan Uses I-81 Project to Resurrect City Center, Combat Poverty." Syracuse.com, December 27, 2016. https://www.syracuse.com/news/2016/12/syracuse_housing_authority_plan_uses_i-81_project_to_resurrect_city_center.html.

Londono, Kenneth. "Pioneer Homes, First Public Housing Complex in New York, Provides Living Space and Hope for a Place of Their Own One Day." My Housing Matters (blog), May 6, 2015. http://myhousingmatters.com/pioneer-homes-first-public-housing-complex-in-new-york-provides-living-space-and-hope-for-a-place-of-their-own-one-day/.

"Luján, Thune Announce Bipartisan Working Group on the Universal Service Fund and Broadband Access." Lujan.senate.gov, May 11, 2023. https://www.lujan.senate.gov/newsroom/press-releases/lujan-thune-announce-bipartisan-working-group-on-the-universal-service-fund-and-broadband-access/.

Lung-Aman, Willow. "The Next New Deal Must Be for Black Americans, Too." Bloomberg, January 18, 2021. https://www.bloomberg.com/news/articles/2021-01-18/the-next-new-deal-must-be-for-black-americans-too.

Macy, Beth. *Dopesick: Dealers, Doctors, and the Drug Company That Addicted America*. Boston: Little, Brown, 2018.

Maryland Department of Labor. "Garrett County Major Employers Size Category." https://dllr.state.md.us/lmi/emplists/garrett.shtml.

Maryland State Department of Education. "Maryland Report Card." https://reportcard.msde.maryland.gov/Graphs/#/ReportCards/ReportCardSchool/1/E/1/11/1812/2019.

McBride, Brandon. "Celebrating the 80th Anniversary of the Rural Electrification Administration." U.S. Department of Agriculture, February 21, 2017. https://www.usda.gov/media/blog/2016/05/20/celebrating-80th-anniversary-rural-electrification-administration.

Microsoft. "Declaration Networks Group and Microsoft Announce Agreement to Deliver Broadband Internet to Rural Communities in Virginia and Maryland." April 24, 2018.

https://news.microsoft.com/2018/04/24/declaration-networks-group-and-microsoft-announce-agreement-to-deliver-broadband-internet-to-rural-communities-in-virginia-and-maryland/.

"Microsoft Airband Initiative." Microsoft: Corporate Social Responsibility. https://www.microsoft.com/en-us/corporate-responsibility/airband-initiative.

Mock, Brentin. "What 'Livability' Looks Like for Black Women." Bloomberg, January 9, 2020. https://www.bloomberg.com/news/articles/2020-01-09/the-best-and-worst-cities-for-black-women.

"More Than $1.1 Million Awarded to 'Fight' Opioid Crisis in Garrett County." *Garrett County Republican*, August 23, 2019. https://www.wvnews.com/garrettrepublican/news/more-than-1-1-million-awarded-to-fight-opioid-crisis-in-garrett-county/article_e078799a-51f0-5536-a8b0-d8363e973729.html.

Morin, Rich. "Behind Trump's Win in Rural White America." Pew Research Center, November 17, 2016. https://www.pewresearch.org/fact-tank/2016/11/17/behind-trumps-win-in-rural-white-america-women-joined-men-in-backing-him/.

Morton, Joseph. "John Cornyn Highlights Billions in Broadband Funding for Texas—That He Voted Against." *Dallas Morning News*, June 28, 2023. https://www.dallasnews.com/news/politics/2023/06/28/john-cornyn-highlights-billions-in-broadband-funding-for-texas-that-he-voted-against/.

Mozer, Paul. "Forget TikTok. China's Powerhouse App Is WeChat, and Its Power Is Sweeping." *New York Times*, September 4, 2020. https://www.nytimes.com/2020/09/04/technology/wechat-china-united-states.html.

Mueller, Milton. "Chapter 2: Universal Service: A Concept in Search of a History." In *Universal Service: Competition, Interconnection and Monopoly in the Making of the American Telephone System.* University of Syracuse Press, 2013. https://surface.syr.edu/cgi/viewcontent.cgi?filename=1&article=1017&context=books&type=additional.

Murphy, Mary-Elizabeth B. "African Americans in the Great Depression and New Deal." *Oxford Research Encyclopedias: American History.* November 19, 2020. https://oxfordre.com/americanhistory/display/10.1093/acrefore/9780199329175.001.0001/acrefore-9780199329175-e-632;jsessionid=897C7418627363E4555932A11FE10193.

Nakashima, Ellen. "Trump Administration Moves against Chinese Telecom Firms Citing National Security." *Washington Post*, April 10, 2020. https://www.washingtonpost.com/national-security/trump-administration-moves-against-chinese-telecom-firms-citing-national-security/2020/04/10/33532492-7b24-11ea-9bee-c5bf9d2e3288_story.html.

Nall, Clayton. *The Road to Inequality: How the Federal Highway Program Polarized America and Undermined Cities.* Cambridge University Press, 2018.

National Association of Housing and Redevelopment Officials. "Capital Fund Backlog." https://www.nahro.org/wp-content/uploads/2020/04/CAPITAL_FUND_BACKLOG_One-Pager.pdf.

National Lifeline Association. "Summer 2021 NaLA Lifeline and EBB Subscriber Survey Results." https://ecfsapi.fcc.gov/file/1007003413241/NaLA%20Lifeline%20and%20EBB%20OCH%20Ex%20Parte%20(Oct%202021).pdf.

National Park Service. "The Rural Electrification Act Provides a 'Fair Chance' to Rural Americans: Homestead National Historical Park (U.S. National Park Service)." https://www.nps.gov/home/learn/historyculture/ruralelect.htm.

National Telecommunications and Information Administration. *Falling through the Net: Defining the Digital Divide—A Report on the Telecommunications and Information Gap.* Washington: NTIA, 1999.

"1938: Pioneer Homes Gives Syracuse Families a Chance at a 'Decent' Place to Live." Syracuse.com, May 20, 2021. https://www.syracuse.com/living/2021/05/1938-pioneer-homes-gives-syracuse-families-a-chance-at-a-decent-place-to-live.html.

"No Child Left Behind." U.S. Department of Education. https://www2.ed.gov/nclb/landing. jhtml.

O'Connor, Cozen. "Republican and Democratic AGs Write Opposing Letters to Fortune 100 on DEI Programs." *JDSupra*, July 21, 2023. https://www.jdsupra.com/legalnews/republican-and-democratic-ags-write-8414662/.

Olick, Diana. "A Troubling Tale of a Black Man Trying to Refinance His Mortgage." CNBC, August 19, 2020. https://www.cnbc.com/2020/08/19/lenders-deny-mortgages-for-blacks-at-a-rate-80percent-higher-than-whites.html.

Perano, Ursula. May 12, 2020. "Study Projects Over 100,000 Small Businesses Have Permanently Closed." Axios. https://www.axios.com/2020/05/12/small-businesses-coronavirus-closures.

Powell, Jim. "Why Did FDR's New Deal Harm Blacks?" Cato Institute, December 3, 2003. https://www.cato.org/commentary/why-did-fdrs-new-deal-harm-blacks.

"President Biden Announces American Rescue Plan." White House, January 20, 2021. https://www.whitehouse.gov/briefing-room/legislation/2021/01/20/president-biden-announces-american-rescue-plan/.

"Project Kuiper." Amazon: What We Do. https://www.aboutamazon.com/what-we-do/devices-services/project-kuiper.

Rachfal, Colby Leigh, and Angele A. Gilroy. "Broadband Internet Access and the Digital Divide: Federal Assistance Program." Congressional Research Service, October 25, 2019. https://fas.org/sgp/crs/misc/RL30719.pdf.

Rangarajan, Sinduja. "Jesse Jackson Calls Out Silicon Valley 'Empty Promises' on Diversity." *Reveal*, April 6, 2014. https://revealnews.org/blog/jesse-jackson-calls-out-silicon-valley-empty-promises-on-diversity/.

Rascoe, Ayesha. "Harris' Broadband Push Could Be Political Windfall—or Pitfall." NPR, May 6, 2021. https://www.npr.org/2021/05/06/994017450/harris-broadband-push-could-be-political-windfall-or-pitfall.

Rashid, Tabassum, and Hanan Muhammad Asghar. "Technology Use, Self-Directed Learning, Student Engagement and Academic Performance: Examining the Interrelations." *Computers in Human Behavior* 63 (October 1, 2016): 604–12. https://doi.org/10.1016/j.chb.2016.05.084.

Ray, Rashawn. "Why Are Blacks Dying at Higher Rates from COVID-19?" Brookings, April 9, 2020. https://www.brookings.edu/articles/why-are-blacks-dying-at-higher-rates-from-covid-19/.

Reboot Foundation. "Does Educational Technology Help Students Learn?" June 6, 2019. https://reboot-foundation.org/does-educational-technology-help-students-learn/.

"Rep. Ilhan Omar Introduces Homes for All Act, a New 21st Century Public Housing Vision." Press release, Omar.house.gov, November 20, 2019. https://omar.house.gov/media/press-releases/rep-ilhan-omar-introduces-homes-all-act-new-21st-century-public-housing-vision.

Representative Antonio Delgado. "Rep. Delgado and USDA Under Secretary Torres Small Announce $1.15 Billion Broadband Investment in Rural Communities." October 23, 2021. http://delgado.house.gov/media/press-releases/rep-delgado-and-usda-under-secretary-torres-small-announce-115-billion.

"Reviewing the Implementation of the Infrastructure Investment and Jobs Act | Transportation and Infrastructure Committee," March 28, 2023. https://transportation.house.gov/calendar/eventsingle.aspx?EventID=406231.

Rideout, Victoria, and Vikki Katz. "Opportunity for All? Technology and Learning in Lower-Income Families." Joan Ganz Cooney Center at Sesame Workshop, February 3, 2016. https://joanganzcooneycenter.org/wp-content/uploads/2016/01/jgcc_opportunityforall.pdf.

Rittenberg, Julia. "Square vs. Clover for Businesses." *Forbes Advisor*, October 1, 2021. https://www.forbes.com/advisor/business/software/square-vs-clover/.

"Rolling Study Halls." Google for Education. https://edu.google.com/intl/ALL_us/why-google/our-commitment/rolling-study-halls/.

Rosen, David. "Confronting the Digital Divide: New York City vs. Verizon." *CounterPunch*, February 24, 2021. https://www.counterpunch.org/2021/02/24/confronting-the-digital-divide-new-york-city-vs-verizon/.

Rosenworcel, Jessica. "Closing the Digital Divide." Speech, Aspen Ideas Festival, June 30, 2016.

Sakar, Dibya. "Retailers Will Offer Digital TV Converters." Associated Press, December 11, 2007. https://www.seattlepi.com/business/article/Retailers-will-offer-digital-TV-converters-1258501.php.

Sanchez, Lisa. "Cleveland's Legacy of Housing Discrimination: The Great Migration." Cleveland Public Library, June 7, 2018. https://cpl.org/clevelands-legacy-of-housing-discrimination-the-great-migration/.

Sasso, Brendan. "Republicans: 'Obamaphone' Program Is 'Everything That's Wrong with Washington.'" *The Hill*, October 11, 2013. https://thehill.com/policy/technology/328171-republicans-obamaphone-program-is-everything-thats-wrong-with-washington.

Schwartz, Joel. "The New York City Rent Strikes of 1963–1964." *Social Service Review* 57, no. 4 (1983): 545–64.

Scorse, Yvette. "NDIA Awards 18 National Digital Navigator Corps Grants in Rural & Tribal Areas." NDIA, September 7, 2022. https://www.digitalinclusion.org/blog/2022/09/07/ndia-awards-18-national-digital-navigator-corps-grants-in-rural-tribal-areas/.

"Separate and Unequal: The Legacy of Racial Discrimination in Housing" Statement by Lisa Rice, National Fair Housing Alliance, Before the U.S. Senate Committee on Banking, Housing, and Urban Affairs, 117th Cong., 2021.

Sewall, Sam. "The Switch from Analog to Digital TV." Nielsen, November 2009. https://www.nielsen.com/insights/2009/the-switch-from-analog-to-digital-tv/.

Shreve, Renée. "County Working with Broadband Companies to Expand Service." *Garrett County Republican*, January 16, 2020. https://www.wvnews.com/garrettrepublican/news/county-working-with-broadband-companies-to-expand-service/article_aad7a431-df41-5c4e-bd29-666ff0e1bb85.html.

Smith, Brad, and Carol Ann Browne. *Tools and Weapons: The Promise and the Peril of the Digital Age*. New York: Penguin, 2021.

Smith, Robert L. "Census Data Reveals New Migration Pattern as Black Families Leave Cleveland." Cleveland.com, March 28, 2011. https://www.cleveland.com/metro/2011/03/census_data_reveals_new_migrat.html.

Snider, Annie, and Anthony Adragna. "Trump's Latest Strike against Regulations: His Infrastructure Plan." *Politico*, February 16, 2018. http://politi.co/2EtIVYo.

"State Profiles." Database, Nation's Report Card, 2019. https://www.nationsreportcard.gov/profiles/stateprofile?chort=1&sub=MAT&sj=AL&sfj=NP&st=MN&year=2019R3.

Statista Research Department. "Verizon Communications: Statistics & Facts." Statista, January 19, 2023. https://www.statista.com/topics/2599/verizon-communications/#topicOverview.

Stoll, Julia. "Netflix's Quarterly Revenue 2013–2023." Statista, April 20, 2023. https://www.statista.com/statistics/273883/netflixs-quarterly-revenue/.

"Syracuse Announces $800 Million Housing Project Renovation Plan." WSYR-TV, January 20, 2022. https://www.localsyr.com/news/local-news/syracuse-announces-800-million-housing-project-renovation-plan/.

Syracuse Housing Authority. "Syracuse Housing Authority: Building Neighborhoods, Growing Dreams." https://syracusehousing.org/.

Tadayon, Ali, and Sydney Johnson. "California Schools Build Local Wireless Networks to Bridge Digital Divide." *EdSource*, January 4, 2021. https://edsource.org/2021/california-schools-build-community-wireless-networks-to-bridge-digital-divide/645919.

Taylor, Kiesha. "It's Time to Close the Digital Divide." T-Mobile, May 22, 2020. https://www.t-mobile.com/business/resources/articles/bridge-the-digital-divide.

Taylor, Petroc. "AT&T: Statistics & Facts." Statista, May 2, 2023. https://www.statista.com/topics/1252/atundt/#topicOverview.

———. "Revenue of AT&T Worldwide 2006–2022." Statista, June 9, 2023. https://www.statista.com/statistics/272308/atundts-operating-revenue-since-2006/.

———. "T-Mobile U.S.: Statistics & Facts." Statista, June 13, 2023. https://www.statista.com/topics/996/t-mobile-us/#topicOverview.

———. "T-Mobile U.S. Total Revenue 2009–2022." Statista, June 9, 2023. https://www.statista.com/statistics/219458/total-revenue-of-t-mobile-usa-since-2006/.

———. "Verizon's Revenue by Segment 2012–2022." June 16, 2023. https://www.statista.com/statistics/257309/verizon-communications-revenue-from-wireline-and-wireless-services/.

Teale, Chris. "'Whole Nation' Effort Needed to Build Broadband Workforce." GCN, February 13, 2023. https://gcn.com/cloud-infrastructure/2023/02/whole-nation-effort-needed-build-broadband-workforce/382886/.

"Technology." AAPD. https://www.aapd.com/technology/.

"Telecommunications Workforce: Additional Workers Will Be Needed to Deploy Broadband, but Concerns Exist About Availability." U.S. Government Accountability Office, December 15, 2022. https://www.gao.gov/products/gao-23-105626.

Thomas, William G., Richard G. Healey, and Ian Cottingham. "Reconstructing African American Mobility after Emancipation, 1865–67." *Social Science History* 41, no. 4 (2017): 673–704. https://doi.org/10.1017/ssh.2017.23.

Tibken, Shara. "The Broadband Gap's Dirty Secret: Redlining Still Exists in Digital Form." CNET, June 28, 2021. https://www.cnet.com/home/internet/features/the-broadband-gaps-dirty-secret-redlining-still-exists-in-digital-form/.

Trevor Project. "Research Brief: LGBTQ Youth in Small Towns and Rural Areas." November 2021. https://www.thetrevorproject.org/wp-content/uploads/2021/11/The-Trevor-Project_-Rural-LGBTQ-Youth-November-2021.pdf.

Troustine, Jessica. *Segregation by Design: Local Politics and Inequality in American Cities.* Cambridge University Press, 2018.

Turner-Lee, Nicol. "New Internet Users and Online Privacy Perceptions." March 31, 2012. Social Science Research Network. https://ssrn.com/abstract=2032823.

Turner Lee, Nicol, Rep. "Navigating the U.S.-China 5G Competition." Brookings, April 2020. https://www.brookings.edu/wp-content/uploads/2020/04/FP_20200427_5g_competition_turner_lee_v2.pdf.

Turner Lee, Nicol, and Madelyn Lazorchak. "Digital Divide Creates a New Underclass." NeighborWorks America (blog), August 18, 2021. https://www.neighborworks.org/blog/digital-divide-creates-a-new-underclass.

Turner Lee, Nicol, James Seddon, Brooke Tanner, and Samantha Lai. "Why the Federal Government Needs to Step Up Efforts to Close the Rural Broadband Divide." Brookings, October 4, 2022. https://www.brookings.edu/articles/why-the-federal-government-needs-to-step-up-their-efforts-to-close-the-rural-broadband-divide/.

"Twitter Ad Revenue (2021–2023)." Oberlo. https://www.oberlo.com/statistics/twitter-ad-revenue/.

Tyler-Wood, Tandra L., Deborah Cockerham, and Karen R. Johnson. "Implementing New Technologies in a Middle School Curriculum: A Rural Perspective." *Smart Learning Environments* 5, no. 1 (October 10, 2018): 22. https://doi.org/10.1186/s40561-018-0073-y.

Umeh, Elo. "Three Reasons Why African Mobile Connectivity Is Misleading." *Africa Report*, June 27, 2019. https://www.theafricareport.com/14567/three-reasons-why-african-mobile-connectivity-is-misleading/.

"U.N. Forum Tackles 'Digital Poverty' Facing 2.7 Billion People." *U.N. News*, November 29, 2022. https://news.un.org/en/story/2022/11/1131142.

United States v. Perry County Board of Education, 567 F.2d 277 (5th Cir. 1978).

Universal Service Administrative Company. "Program Data." https://www.usac.org/lifeline/resources/program-data/.

"Universal Service Fund." Federal Communications Commission. https://www.fcc.gov/general/universal-service-fund.

U.S. Census Bureau. "Presence and Types of Internet Subscriptions in Household American Community Survey 1-Year estimates." Census Reporter, 2019. https://censusreporter.org/data/table/?table=B28002&geo_ids=16000US3673000&primary_geo_id=16000US3673000.

———. "QuickFacts: Garrett County, Maryland." https://www.census.gov/quickfacts/fact/table/garrettcountymaryland#.

———. "QuickFacts: Staunton City, Virginia." https://www.census.gov/quickfacts/fact/table/stauntoncityvirginia/PST045219.

———. "QuickFacts: Syracuse City, New York." https://www.census.gov/quickfacts/fact/table/syracusecitynewyork/PST045221.

———. "2013–2017 American Community Survey 5-Year Estimates." https://factfinder.census.gov/faces/tableservices/jsf/pages/productview.xhtml?pid=ACS_17_5YR_GCT2801.ST51&prodType=table.

———. "Why We Ask About . . . Language Spoken at Home." https://www.census.gov/acs/www/about/why-we-ask-each-question/language/.

U.S. Department of Agriculture, Economic Research Service. "Farming and Farm Income." https://www.ers.usda.gov/data-products/ag-and-food-statistics-charting-the-essentials/farming-and-farm-income/.

U.S. Department of Agriculture, Rural Development. "Rural Broadband Access Loan and Loan Guarantee." https://www.rd.usda.gov/programs-services/telecommunications-programs/rural-broadband-access-loan-and-loan-guarantee.

U.S. Department of Education, Office for Civil Rights. "Education in a Pandemic: The Disparate Impacts of COVID-19 on America's Students." June 9, 2021. https://www2.ed.gov/about/offices/list/ocr/docs/20210608-impacts-of-covid19.pdf.

U.S. Department of Housing and Urban Development. "About Neighborhood Networks." https://www.hud.gov/program_offices/public_indian_housing/programs/ph/nnw/nnwaboutnn.

———. "Fair Housing Is 50." https://www.hud.gov/fairhousingis50.

———. "Public Housing." https://www.hud.gov/program_offices/public_indian_housing/programs/ph.

U.S. Equal Employment Opportunity Commission. "Diversity in High Tech." https://www.eeoc.gov/special-report/diversity-high-tech#.

U.S. Federal Communications Commission. "2020 Communications Marketplace Report." FCC-20-188 [36 FCC Rcd 2945 (6)], December 31, 2020. https://www.fcc.gov/document/fcc-releases-2020-communications-marketplace-report.

U.S. Senator Amy Klobuchar. "Klobuchar, Clyburn Introduce Comprehensive Broadband Infrastructure Legislation to Expand Access to Affordable High-Speed Internet." March 11, 2021. https://www.klobuchar.senate.gov/public/index.cfm/2021/3/klobuchar-clyburn-introduce-comprehensive-broadband-infrastructure-legislation-to-expand-access-to-affordable-high-speed-internet.

"User Clip: Larry Irving on Digital Divide." C-Span, June 7, 2023. https://www.c-span.org/video/?c5073707/user-clip-larry-irving-digital-divide.

Valley Project. "A Brief History of Staunton, Virginia." http://www2.iath.virginia.edu/staunton/history.html.

van Schewick, Barbara. "Setting the Record Straight: Carriers Can Help Veterans and Comply with California's Net Neutrality Law." *Medium*, March 25, 2021. https://schewick.medium.com/setting-the-record-straight-carriers-can-help-veterans-and-comply-with-californias-net-neutrality-b25fdd2fa1ff.

Vogels, Emily A. "Digital Divide Persists Even as Americans with Lower Incomes Make Gains in Tech Adoption." Pew Research Center, June 22, 2021. https://www.pewresearch.org/short-reads/2021/06/22/digital-divide-persists-even-as-americans-with-lower-incomes-make-gains-in-tech-adoption/.

Wang, Cecilia. "How the People of Maricopa County Brought Down 'America's Toughest Sheriff.'" American Civil Liberties Union (blog), August 3, 2017. https://www.aclu.org/blog/immigrants-rights/state-and-local-immigration-laws/how-people-maricopa-county-brought-down.

Washington Post. "The Attack: Before, During and After." https://www.washingtonpost.com/politics/interactive/2021/jan-6-insurrection-capitol/.

Weaver, Teri. "I-81 Construction Could Force Hundreds of Syracuse Public Housing Residents to Move, Director Says." Syracuse.com, July 16, 2014. https://www.syracuse.com/news/2014/07/i-81_construction_could_displace_hundreds_of_syracuse_public_housing_residents_d.html.

Weinberg, Matthew. "Saving the Universal Service Fund: Time for Big Tech to Pay Up." *The Hill*, August 25, 2022. https://thehill.com/opinion/congress-blog/3616131-saving-the-universal-service-fund-time-for-big-tech-to-pay-up/.

"What You Need to Know About Naloxone." https://howtoadministernaloxone.maryland.gov/en/drawer.html.

Wheeler, Tom. "A Lifeline for Low-Income Americans." FCC Blog, May 28, 2015. https://www.fcc.gov/news-events/blog/2015/05/28/lifeline-low-income-americans.

White House. "Fact Sheet: Biden-Harris Administration Announces Over $40 Billion to Connect Everyone in America to Affordable, Reliable, High-Speed Internet." June 26, 2023. https://www.whitehouse.gov/briefing-room/statements-releases/2023/06/26/fact-sheet-biden-harris-administration-announces-over-40-billion-to-connect-everyone-in-america-to-affordable-reliable-high-speed-internet/.

"Wicker, Luján, Young, Kelly Reintroduce Bill to Explore Collecting USF Contributions from Big Tech." Press release, Wicker.senate.gov, March 16, 2023. https://www.wicker.senate.gov/2023/3/wicker-luj-n-young-kelly-reintroduce-bill-to-explore-collecting-usf-contributions-from-big-tech.

Will, Madeline. April 29, 2020. "Teachers Without Internet Work in Parking Lots, Empty School Buildings During COVID-19." *Education Week*, April 29, 2020. https://www.edweek.org/technology/teachers-without-internet-work-in-parking-lots-empty-school-buildings-during-covid-19/2020/04.

Wotipka, Sam. "How Racism Reshaped the Civilian Conservation Corps." *Crosscut*, March 29, 2023. https://crosscut.com/equity/2023/03/how-racism-reshaped-civilian-conservation-corps.

Young, Rich. "The Facts on Verizon's Broadband Deployment." Verizon, January 20, 2023. https://www.verizon.com/about/news/facts-verizons-broadband-deployment.

Index